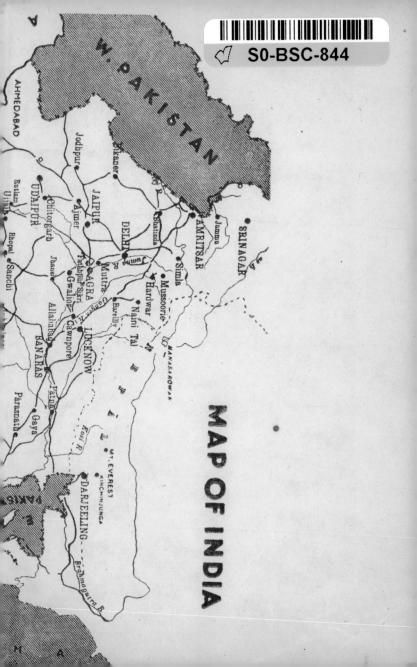

MAP OF INDIA

W. PAKISTAN

AHMEDABAD

Jodhpur

Bikaner

JAIPUR

Ajmer

UDAIPUR

Chitorgarh

Ratlam

Ujjain

Bhopal

Sanchi

DELHI

Jammu

SRINAGAR

AMRITSAR

Bhatinda

Muttra

Simla

Mussoorie

AGRA

Hardwar

Fatehpur Sikri

Gwalior

Naini Tal

Jhansi

Bareilly

Allahabad

Cawnpore

LUCKNOW

BANARAS

Patna

Parasnath

Gaya

MANASAROWAR

MT. EVEREST

KINCHINJUNGA

DARJEELING

Kosi R.

Brahmaputra R.

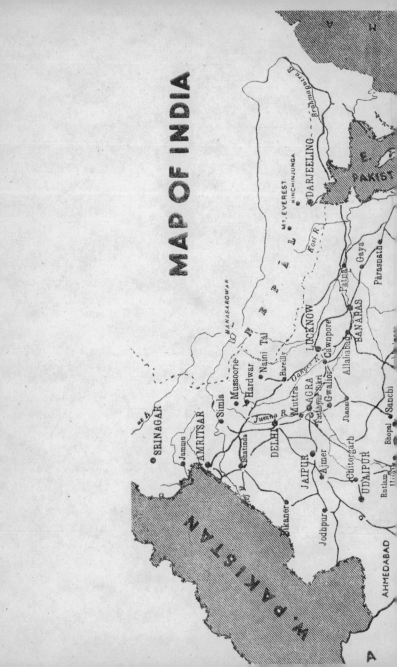

# INDIA : A HANDBOOK OF TRAVEL

# INDIA

## A HANDBOOK OF TRAVEL

P. B. ROY

WITH AN INTRODUCTION BY
**T. S. CALDWELL**
MANAGER : THOS. COOK & SON
(C. AND O.) LTD.

SATURDAY MAIL PUBLICATIONS
24 RIPON STREET, CALCUTTA-16

*First Published 1954*
*Second Revised Edition 1958*

*Price : Rupees Ten*

*Distributors :*
**Motilal Banarsidass**
**Post Box 1586 : Bungalow Road**
**Delhi-6**

*Printed by Naya Hindustan*
*Press, Chandni Chowk, Delhi.*

# INTRODUCTION

Mr. P. B. Roy has already published small guide books on Calcutta, Banaras and Darjeeling, all of which are well written and extremely useful to the traveller.

In the present volume, "India : A Handbook of Travel", Mr. Roy has been far more ambitious and has covered the whole of India. This, it will be realized, is a gigantic task, but Mr. Roy has tackled it manfully and, in my opinion, very successfully. He has travelled the length and breadth of this vast land in search of material. He has written hundreds of letters to Railway and Airway Authorities, Motor car hire contractors and Transport organisations with a view to obtaining comprehensive and up-to-date information on means of transport to the numerous resorts and places of historical, religious and scenic interest. He has interviewed scores of Hoteliers, inspected untold Dak Bungalows, Circuit Houses, and Caravanserais, and the information on communications and on availability and suitability of places to stay will be found most useful, particularly to the traveller who is interested in the lesser known out of the way places.

The brief sketches on historical places and events will be found most interesting and as Mr. Roy, apart from being a student of history, has also had the benefit of the advice of an eminent professor of Indian History, it can be taken that his facts are correct.

The idea of dividing the book into two separate parts is excellent and I recommend the reader to study the first part most carefully before setting out to see India, as an understanding of Indian religions, customs, and arts will increase immeasurably the pleasure derived from the many beautiful and extraordinary sights that he will encounter on his travels.

I commend this "India : A Handbook of Travel" to anyone planning a visit to this historic land of Hind.

T. S. CALDWELL

Thos. Cook & Son
(C. and O.) Ltd.
Calcutta, 1954

# AUTHOR'S NOTE

This book was first published at the close of 1954 and was sold out within a year. Demand for the book has since continued to mount, which has encouraged me to publish a second edition with an wider scope and extent. Many new places of tourist and historical interest have been included and necessary informative data added in order to bring the book up-to-date. Unhappily, the present edition has been somewhat delayed owing to my other preoccupations.

I take this opportunity to express my gratitude to the distinguished scholars, travellers and experts in the travel trade whose considered advice and suggestions have helped to enhance the value of the book.

P. B. ROY

Delhi
October, 1958

# CONTENTS

## PART ONE

## RAJASTHAN

## CENTRAL INDIA

## WESTERN INDIA

# SOUTHERN INDIA

*We take within our own, this hand which India extends to us. Our cause is one : the saving of humanity and its full accord. Europe, Asia, our strengths are different. Let us unite them for the accomplishment of a common task, for the achievement of human genius. Teach us to understand all things, Asia, teach us your knowledge of life! And learn of us action, achievement !*

ROMAIN ROLLAND

# CHAPTER I

# INDIA AWAITS YOU

To know India is a privilege ; it is to drink at the fountainhead of the oldest civilisation and culture of the world. The romance of Indian history, adorned with the lives and achievements of the saints and sages of the great past and the gallant deeds of her kings and emperors, is indeed very great.

With her culture going back more than 5,000 years, her history written in superb stone and marble thousands of years ago and with her many-sided achievements, India has always attracted innumerable visitors from all lands. For, no other country in the world can provide such absorbing interests for the senses as well as the soul such as the unrehearsed beauty of ever-changing countryside, the bewildering variety of races and customs, festivals and folk-lore, religion and philosophy, art and architecture, monuments and memorials of one of the oldest civilisations. India, in short, is at once one and mani-fold, a unique world in herself, and in an historical sense represents a synthesis of many cultures old and new.

The greatest attraction for the visitor to India is the great diversity to be found in every respect—in mode of living, dress, food, language, character and religion. And yet underlying this apparent diversity there is a fundamental bond of unity which welds the people into a solid racial mosaic, a unique unity, deep and abiding. This is the legacy of India which is the proud heritage of all Indian, whatever his social status or geographical position. And again the legacy she bequeathes is characterized by a particular attitude towards life on the part of her people and the deep waters of spiritual life that flows beneath the surface of everyday life. In fact, a traveller would never be bored. Here life surges past in a picturesque procession. You will hear a medley of strange sounds, the tinkle of the temple bells, the throb of the drum, the chant of the 'muezzin', the song of a nightingale, the cries of the beasts in the jungle.

"The East has a glamour of its own and perhaps it is found at its best away from cities, in scenes and places as yet scarcely touched by modern progress and Western influence, where life is still of arcadian simplicity and wholly Oriental. Or it may be found again among the many wondrous buildings designed by master-architects of bygone days where echoes from the vanished centuries ring in the ear like distant music".

Men of culture, poets, artists, philosophers, those who love beauty in any form, will find in this admirable country just the place for an enjoyable and instructive holiday. "It is impossible to belittle," says Prof. Rawlinson, "or ignore a culture which gave the world a religious teacher such as Buddha, rulers like Asoka and Akbar, Kalidasa's *Sakuntala*, the superb plastic masterpieces of Sanchi and Borobuder, the South Indian bronzes, the Hindu temples of Orissa and the Muslim palaces and mosques of Hindustan."

To the lover of nature, the naturalist and the anthropologist, India offers the endless scenic splendours of her peninsular landscape, desert wastes and forests, sunshine and colour, rivers and lakes, flora and fauna and a picturesque assortment of ethnic groups which make up India. This wondrous variety of sights and scenes, faces and places, customs and colours has no equal in the world. What vocabulary can adequately describe the beauty of Travancore's fascinating back-waters; the famous Periyar Lake which

18

abounds in exciting wild life, the mighty majesty of the Himalayas, the world's greatest range of mountains rising almost five and a half miles towards the sky, the object of perennial awe? And Kashmir ! the land of majestic mountain scenery, with a capital city comparable to a "Venice set in the heart of Switzerland".

To the lover of art and the aesthete, India offers a rich variety—temples and mosques, monuments and memorials, many of them belonging to remote prehistoric times. Ancient India's skill in architecture, sculpture and painting, however, found its ultimate expression in the numerous great temples and caves scattered all over the country. Among them mention may be made of the thousand-pillared temple of Rameswaram, the Meenakshi temple of Madura, the Brihadesvara temple of Tanjore, the rock-cut temples of Mahabalipuram, the caves of Ajanta, Ellora and Karli, the Kailasa temple of Ellora, the great temple of Bhubaneswar, the Sun temple of Konarak—all splendid specimens of art expressive of the religion and culture of an ancient people. The other architectural wonders of comparatively recent times are the Hawa Mahal of Jaipur; the Gol Gumbuz of Bijapur with the second largest dome in the world, bigger than that of the Roman Pantheon ; the sky-rocketing Kutb Minar in Delhi, standing for over eight centuries up to the assaults of Time ; and, of course, the Taj Mahal, peerless marble tribute of a great Emperor to his beloved Queen, a masterpiece of architecture, exquisite beyond words.

To the sportsman and the adventurous tourists, India, offers unlimited opportunities. Its forests and hills teem with tigers, bisons, wild elephants, leopards, bears, foxes pigs and snakes; lakes and marshes full of geese, ducks, and a host of other birds ; rivers and lakes abundantly stocked with a large variety of edible fish. Then there is jungle life in its enchanting variety. Natural wild life and the game sanctuary around Periyer in Travancore, and the Rajaji Sanctuary near Dehra Dun and the elephant-catching operations held from time in the forests of Assam and Mysore are among the most thrilling sights for tourists.

To the mountaineer, India is a paradise. There are the majestic Himalayas, stretching for two thousand miles across Asia, and forming India's northern bastion. Its seventy giant peaks, ranging from 25,000 ft. to over 28,000 ft. hurl an eternal challange to the skies. The romance of successive parties of climbers trying to scale their summits has formed a library of most fascinating literature of man's quest for knowledge and dreary endeavour to know the unknown. Dotting the Himalayan slopes there are many hill stations which are second to none in the world in romantic beauty and attractiveness. In summer, it is a unique experience to travel from the sweltering heat and dust-hazy horizon of the plains to these delightfully cool and peaceful valleys. Abounding in Alpine flowers, fragrant forest glades with quaint little villages and hill people and magnificent with glistening waterfalls and scenic beauty these make an ideal setting where one can ride, walk, fish, swim, yacht, ski and climb or simply laze amidst beautiful surroundings and forget all about the worries of work or the prickly heat below.

To the antiquarian, India furnishes a wide field of study. Timeless and enduring, India 'enjoyed an advanced and singularly uniform civilization about six thousand years ago'. The Indus Valley civilisation which forms the basis of modern Indian culture, Sir John Marshall tells us, "is not an incipient civilisation, but one already age-old and stereotyped on Indian soil, with many millennia of human endeavour behind it." There is something unique about the continuity of this heritage and culture through five thousand years of chequered history. Only China can boast of such a continuity of tradition and cultural life. "There was something living and dynamic", writes Jawaharlal Nehru, "about this heritage which showed itself in ways of living and a philosophical attitude to life and its problems. Ancient India, like ancient China, was a world in itself, a culture and a civilisation which gave shape to all things".

And here again you find a literature and culture that coming down the ages have now attained the pinnacle of glory. In the words of Dr. F. W. Thomas, "there is no country where the love of learning had so early an origin or has so lasting and powerful an influence." In few lands can the climate and the soil be more friendly to the growth of great literature." Sanskrit drama has a particularly distinguished history; here Kalidasa is the master and *Sakuntala* his masterpiece. Mention must also be made of the famous books of animal fables, the *Panchatantra* and the *Hitopadesa*. "Chaucer, Shakespeare and, in modern time, Rudyard Kipling." says Prof. Rawlinson, "have borrowed indirectly from this source."

In short, no other land in the world is more colourful, picturesque and instructive than India; and wherever he may go the visitor will find something to delight his eye and stimulate his interest. It is not unappropriately therefore, that the great Orientalist, Max Muller said : "If we were to look over the whole world to find out the country most richly endowed with all the wealth, power and beauty that nature can bestow —in some parts a very paradise on earth—I should point to India. If I were asked under what sky the human mind has most fully developed some of its choicest gifts, has most deeply pondered over the greatest problems of life, and has found solutions of some of them which well deserve the attention even of those who have studied Plato and Kant—I should point to India."

Again, the French savant Romain Rolland said : "If there is one place on the face of the earth where all the dreams of living men have found a home from the very earliest days when man began the dream of existence, it is India."

# CHAPTER II

# AN OUTLINE OF INDIAN HISTORY

In the whole history of the human race, India, more than any other country, can boast of an uninterrupted continuity of heritage and culture through five thousand years of history, of invasions and upheavals, and of rise and fall of empires. "The verses of the Rig Veda", writes an English historian, "are still recited by the Hindus at their morning and evening prayers and at their marriage ceremonies, as they were three thousand years ago. The foundations of their legal and social systems were laid before the foundations of Rome. There were Indian philosophers before Socrates was born. Universities flourished and great buildings arose in India before the British Isles emerged from a state of barbarism."

## Indus Valley Civilisation

The Indus Valley Civilisation which flourished five to six thousand years ago is the earliest picture of India's great past. Although there is no recorded history of the growth and development of that civilisation, it has been conclusively proved that that civilisation was of a very high order, "in some respects even superior to that of contemporary Mesopotamia and Egypt". From the extensive excavations carried out at Mohenjo-daro and Harappa (now in Pakistan) it has been found that there was a highly planned township with public and private baths as well as an excellent drainage system. The use of cotton for textiles at this period was exclusively confined to India and was not extended to the world until 2,000 or 3,000 years later ; there was considerable technical progress in the arts and the amenities of life which gradually culminated in the modern civilisation of India.

## The Vedas, Upanishads, Bhagvat Gita

Before we can find a basis for a systematic and scientific history of the ancient Indian civilisation we must depend on the Vedic literature for the earliest records of the Indian people and culture. The Rig Veda, the first of the Vedas, is the oldest book that humanity possesses and is supposed to date from 4,000 B. C. which brings us very near the Mohenjo-daro period. The Vedic hymns were the outpourings of the Aryans as they streamed into the rich land of India from the north of Hindukush. They arrived in India and conquered a race called the Dravidians who had a long background of civilisation behind them. The religion and metaphysics of the Indo-Aryans are to be found in the Vedas, the Upanishads and the Bhagvat Gita.

In the Upanishads the emphasis is essentially on self-realisation, on knowledge of the individual self and Absolute self, both of which are said to be the same in essence ; while the Gita deals essentially with the spiritual background of human existence and it is in this context that the practical problems of everyday life appear.

## Hinduism

Hinduism, as a faith, is many-sided—all things to all men. In its present form, and even in the past, it embraces high philosophy, moral teachings, rituals and practices. It is a philosophy, more than a codified religion, and it has grown with the advance of time into a system of ethics under which there is room for human beings of widely different beliefs and practices.

The two great epics, Ramayana and Mahabharata extol the mythical heroes, record their conquests and civil wars in the process of consolidation and incidentally impart lessons for a noble and ethical living. Dating back to a remote antiquity they are still a living force in the life of the Indian nation ; while the Laws of Manu, the great law-giver of ancient India, gives a picture of civilised society as it should be.

The Aryan settlements gradually spread over the Punjab and the Gangetic valley of Northern India. Their religious and social development took place along with their expansion, although the Dravidian South mainly remained aboriginal but was ultimately absorbed into the Hindu pale. The Aryans considered themselves vastly superior to others and out of this conflict and intersection of races gradually arose the caste system which during the following centuries profoundly affected Indian life and society. Life was graded according to occupations, out of which evolved the Vaishyas, the artisans and merchants ; the Khatriyas, or rulers and warriors ; and the Brahmins, priests, statesmen and thinkers who were to guide policy and preserve the ideals of the nation. At the lowest level of society were the Sudras, the labourers and unskilled workers. During the later centuries the institution lost its earlier flexibility, and caste-system became a rigid institution which governed the life of every Hindu from cradle to grave.

## Jainism and Buddhism

In the sixth century B.C. two new religions arose— Jainism and Buddhism which were breakaways from Vedic religion and Brahmanical ascendency although they had grown out of them. Dr. Radhakrishnan observes that both are creation of Indian mind and represent reform movements from within the fold of Hinduism put forth to meet the special demands of the various stages of the Hindu faith. Both Mahavira, the historical founder of Jainism and Gautama Buddha, the founder of Buddhism, came from the Kshatriya warrior caste. Gautama renounced his kingdom, wandered in search of truth, sat in long meditation till he attained 'Enlghten-ment', preached among high and low for 45 years and attained Nirvana about 544 B. C.

24

His tenets are contained in the Tripitaka, the Buddhist gospel. Buddhism, mainly a social reform, a revolt against the pride and the caste exclusiveness of the Brahman priesthood and more independent in thought and outlook, prevailed widely from 250 B.C. to 180 A.D., but was never quite general and existed side by side with Brahmanism. At length it lost ground and before the twelfth century it pratically disappeared from India, though it influenced India and Hinduism profoundly. Jainism, also a rebel against the parent religion, and in many ways utterly different from it, was yet tolerant of the caste system, and so it survives in India today almost as an offshoot of Hinduism.

## Maurya Empire

Alexander's invasion of India (326 B.C.) is the first landmark of an authentic history of India. Alexander invaded India to consolidate his Persian empire and extended his dominion right up to Taxila which was then a great centre of Brahmanical learning. On his death at Babylon in 323 B.C., Chandragupta Maurya, the founder of the Great Maurya Empire, assisted by his able minister Kautilya drove away the Greek garrison and captured Taxila. Alexander's general, Seleucus, who inherited his chief's possessions from Asia Minor to India, was defeated by Chandragupta and had to cede a part of Afghanistan, up to Kabul and Herat, to Chandragupta, who also married the daughter of Seleucus. Out of small kingdoms and petty republics thus grew up, for the first time, a mighty Indian empire which extended to the Narbada river on the south with its capital at Pataliputra or modern Patna.

Magasthenes (306 B.C.), ambassador to the court of Patliputra, has left an account of the people and the government under the rule of Chandragupta. Another record of inestimable value of the time is Kautilya's Arthshastra, the 'Science of Polity', which gives details of the political, social, economic and military system of the Maurya Empire.

# Emperor Asoka

But by far the grandest figure in the long line of mighty emperors and captains of history is Asoka (273-232 B.C.), grandson of Chandergupta, who, for the first time, brought the whole of India, Afghanistan and Baluchistan into a single political entity. The bloody victory in the campaign of Kalinga filled his heart with remorse, and this was the turning point of his career and a great land mark in the history of India as well. Henceforth the great emperor refrained from further aggression and under the influence of Buddha's gospel turned his mind to conquests in other fields—the conquest of men's heart by piety.

So his Sacred Majesty, still beloved in India and in many other parts of Asia, devoted all his energies to the spread of Dharma and to the moral and material uplift of his people. He maintained the old foreign contacts of Chandragupta and his messengers and ambassadors went to Syria, Egypt, Mecedonia. Cyrene and Epirus, and to the countries of Central Asia, to Burma, Ceylon and Siam conveying his greetings and the Gospel of Lord Buddha. His many edicts carved on rocks and stone pillars spread all over India, throw a floodlight upon this proud chapter of Indian history. These edicts have a high human interest. Some set forth the Buddhist moral code : obedience to parents, respect for living creatures and truth. In others Asoka enjoins justice and mercy on governors and officials or records his visit to Gautama's birth place or places of pilgrimage. "All men are my children". "At all hour and any place work I must for the common weal". "His Sacred Majesty desires that all animate beings should live in security, peace of mind and joyousness". These are Asoka's own words and no one has ever doubted their sincerity.

Emperor Asoka was a great builder ; and it was during his reign that Indian masons displayed unparalleled excellence in stone architecture and carving which shows 'a mastery over material never afterwards equalled by Indian masons and which is not surpassed even in the marble work of Parthenon'.

After a strenuous rule of forty-two years Asoka died in 232 B. C. Of this astonishing ruler H. G. Wells says in his 'Outline of History' : "Amidst the tens of thousands of names of monarchs that crowd the columns of history, their majesties and graciousness and serenities and royal highnesses and the like, the name of Asoka shines, and shines almost alone, a star. From the Volga to Japan his name is still honoured. China, Tibet, and even India though it has left his doctrine, preserve the tradition of his greatness. More living men cherish his memory today than have ever heard the names of Constantine or Charlemagne".

## The Sungas and the Andhras

Fifty years after Asoka's death, the Maurya empire faded away and was followed by the Sunga dynasty (185-73 B. C.) which ruled over a much smaller area. In the south great states were rising and the Andhras of the south having extended their sway along the Godavari reached northward and occupied Ujjain. The Roman Peace encouraged sea-borne trade and the Andhra kings earned fabulous wealth from the export of pepper, pearls and silken fabrics. There were other independent states; King Kharavala established a powerful dynasty in Kalinga (Ganjam), in 155 B. C.

The Greek successors of Alexander in Bactria spread from Kabul to the Punjab (206 B. C.). Antiochus II subdued the Punjab and later a Greek capital was established in Taxila. In 155 B. C., Menander had established a capital at Sialkot and under him the Greek army advanced right up to Pataliputra but was defeated and repulsed. Menander himself became an ardent Buddhist. From the fusion of Indian and Greek cultures evolved the Graeco-Buddhist art of Gandhara, the region covering part of the Frontier. The Sunga period and the following centuries produced highly decorative works in stone. While some of the monuments at Sanchi are attributed to the Andhras the earliest caves near Bombay are also possibly their work. The

27

Besnagar pillar near Sanchi, erected by a Greek ambassador to the court of Vidisa towards the end of the Sunga period (90 B. C.) gives us a glimpse of the Indianization of the Greeks and their absorption in Indian culture.

## The Sakas

The influence of the Greek conquest was swept away by the Sakas or Scythians who poured in many waves into Northern India about 75 B. C. The Sakas, who become converts to Buddhism and Hinduism, left a lasting influence on the character of the population and profoundly modified the religious and domestic institutions of the Hindus. A vigorous school of sculpture and painting arose as a result of intersection of various races —Greeks, Iranians, Indians, Scythians—and its examples are found spread all over India, and notably in the museum at Mathura.

## The Kushans

The rule of the Sakas was replaced by that of the Kushans (48-180 A. D.), who established an extensive and durable empire over the whole of Northern India. They also became converts to Hinduism and their most famous king, Kanishka, is one of the heroes of Buddhist legend. During this period a great schism divided Buddhism into two sections—Hinayana and Mahayana, and this, followed by the revival of Brahmanism under the Imperial Guptas, led to the decline of Buddhism in India. It was during this period, again, that the first diplomatic contact was made with China. A Chinese embassy came to India in 64 A. D.

## The Imperial Guptas : "Golden Period"

The Kushans had indianized themselves and had become patrons of Indian culture. But, when later, fresh tribes poured into India, the nationalist movement took shape at the beginning of the fourth century A. D., Seizing this opportunity, Chandragupta I drove out the new intruders and established a powerful and widespread empire. Thus began the era of the Imperial Guptas

(320-474 A. D.) who ruled for hundred and fifty years over a prosperous state with their capital at Kanauj and produced a remarkable succession of great rulers successful in war and in the arts of peace. Samudragupta (330-75) extended his empire to Assam and annexed the Deccan, Malwa and Bundelkhand. Vikramaditya Chandragupta II (380-415) further added Kathiawar, Gujrat and parts of the south. During the reign of Chandragupta II there was a great advance in art and literature and Kalidasa, the greatest poet of all times, wrote the famous *Sakuntala*. During the Gupta period, ' Golden Period" of India as it is called, Indian art and literature were at their best. The caves of Ajanta were dug out and the frescoes painted. Bagh and Badami also belong to this period. Fa-Hien, the Buddhist pilgrim from China who visited India about 400 A. D. give a striking picture of a peaceful, prosperous and well-governed state. Chandragupta II was succeeded by Kumaragupta (415-455) and Skandagupta (455-467). Towards the end of the reign of Skandagupta the White Huns raided India in successive waves and as a result the Gupta empire declined and confusion prevailed for a time.

But the Hun ascendency in Northern India was a short phase. The Huns and the Gurjara chiefs were all crushed by Harshavardhana (606-47), the king of Thaneswar, who after many years of fighting, made himself master of Northern India, with the Narbada river as his southern boundary with the Chalukyans, and ended his reign in piety and peace. During his reign the famous Chinese pilgrim, Hiuen Tsang came to India to study at the University of Nalanda. After Harsha's death, the north became disintegrated into small independent states although in the south the Cholas ruled over a powerful and wide empire. But this did not save the north from the impending Muslim invasion.

## Muslim Conquest

The Arab conquest of Persia, in the middle of the seventh century, brought the Muslims to India, and in Sind they made some temporary acquisitions. Three centuries were to pass before the foundations of a durable Muslim empire was laid. It was in 999 A. D. that Mahmud of Ghazni began a long series of raids into India, no fewer than fifteen incursions taking place between 999 and 1027, in one of which he plundered and devastated Mathura, while another ended with the capture of Somnath in Kathiawar. The successive dynasties of Afghan kings held power in India for 300 years; but their advance was gradual, for it was not till 1206 that Delhi was taken and the greater part of India annexed by Kutb-ud-din, whose memory is perpetuated by the Kutb Minar at Delhi. Alauddin Khilji, a great ruler, finally established the Sultanate of Delhi. The first Mohammedan invasion of the Deccan took place under him in 1297. But this did not mean the subjugation of entire India; the Cholas were still powerful in the South and there were the Hindu kingdom of Vijaynagar and the Muslim Bahamani kingdom of the Deccan. But Delhi was symbolical of the new power.

## The Imperial Moghuls

Late in the fourteenth century, the famous Tamerlane (Timur the Lame) burst into India at the head of a mighty host, smashed the Sultanate of Delhi, and laid waste a great part of Hindusthan. Fortunately for India, Timur went back; but his devastating blow weakened India and the general misrule and anarchy that followed paved the way for larger and more permanent conquest by the Moghul emperors. Babar, a direct descendent of Timur, overthrew the last of the Lodi kings at the famous battle of Panipat (1526), and founded the Moghul empire. Humayun (1530-56), lost the whole of the territory conquered by Babar, but recovered a portion of it shortly before his death. His victor was Sher Shah, the ablest among the Afghan rulers, who reigned from 1540-1545.

Akbar (1556-1605) spent a long reign in firmly establishing the Moghul empire. During the benign rule of this Great Moghul, the Moghul empire reached

the greatest height of power. Akbar followed up
his conquests by important financial and agrarian
reforms. He gathered around him a brilliant group of
men of all religion : poets, painters, writers, mathematicians and saints of all faith flocked to his court and sought
his patronage. Among the great men of his time were
Raja Todar Mall, his able finance minister; Abul Fazl,
the historian of his reign; and Faizi, the poet. Akbar was
beloved by the Hindus and the Muslims alike. The
Moghul dynasty became firmly established as India's
own. Jahangir (1605-27) received in 1616 Sir Thomas
Roe, the ambassador of James I of England.

Under Shah Jahan (1627) the Moghul Empire
reached the zenith of its glory. Many stately palaces and
forts, including the Taj Mahal at Agra, testify to his
magnificence and taste. The close of Shah Jahan's reign
was embittered by the rivalries of his four sons. Aurangzeb (1658-1707) defeated and killed his brothers and kept
his father a prisoner till death (1666). His reign, in
some respects splendid, ended in failure. His conquest
of the Deccan as far south as Tanjore marked the height
of Muslim conquest. But from this time the Moghul
Empire was visibly declining. Sir Thomas Roe had already succeeded in establishing an English factory at
Surat. Madras was founded in 1639. Bombay was presented to Charles II of England by way of dowry from
Portugal and he transferred it to the East India Company.
Calcutta was founded by Job Charnock in 1690. Thus
by the end of the seventeenth century the British had
gained a number of footholds in India and even during
the reign of Aurangzeb the British made an unsuccessful
attempt to increase (1685) their possessions in India by
military power.

The French had already established footholds in
India. The overflowing energies of Europe were spreading out to India just when India's political and economic
condition was rapidly declining. Aurangzeb's sons dispu-
ted the right of succession, and Bahadar Shah (1707-12)
secured the crown. After four short-lived emperors
Muhamad Shah (1719-48), grandson of Bahadur came

to the throne. His viceroys because rebellious, and so contributed to the success of the Mahrattas who subdued the Deccan. About 1738, part of the Deccan became practically independent under Nizam-ul-Mulk (ancestor of the present Nizam). In 1739, to avenge an alleged insult, Nadir Shah of Persia invaded India, captured Delhi, gave orders for a general slaughter of the inhabitants and carried off enormous plunder including the Peacock Throne. All the country west of the Indus was lost to the empire. On the death of Muhamad, the phontom rulers, Ahmad Shah (1748-1754) and Alamgir I1 (1754-1759) occupied the throne, and was succeeded by Shah Alam (1759-1806) who, after his defeat in the battle of Buxar, surrendered himself to the protection of the British, and ceded, by a royal firman, the Dewani of Bengal, Bihar and Orissa to the East India Company.

## The Mahrattas & the British

While the Moghul empire was declining by strife and revolt, the Maharatta power was growing and consolidating itself in western India, east of Bombay. The founder of the power was Shivaji, a staunch Hindu nationalist who, drawing inspiration from the old classics and religious lores, aimed at founding a united Hindu empire on the ruins of Moghuls. After a career of unparalleled military achievement and chivalry, Shivaji died in 1680; but the Mahratta power continued to grow till it dominated India. Under the Peshwas, the Mahrattas rapidly extended their territory and influence conquering Gujrat, Malwa, Bihar and Orissa and exacting *chauth* of Bengal from the local Viceroy, Ali Vardi Khan. In 1737, the Mahratta troops burst forth at the gates of Delhi and there was no power strong enough to oppose them.

Betweeen 1707 to 1758, the Mahratta power was at its zenith when the Mahratta people under the leadership of the Peshwas almost established a Hindu empire. Although they were severely defeated at Panipat in 1761 by Ahmed Shah Durrani, the Afghan invader, they remained for sometime the first power in India and were the most dangerous opponents of the British. For a time there were only two protagonists for supreme power in India—the Mahrattas and the British. But the seeds of disintegration of the Mahratta power were already at work. Under the fourth Peshwa, Madho Rao (1761-72), the Mahratta chiefs became almost independent and this coupled with internal feud and intrigue greatly weakened the Mahratta power at a time when the English Company was making a supreme bid for power in India. The struggle between the French and the English in the south, a part of the Seven Years War of Europe, ended in triumph for the British at Wandiwash in 1760 ; and the French power finally took leave from the political scene of India.

## English Domination

In Bengal, Lord Clive, by taking advantage of internal rivalry and with very little fighting, had won the battle of Plassey in 1757, a date which is said to mark the beginning of the British rule in India. This was followed by a decisive victory at Buxur in 1764 when Major Hector Munro completely defeated the combined force of Shah Alam, the Emperor of Delhi and Sujauddaullah, the Nawab of Oudh. In 1739, Nadir Shah had shattered the pride and magnificence of the Moghul Empire ; now it was altogether lost. The Dewani of Bengal, Bihar and Orissa, that the Emperor granted as the price of peace, made the British masters of a great part of India and their subsequent expansion to other parts was a question of time and expediency. Warren Hastings (1774—85) took upon himself that task of consolidation and expansion. By repelling Hyder Ali's memorable invasion of the Carnatic (1780), and defeating the triple alliance of the Nizam, the Mahrattas and Hyder Ali, Hastings probably saved British India. The fourth Mysore war, under Lord Wellesley, ended in the capture of Seringapatam (1799), the death of Tipu and the conquest and restoration of Mysore to a representative of the Hindu Raja whom Hyder Ali had dethroned. The second Mahratta war definitely established the British ascendancy in both Hindustan and Deccan. By 1818 the Mahratta power was finally crushed and almost all great chiefs were forced to accept the overlordship of the East India Company. In 1827, Lord Amherst insisted on meeting Shah Alam's successor as an equal. The Emperor seated himself on his throne in the Hall of Audience, and the Governor-General sat by his side on a chair. The dissolution of the Moghul empire was complete. The Punjab and some outlying parts were still beyond the reach of the British, but subsequent wars with the Sikhs (1846-1849) and the Gurkhas and in Burma resulted in firmly establishing the British empire in India.

## The Sikhs

The decay of the Moghul empire gave opportunity to the Sikhs to establish a territorial domain. The founder of the sect, Guru Nanak, a Hindu reformer, was born near Lahore in 1469. The sect, though cruelly persecuted by Aurangzeb, survived and gradually adopted a strong military and political organisation under Guru Gobind Singh. It became a great power under Maharaja Ranjit Singh ( 1780-1839 ) who founded the kingdom of the Punjab which susequently spread to Kashmir and the Frontier Province. Ranjit Singh was altogether an extraordinary figure, extremely brave, remarkably humane and a born leader of men. He was concerned about the British whose growing power he distrusted and feared. It is said that, on being shown a map of India, he exclaimed in disgust : *"Sab lal ho jayega"* ! (Soon it will *all* be red). But he had the prudence to conclude a 'treaty of amity' with the British, recognising the Sutlej as the boundary between the two powers. After his death in 1839, his unworthy successors came in conflict with the British ; and after two wars the Sikh kingdom was annexed, and became the Province of the Punjab (1850). The Maharaja's forebodings had come true. England was now mistress of India from Cape Comorin to the Khyber Pass.

# The Game of the British

Following the break-up of the Moghul empire India was broken into a thousand pieces and the field was left open to adventurers and new claimants for power. "Among these adventurers and claimants", says Nehru, "the British and the British alone at the time, possessed many of the qualities necessary for success".

"The East India Company", the same authority adds, "had originally established itself for trading purposes and its military establishment was meant to protect this trade. Gradually and almost unnoticed by others, it had extended the territory under its control, chiefly by taking sides in local disputes, helping one rival against another. The Company's troops were better trained and were an asset to any side ; and the Company extracted heavy payment for the help. So the Company's power grew and its military establishments increased. People looked upon these troops as mercenaries to be hired. When it was realised that the British were playing nobody's game but their own and were out for political domination of India, they had already established themselves firmly in the country".

## The British Period

The East India Company enjoyed a monopoly of Indian trade until 1813. They bought goods at prices they were willing to pay and sold goods at prices they were willing to extract. Honest historians including the British have disparaged this, while Nehru calls it 'pure loot'. "This process", continues Nehru, "was called trade later on, but that made little difference. Government was this so-called trade and trade was plunder. There are few instances in history of anything like it. And it must be remembered that this lasted, under various names and under various forms, not for a few years but for generations. This outright plunder gradually took shape of legalised exploitation, which, though not obvious, was really worse". Famous English historians, Edward Thompson and G. T. Garret in their "Rise and Fulfilment of the British Rule in India" tells us that "gold-lust unequalled since the hysteria that took hold of the Spaniards of Cortes' and Pizarro's age filled the English mind. Bengal, in particular, was to know no peace until she had been bled white".

This was inherent in the state of things. For, whereas, the earlier conquerors completely indianized themselves, struck roots in the soil of the country and made India their home, "the new rulers were entirely different, with their bases elsewhere, and between them and the average Indian there was a vast, unbridgeable gulf—a difference in tradition, in outlook, in income and ways of living. It was felt that the British ruling class must maintain its prestige in India by keeping aloof, exclusive, apart from the Indians, living in a superior world of its own". So it is that after 167 years of British rule, accompanied, as we are told, by strenuous and constant attempts on the part of the British to improve its condition and to teach its people the art of self-government, India, when the British were forced to withdraw in 1947 under the pressure of a militant nationalism, was a miserable mass of poverty-stricken, starving and dying people.

## India's Debt to Britain

And yet it would be wrong to conclude that the British rule in India was all a story of exploitation and evil. There was the other side, indeed a very bright side. The British respected our religion, age-old customs and social institutions and never interfered with them ; and yet they proceeded with caution to eradicate many anti-social practices that beset our social life. Although no attempt was made to impart education to the masses and improve their condition for obvious reasons, the fact can be emphasised that the British gave us 16 modern universities one of which—the Calcutta University—can claim to be the largest university in the world, a number of higher institutes for scientific and cultural researches and an advanced system of administration and judiciary which India largely follows even after independence.

To the great friend of India, Sir William Jones, the

founder of the Asiatic Society, to the great Orientalist, Max Mullar, to Princep and Sir John Marshall and a galaxy of European scholars India owes a deep gratitude of debt for the rediscovery of India's past literature and art and their interpretation to the world at large. And crowning them all comes the English language about which the Marquess of Zetland once wrote with justifiable pride : "And with all its drawbacks from educational point of view, the imposition and wide diffiusion of the English tongue has had undying influence of remarkable effect. No more striking proof of its value from this point of view could be desired than is provided by the fact that all the proceedings of conferences of all kinds held by Indians from all parts of the continent are conducted as a matter of course in English. Whatever significance we may attach to the favourite catch-cry of the Indian politicians of today —"India a nation"—is derived from the genius which the British have shown for breaking down the barriers with which the many fragments—racial, religious, linguistic, and cultural—of which the population is composed and hedged around".

## HINDU INDIA

| | | |
|---|---|---|
| B. C. 4,000 | Rik Veda | |
| | 599-527 | Vardhamana Mahavira, the founder of Jainism |
| | 563-480 | Siddhartha Gautama, the founder of Buddhism |
| | 326 | Alexander the Great invades India |
| | 322 | Chandragupta founds Maurya Empire |
| | 273 | Accession of Emperor Asoka |
| | 261 | Kalinga War : Asoka's conversion to Buddhism |
| | 259 | Despatch of Buddhist missionaries abroad |
| | 202 | Andhras in Upper Godavari valley |
| | 180-60 | Menander. Greek king of Sialkot |
| | 100 | The Sakas in Northern India |
| A. D. 68 | Kushans replace the Sakas | |
| | 120 | Accession of Kanishka |
| | 182 | Break-up of the Kushan empire |
| | 320 | Accession of Chandragupta I: Gupta Era begins |
| | 330 | Accession of Samudragupta |
| | 380 | Accession of Chandragupta II |
| | 401-11 | Fa-Hian visits India |
| | 455 | Accession of Skandagupta : the Huns invade India |
| | 480-90 | Break-up of the Gupta Empire |

| 528 | Defeat of the Huns by Hindu Confederacy |
| 506 | Accession of Harsha to the throne of Kanauj |
| 630-45 | Hiuen Tsang in India |
| 608-642 | Pulakeshi II, the Chalukya |
| 647 | Death of Harsha |
| 711 | Muslim invasion of Sind |
| 788-820 | Sankaracharya, the Vedanta Philosopher |
| 1001-19 | Mahmud of Ghazni's annual raids |
| 1026 | Sack of Sommath by Mahmud of Ghazni |
| 937-1048 | al-Biruni, the Muslim traveller. |
| 1176-6 | Mahammad Ghori commences to invade India |
| 1192 | Battle of Tarain : Prithvi Raj slain |

## MUSLIM RULE

| 1192 | Sultanate of Delhi established |
| 1193 | Capture Northern India and Banaras |
| 1197-9 | Conquest of Bihar and Bengal |
| 1206 | Kutb-ud-din Ibak |
| 1236 | Raziya : Firoz Shah (1290) |
| 1296 | Allauddin Khilji |
| 1303 | Sack of Chitor |
| 1321 | Gias-ud-din Tuglak |
| 1325 | Muhamad Adil |
| 1398 | Sack of Delhi by Timur |
| 1489 | Sikandar Lodi |
| 1517 | Ibrahim Lodi ; Babar's invasion of India (1524) |
| 1526 | Battle of Panipat : Moghul empire founded |
| 1540 | Defeat of Humayun at Kanauj |
| 1540 | Accession of Sher Shah |
| 1545 | Death of Sher Shah : restoration of Humayun |
| 1556 | Death of Humayun : accession of Akbar |
| 1567-8 | Siege of Chitor by Akbar |
| 1569 | Building of Fatehpur Sikri |
| 1585 | Akbar shifts his capital to Lahore |
| 1600 | The Foundation of the East India Company |
| 1605 | Death of Akbar : coronation of Jahangir |
| 1615-18 | Embassy of Sir Thomus Roe |
| 1627 | Death of Jahangir |
| 1628 | Accession of Shah Jahan |
| 1646 | Shivaji captures the hill-forts round Poona |
| 1653-80 | Shivaji's career : foundation of Mahratta power |
| 1659-1707 | Reign of Aurangzeb : rise of the East India Co. |
| 1707-58 | Mahratta power at its zenith |
| 1739 | Nadir Shah's sack of Delhi : fall of Moghul empire |
| 1746-61 | Struggle between English and French in India |
| 1758-67 | Clive, Governor of Bengal for the East India Co. |
| 1756 | Ahmed Shah Durrani's invasion |
| 1757 | Battle of Plassey |
| 1761 | Defeat of the Mahrattas at Panipat |

# BRITISH RULE

| 1764 | Battle of Baxar : Dewani of Bengal Bihar and Orissa for the East India Co. |
| 1774-85 | Warren Hastings consolidates British gains |
| 1799 | Rise of Maharaja Ranjit Singh |
| 1804 | Delhi Emperor under British Protectorate |
| 1818 | Final overthrow of the Mahrattas : establishment of the British as the paramount power |
| 1849 | Second Sikh War : annexation of the Punjab |
| 1858 | Out-break of the Mutiny ; third Sack of Delhi by the British |

# CHAPTER III

# THE LAND AND PEOPLE

## Geography

From the Himalayas in the north, India stretches her enormous surface to the sea at Cape Comorin covering a length of 2000 miles. The breadth of India, from Assam to Bombay, is about 1700 miles. Its land frontier is about 8,200 miles long and the sea coast about 3,500 miles. The total area of the Indian Republic is 15.81,410 sq. miles which is roughly two thirds the size of Europe excluding Russia. The Indian peninsula which lies north of the equator can be divided into three geographical units : (i) the great mountain wall formed by the Himalayas with beautiful valleys running along it from Kashmir to Assam : (ii) the great lowland plain of Hindustan through which flow the rivers Ganga, Jamuna, Brahmaputra and the tributaries : and (iii) the great plateau of peninsular India with the Western and Eastern ghats skirting the west and east coasts and the Vindya hills at the base.

## Population

India's vast population of 362 million people represents about a fifth of the entire human race. Of it Hinduism alone counts for 242 million adherents. The rest are Muslims (43 mls.), Sikhs (4½ mls.), Budhhists, Christian (5½ mls.), Jews and others—representing almost all the religions of the world. This population represents a great racial mosaic, only comparable to Soviet Russia in this respect.

The density of population is 296 per sq. mile. Birth rate is approximately 26.7 per mill. and death rate 16 per mill.

Since India is referred to as a land of villages the real dimension of her urban population is often missed. About 62 million live in towns, that is, 12 mls. more than the total population of Great Britain which is reckoned as the most urbanized country in the world.

## Climate

Few lands of the earth can rival India in the diversity of her climate. About half of India is within the tropics, but the greatest extremes of heat and cold are in Northern India. In the Himalayas climate is moist and cold. In the tropical south the climate is more equable. Calcutta, Bombay and Madras all have an equable climate, owing to proximity to the sea. Meteorologically, the Indian year can be broadly classified under three heads : (I) the cold season from October to February; (II) the summer from the end of March to June; and (III) the monsoon from July to September leading to a drop in temperature.

The winter (October-March) is extremely pleasant throughout India. In Eastern India however the cold spell lasts only from December to the end of January. In Bombay and the south, there is no cold weather as such, but the climate is cool and bracing. The summer in India is very hot, particularly in Nothern India where it is unbearable at times. But even in the hottest summer one can find cool and healthy resorts in the hill stations of India which are second to none in the world. Places like Kashmir, Simla, Mossourie, Dalhousie, Nainital, Darjeeling Ranchi, Panchmari, Abu, Mahabaleswar, Ooty and Kodaikanal are delightfully cool during the summer months when they are haunted by thousands of holiday-seekers from the plains. In the month of June when most of the country appears brown, the monsoon breaks out and small patches of green fields appear even in the sandy deserts of Rajasthan. The rainfall which lasts till the end of September average 60 inches in the sub-Himalayan region, 39 inches in the Indo-Gangetic plain and 30 inches in the Deccan but is very poor in Rajasthan. In short, one can find just the climate he likes, all the year round, at one place or the other.

## Language

No fewer than 250 languages are spoken in the Indian Union. The principal languages are Hindi, spoken by nearly 44 per cent of the population in Northern and Central India, the Punjab and Rajasthan; Bengali, spoken by 7.8 per cent in Bengal; Telugu 10.2 per cent and Tamil 8.2 per cent spoken in Madras and southern India; Marathi 8.3 per cent and Gujrati 5.1 per cent spoken in western India. Then there are Punjabi, Behari, Oriya, Assamese which indicate the area in which they are spoken. Urdu a dialect of Hindi, containing a large number of Persian and Arabic words, is widely spoken by the Muslims in the North.

## Role of English

Hindi is the national language of India and is increasingly taking part in government dealings, notifications and publications. Bengali is the most literary language of India. English is the medium of all higher education, literary and scientific researches and governmental communication and is spoken exceedingly well by the educated sections of the country. It has been the common language of India and the only medium of inter-state communication.

## Agriculture

Although industrialization is increasing at a rapid pace, agriculture is still the mainstay of nearly 70 per cent of the population and the principal source of national wealth. The chief crops are wheat, rice, jute, cotton, millet, tobacco, oilseeds, tea, rubber and sugarcane.

India has a total area of 811 million acres. Leaving aside 196 million acres, for which no statistics are available, the remaining 615 million acres comprise 93 million acres of forests, 324 million acres of cultivated land, 98 millions of cultivable waste and 96 million acres of land (about 16 per cent) which is not available for cultivation.

Commercial crops form the bulk of the country's export. India is an important producer of oilseeds and vegetable oil. More than 50 per cent of the tea produced in the world comes from India, which brings in about Rs 1000 to 1250 million of foreign exchange annually. Among the other cash crops grown in India are tobacco, cotton and jute. India is the third largest producer of tobacco. Cotton, jute, pepper and tobacco bring in about 2500 million to the country's income from foreign trade.

Covering 22 per cent of the country's area, forests are an important source of wealth. Teak, *sal, deodar,* and *shisham* and many other varieties of useful timber comes from the forests. Besides yielding products like lac, tanning material, gums and resins and medical herbs, they are an important source of raw material for the match-wood, ply-wood and paper industries.

## Minerals

The mineral wealth of India is unlimited. The country has enormous resources of iron ore ; in fact, its deposits of high-grade ore are among the richest in the world ; her coal reserves are estimated at 66,000 million tons. There are also large deposits of manganese. India produces between 70 to 80 per cent of the world's output of sheet mica ; there are large resources of titanium and thoriam ores, ilmenite and monazite. The gold and silver mines of India are among the oldest in the world.

The country is, however, deficient in copper, tin, lead, zinc, nickel, and above all petroleum.

# CHAPTER IV

# CUSTOMS & MANNERS

From the earliest times waves of foreigners and conquerors have entered India : kingdoms and dynasties have risen and fallen but the larger structure of Hindu society and culture has remained the same throughout the ages. In no other country does religion and social system govern the life and thought of the people so vitally as in India. Hinduism, timeless, durable and catholic as it is, has absorbed many religions and foreign influences and this coupled with regional climate, tradition, myth and legend has given rise to a variety of customs and manners that prevail in India today. So there is in India a great contrast in physical features, mental habits and traits, food and clothing. There is very little in common between Northern India, the original seat of Indo-Aryan culture, the meeting place of various civilisations, cultures and religions and the far South, the cradle of Dravidian civilisation, unaffected for centuries by influence and turmoils of the north.

## Unity in Diversity

"It is difficult, for instance, to trace any racial kinship between the high-caste Hindu from Madras and the high-caste Hindu from Kashmir. The Kashmiri Brahmin eats meat, which is anathema to the orthodox Brahmin of south India ; indeed, in appearance, dress, language, manners and customs each represents a distinct type." India is a land of infinite diversity; so customs differ from place to place as do the minor practices and ways of life. The Bengalees, the Mahrattas, the Gujratis, the Tamils, the Andhras, the Oriyas, the Assamese, the Canarese, the Malayalis, the Sindhis, the Punjabis, the Kashmiris, the Rajputs all have their distinctive features. And fashion and dress often vary with climate and occupation. So the people wear robes of every type and shade. And yet beyond these physical diversities, customs and tradition, there is one supreme bond that binds them firmly together — the bond of religion and the great national heritage of the timeless past.

Again Hindusthan is a land of tolerance where many religions and beliefs flourish. There are the Muslims, who count for a large section of the Indian population, Jews, Parsees, Tibetans, Chinese, and a score of other nationalities with their peculiar customs and institutions which add to the varied panorama of Indian life.

Then there are the aboriginals, 10,000,000 of those primitive people, who were in this land before the dawn of history. They are to be found in the hills and jungles throughout the land. Animist by religion, they worship the hills, the rivers and flowers of their countryside and live mainly on jungle fruits and animal flock. In the hill tracts of Assam and towards Tibet there are the Abots and the Nagas, who retain their own primitive habits; and in the heart of India, in forests and hills, there are the Santals, the Gonds and Todas and other aborigines, who hunt with bows and arrows and keep alive the pagan fire.

Besides colour, Hindusthan is a land of many contrasts; and this is nowhere so vividly evident than in the varying living standard of the people, the vast majority of whom are too poor to provide themselves the ordinary amenities of life. Various factors have contributed to create this gulf, and of them the caste system which makes profession generally hereditary is the principal. Then there was the lack of opportunity

45

and education ; and, above all, about 200 years of foreign
domination which failed to provide a fair standard of
living. So whether he is a tiller, or a carpenter, or a
weaver, or a cobbler or a menial the average Indian
finds life a hard business and a wide gulf separates
them from the educated and the commercial classes and
those fortunate feudal lords favoured by the British. Altogether, life will be found in India in its most modern
form together with customs and beliefs which have not
changed for hundreds of years. It is a unique blend of
the old and the new.

## RURAL LIFE

Eightyfive per cent of the total population of India
live by agriculture and allied pursuits. There are
throughout India some 600,000 villages, which constitute
the economic back-bone of India. It is again in the
countryside that the visitor will find the true India
where old traditions and customs still flourish down the
ages. According to Indian law, land is divided equally
among the sons with the result that the small holdings
are often uneconomic. The farmers of India pay more
to the money-lender by way of interest than they pay to
the Government by way of taxes. The subserviency of
Indian village economy to the money-lender is still one
of problems of the country.

All professions are usually hereditary. The carpenter's son will be a carpenter, the ministrel's son a ministrel. Here one sees that the life of India is unchanging.
The villagers and their womenfolk wear the coarse
cloth made by hand on the village looms. The somewhat rough jewellery they wear is made by the village
goldsmith. They eat simple food consisting of cereals
and vegetables, supplemented, if he has a cow, with
milk and ghee. The vast majority seldom eat meat ;
for, religious prejudices apart, it is beyond their means.
They eat, morning and evening, rice or *chapattis* with
a little curry made of vegetables or cereals. The villagers invariably live in mud houses and have practi-

cally no ventilation. They cook, eat and sleep in the same room. The richer, of course, have better houses and the landlords live in their palatial buildings. The average village consists of a cluster of mud and semi-pucca houses with twisting, dusty narrow streets. Morning and evening, the villages are clouded by dust from the cattle as they move in and out.

The general standard of living in the village is very low. The income per head per annum averages Rs. 280 as against approximately £100 in England. But the villager is contented, peaceful and law abiding.

His religion has not a little to do with his contentment. The average Indian has a blind faith in God, and seems to live in the belief that all that happens in this world occurs according to the will of God. Although technically illiterate, the Indian peasant has a true cultural background and a high outlook on life. This is due to his intimate understanding of the lessons of Ramayana, Mahabharata and the Gita which are often discoursed and sung by a roving saint or the village priest.

The social life of the villages is enjoyed mostly by men, for, the women, except when they gather round the wells or at the baker's oven or at the corn grinding parlour, remain at home. But the men gather in the evenings at the headman's home to smoke and exchange news or perhaps to settle disputes by simple methods of arbitration. Rural Broadcasting and newspapers are gradually penetrating into the rural areas ; and it is not uncommon to see the village schoolmaster or the doctor reading out the news to his unlettered neighbours. The Indian peasant bothers very little with politics and cares less who are his rulers. *Dilli dur ast*—'It's a far cry to Delhi'. All he demands is justice, light taxation and non-interference.

The vast majority of Indian farmers who produce enormous wealth for Hindustan depend for their prosperity on the vagaries of the monsoon ; but owing to the number of river barrages and dams and controlled irrigation that are now being built, famines, as they were known in the days of the East India Company, are unknown and before long they may be entirely things of the past.

## CITY LIFE

The cities and towns of India offer an almost bewildering medley of sights and sounds and present many strange contrasts between the ancient and the ultra-modern.

There is the mediaeval beauty of twisted streets where a hundred shades of every colour meet and mingle, and on the other hand the broad thoroughfares and stately edifices of a modern commercial city displaying its varied commodities in the blaze of a thousand neons and lamps of every colour and hue. "Motor-cars thread their way jerkily through the crowd. There is a clatter of trams : buses rumble past : bicycle bells tinkle urgently. Pedestrians overflow from the sidewalks into the streets. Hawkers trundle their carts, shouting their wares. Everywhere there is bustle and variety. Sometimes a bullock cart goes noisily by and a cow saunters across the street oblivious of the traffic and, if the mood seizes her. calmly stops to sit down plumb in the middle of a crowded thoroughfare".

An Indian bazar is always filled with throngs of merchants, buyers, sellers, newsmongers and sightseers who gather round the shops in close-packed rows on either side of the narrow ways. It is a scene of wonderful colour and movement. This is also the place for idle loungers, fortune-tellers—all flotsam and jetsam of the city—and those who have no money to buy, for, here ebbs and flows in one unending flood the news, the rumours and the gossip of the town and the country.

Most conspicuous of them all are the snake charmers, monkey-players and beggars—many of them deformed skeletons hired for the purpose—who continually clamour for patronage and pity : and the Sikh soothsayers who trot along the pavement with mutterings of "a very fortunate face" at the sight of an innocent pedestrian.

"From Rajputana comes also the Marwaris, orthodox Hindus born with flair for profit in business and a passion for taking risks. From Bikaner, in the desert, they travel more than a thousand miles to Calcutta, even as Aberdonians fare to London, and there they oust from his own business the legally-minded Bengali. The Sikh drives the Bengali out of the taxi trade and other occupations, and the Pathan comes with a big stick to lend him money or make him pay interest.

"Hindusthan is a world of movement. Pilgrims of religion or politics or business are for ever on the road or the trains : here today, gone tomorrow. People of every colour and stock jostle each other in the crowded ways, and there is a bewildering variety of tint and form in the striking and picturesque scene."

In cities, too, religion dominates—and here and there a small wayside temple offers a peaceful retreat from the noise of city life.

## INDIAN WOMEN

From the earliest times the women of India have occupied position of honour and reverence in home and society. Manu, the ancient law-giver lays down : "Where women are honoured, the gods dwell." That tradition is as powerful today as it was during the old ages. Women are regarded as the epitome of the best virtues of Vedic Hinduism. Throughout the ages, they have profoundly shaped the thoughts and activities of men and many a great man of India have drawn inspirations from their mothers to whom they pledged unquestioned obedience.

In ancient and mediaeval literature there are numerous instances of women scholars, mathematicians.

astronomers and the like many of whom excelled men with their proverbial accomplishment. In the nineteenth century there has been a phenomenal improvement in the higher education of women and since then a galaxy of distinguished women have adorned the social and political life of India. Today a great woman of India, Shrimati Vijaylakshmi Pandit, occupies the exalted position of the High Commissioner for India in London. There are others who function as cabinet ministers, governors, university professors, magistrates, doctors, lawyers and high government officers; hundreds of them occupy positions of responsibility in public offices and commercial houses. Their contribution in the struggle for Indian freedom is no small.

Shrimati Sarojini Naidu, a trusted colleague of Mahatma Gandhi who was elected Congress President at a bitter phase of the nation's fight for freedom, had a gift of oratory which was considered unsurpassed in the English-speaking world.

But in spite of this high progress and accomplishment, the Indian woman is turned more inwardly than outwardly, more eminently suited, by traditions and traits of character, to become ideal wives and mothers than politicians and wage-earners. And once married they build happy homes where they reign supreme with all their majesty and serenity. A deep concern of the household is their first love and they make great sacrifice to make their children and husbands comfortable and happy.

A Hindu marriage is no trifle of a civil contract; it is an integral part of Hindu religion which through a process of elaborate rituals binds the couple in eternal ties, make them equal partners in the joys and sorrows of life. The standard of morality in India is very high, and divorce is almost unknown among the masses. This again, can be traced to the deep religious feeling that pervades Indian life.

## FESTIVALS

Religious festivals play an important part in the life

of the nation. There are twenty-six official religious holidays in India which are occasions for festivities and impressive rites. Ranging from austere fast and practices to exuberant fairs the festivals of India are as varied and colourful as its land and people. Hinduism, Islam and Christianity are the three main religions, and since each has its own particular observances and customs, the total number of festivals is quite large.

Of the Hindu festivals *Durga Puja* and *Diwali* are occasions for great rejoicings. *Durga Puja,* the national festival of Bengal, which spreads over four days in September-October, signifies the victory of the Goddess Durga, the embodiment of Divine power, over the demon Mahisasura who threatened gods and men—the triumph of good over evil and the subjugation of animal passions by Divine power. In other parts of India, particularly in South India, the festival is called *Dusserah*. In Mysore it is celebrated with great pageantry and pomp.

*Diwali,* the festival of lights, occurs in October-November and is most popular throughout India. According to legend, its celebration began with the coronation of Rama, the hero of Ramayana. Fireworks, candles and oil-lamps worth over a million rupees are sold and burnt on this occasion.

The other great Hindu festival is *Holi,* celebrated in honour of Lord Krishna in March. The day is celebrated with great revelry and fun; coloured water is sprinkled over everyone's clothes and endless processions of merry-makers make their way round the town. The usual rules of decorum are relaxed for the day and crowds equipped with sprays take complete possession of the thoroughfares. There is no consideration, even a stranger is not spared a drenching.

*Ganesh Chaturthi,* a great festival of Western India, takes place in September in honour of god Ganesh. Picturesque processions accompany the images to the water-front. There are music and dancing. The festival is also known as Ganapati Day or Coconut Day.

*Sivaratri* is devoted to the worship of Lord Siva, one of the Hindu Trinity, and is preceded by an austere all-day fast. Great fairs are held on the occasion of the festival which takes place in March.

There are as many as seventy Hindu festivals. During the season from September to March, particularly, there is a whole chain of religious festivals and national celebrations when the nation goes on holiday in a spirit of prolific abandon. Then there are Tagore's Birthday (May 7), Gandhi Jayanti (October 2), Netaji's Birthday (January 23), and Republic Day (January 26) when there are grand parades of India's armed forces in New Delhi and public meetings and cultural functions in villages, towns and cities.

*Vaisakhi Purnima* (April) is the most auspicious day in the Buddhist calendar. On this day was born of Queen Maya, in the beautiful garden of Lumbini, Prince Siddhartha Gautama, afterwards Lord Buddha.

*Ashada Purnima* is celebrated in the middle of November at Sarnath in commemoration of the first sermon delivered by Lord Buddha there.

The chief Muslim festivals are Id at the end of the month of Ramzan (fasting), and Moharram which are celebrated with equal exuberance. On the day of the Id, vast congregational prayers are held in mosques and maidans, alms are distributed and the day is spent in rejoicing and merriment. Moharram, however, is observed only among the Shia Muslims in memory of the martyrdom of Hazrat Imam Hussain, the Prophet's grandson who was murdered at Karbala ( Iraq ). Moharram at Lucknow is famous.

The Christian festivals—Christmas, Easter and Good Friday—are celebrated in India with great zeal. Christmas, incidentally, is widely celebrated throughout India by members of all communities and is regarded as a festival of great rejoicing and feasting.

CHAPTER V

# HOW INDIA IS GOVERNED

India is a sovereign democratic republic composed of 14 States and 6 Union Territories. It is the largest democracy in the world, the next being the United States. The Constitution of the Indian Republic, the first charter of her freedom, came into force on January 26, 1950.

The President, who is elected for a term of 5 years, is the head of the Indian Republic. The executive authority of Republic, however, vests in a Council of Ministers, with the Prime Minister at the head, which is collectively responsible to the Parliament which consists of an Upper House (Rajya Sabha) and a Lower House (Lok Sabha). The Lower House or the House of the People consists of 500 members elected by the people, on the basis of adult franchise, for a term of five years. The Government of the Indian Union is a government by the people, both at the Centre and in the States. It is a parliamentary form of government. All the adult citizens have the right to vote, which makes India the largest among the existing democracies of the world.

For the first time in Indian history, the country has achieved complete political unity and territorial integrity. India is a federation of States which have no right to secede from the Union. The country has a unified administration under a single Constitution.

India is a truly secular state where the Constitution

guarantees to all its people religious and political freedom regardless of race, caste or creed. The Constitution includes a very elaborate declaration of Human Rights which guarantees to all citizens the Right to equality, Right to freedom, Right against exploitation, Right to freedom of religion, Cultural and educational rights and Rights to property. In respect of civic rights, services and obligations, no discrimination is made on grounds of religion, race, caste or sex.

## The States

| | Names of States | Capital | Population | Area in sq. miles |
|---|---|---|---|---|
| 1. | Andhra Pradesh | Hyderabad | 31,253 | 105,677 |
| 2. | Assam | Shillong | 9,044 | 85,012 |
| 3. | Bihar | Patna | 38,355 | 66,161 |
| 4. | Bombay | Bombay | 48,272 | 191,367 |
| 5. | Kerala | Trivandrum | 13,544 | 14,601 |
| 6. | Madhya Pradesh | Bhopal | 26,102 | 170,909 |
| 7. | Madras | Madras | 29,980 | 50,171 |
| 8. | Mysore | Bangalore | 19,401 | 74,093 |
| 9. | Orissa | Bhuvaneswar | 14,646 | 60,136 |
| 10. | Punjab | Chandigarh | 16,135 | 47,427 |
| 11. | Rajasthan | Jaipur | 15,940 | 132,439 |
| 12. | Uttar Pradesh | Lucknow | 63,216 | 113,433 |
| 13. | West Bengal | Calcutta | 26,681 | 34,944 |
| 14. | Jammu & Kashmir | Srinagar | 4,410 | 92,780 |

## Union Territories

| | | | |
|---|---|---|---|
| 1. | Delhi | 1,744 | 578 |
| 2. | Himachal Pradesh | 1,109 | 10,909 |
| 3. | Manipur | 578 | 8,622 |
| 4. | Tripura | 639 | 4,032 |
| 5. | Andamans and Nicobar Islands | 31 | 3,215 |
| 6. | Laccadive, Minicoy and Amindivi | 21 | 384 |

# CHAPTER VI

# INDIAN ART

## ARCHITECTURE

Indian art is intimately connected with Indian religion and philosophy ; architecture, sculpture, music and dancing all are expressions more of religious urge than of secular culture. An important influence in the development of art in ancient India was the religious pre-judice against graven images. The Vedas did not coun-tenance image worship in any form, and it was at a com-paratively late period in Buddhism that Buddha's person began to be represented in sculpture and painting. This was due to the effect of Greek influence on Indian art, typified in Graeco-Buddhist art of Gandhara which large-ly influenced the sculptures of the Maurya and post Maurya period. The Apollo-like statutes of Boddhisatt-vas are good examples. But the Greek influence on Indian art was in externals only—in matter of form, but never in spirit.

### Buddhist Architecture

Of the standing Buddhist monuments which primarily interest the tourists, none dates later than 260 B.C., when the great king Asoka carved on rocks and pillars the main precepts of Buddhist faith. Two of the pillars are to be seen at Delhi. A better pillar, which also bears later Gupta and Moghul inscriptions, rises in the fort of Allahabad.

The finest specimen of Buddhist building, however, are the topes (stupas) which mark some spot sacred to Buddha, or were meant to contain some relics of His, the rails which surrounded these and other holy places, the *chaityas* or churches, and the *viharas* or monasteries. The most impressive group that survives is that at Sanchi near Bhopal. Topes, rails, monasteries, and some later temples are nobly set on a hill commanding wide and beautiful views, and the visitor will indeed be of dull of imagination if he does not feel the sanctity and grandeur of a place that is almost comparable with the Acropolis of Athens. Less impressive than Sanchi but not less interesting, is the stupa at Sarnath, near Banaras, which marks the beginning of Buddha's mission. Holier than either of these is the temple at Buddha-Gaya, nearby the Bodhi-tree where Buddha meditated and attained enlightenment, a lofty pyramid-like building said to have been built by a Brahmin in the days of religious tolerance about 1100 A.D. The early specimens of the characteristic Buddhist railing can be studied best at Bharhut and Amaravati, but the best specimens of chaityas are the rock hewn caves of the Bombay State, of which the most famous are those at Karli, Bedda, Nasik, Ajanta and Ellora. These are generally regarded as the crowning glory of Bhudhist art in India. Karli is architecturally the finest, but the fresco paintings of Ajanta have a nobility which the art of painting never again attained in India, and from them some of the best Indian artists of today draw inspiration.

## Hindu Architecture

With the revival of Brahminism during the Gupta period, the 'Golden Period' of India, art became more purely Indian in intention and assumed a rich and varied character. To the Jains belong the credit for introduction of the dome. It is characteristic of the Jains that they mass their temples together on hill-tops, as at Palitana in Saurastra or Mount Abu in Bombay, where the temple of Vimala Sah is one of the noblest examples of the style. There are notable groups also at Khajuraho in Madhya Pradesh and at Deoghar in

Jhansi district. Later Jain work is to be seen at Sunagir, near Datia, but by this time the bulbous Moghul dome has mingled with the pyramidal spire of earlier days.

Fergusson lays it down that all that is intellectually great in India pertains to the Aryans, and all that is artistically great belongs to other stocks, notably the Dravidians. The period from the 8th century to the 13th century was a great age of temple building in India, comparable in its achievements only to the age of Gothic cathedral building in Europe. The great Hindu temples are to be found in the Dravidian south in amazing numbers and variety. The main styles are now clearly differentiated ; the northern or Brahmanical style emphasising the perpendicular, the southern or Dravidian style emphasising the horizontal, while the later Dravidian or Chalukyan style is a mixture of northern and southern styles.

The *gopurams* or gate-towers first appeared under the Cholas and are a distinctive feature of Dravidian architecture ; later they assumed gigantic proportions almost dwarfing the main building. The general impression of Chalukyan architecture is one of colossal labour and effort with a profusion of ornament which is sometimes astounding. The famous Dravidian temples are the Kailashnath of Kanchipuram, the Great Temple of Tanjore, the Vithala temple of Vijaynagar and the Meenakshi temple of Madura. The Hoysala style reaches its climax in the profusely carved temples of Mysore, at Belur, Halebid and Somnathpura.

Time was of little value when many of these buildings which we now look at with wonder were built ; and many an artist only lived that his handiwork might do honour to his god.

Apart from Bhubneswar the northern style comes into full flower in Khajuraho, in Mount Abu, in Ambarnath and, comparatively recently, in the two towers of Fame and Victory at Chittorgarh, in the palaces of Gwalior, Udaipur, Ambar and at many other places.

Hindu temples in northern India are generally smaller, simpler, and more scattered. There are few pleasanter sights in the northern plains than that of the flame-like spike of the *Sivalaya* peeping over the village trees like some country church spire in England. But the pulse of Hindu worship at its strongest is to be felt at a few famous places along the holy rivers ; notably at Hardwar where the Ganga breaks into the plain through the outer hills ; at Mathura and Brindavan where Lord Krishna descended on earth and played with His devotees ; and above all, at holy Banaras, the centre and crown of Hindu India, where there are no less than 1500 temples, all of them of smaller and simpler style.

## Muslim Style

The main development of Muslim building in India can be observed at Delhi and Agra. Nearly 800 years ago Kutb-uddin proclaimed himself emperor and built the noble Kutub Minar. To this time belongs also the Qwwatul Islam mosque, the first mosque in India, and finely decorated tomb of Altamash. The Alai Darwaza close by the Kutb pertains to the next dynasty. A few miles east are the ruins of Tuglakabad and the solitary tomb of Tuglak Shah, the outstanding figure of the 14th century. In the heart of New Delhi rise the tombs of the Lodi kings, with their low strong domes and buttressed octagonal walls. But meanwhile the Adil Shahi dynasty of Bijapur, who had a great passion for architectural edifices of every kind and purpose, built the Jama Masjid, Atala Masjid and Gol Gumbaz, splendid massive creations which rank among the finest in India.

At Mandu, in the early 15th, century the Hushang Shah dynasty built a splendid capital, which till today is majestic in ruins; and at Gujrat Ahmed Shah and his successors have left notable monuments, only surpassed by those of Bijapur.

With the coming of the Moghul the great age of Muslim building was reached. Babar certainly built, though no work of his has been identified. His son

Humayun's tomb stands out majestically in Delhi; and to Sher Shah is attributed a beautiful mosque in the Purana Kila and his own solemn tomb at Sasaram. Akbar the Great has left us not merely the great forts of Agra, Delhi and Allahabad, but the old palaces in the Agra Fort and the immortal city of Fatehpur Sikri, and his own stately tomb at Sikandra. Jahangir built himself a mosque and tomb in Lahore as well as a tomb for his minister Itimad-uddalua at Agra. But the greatest of builders was Shah Jahan who gave us not only the unequalled Taj and the great mosques both at Delhi and Agra, but also the imperial places within the fort of both capitals. (Based on an article in the Indian Number of *The Times*, 1930).

## SCULPTURE

Indian sculpture was a component part of architecture and was inspired by the same religious fervour that inspired the other arts of India. As in architecture and painting, its intention was to make the central ideas of religion and philosophy intelligible to the masses. Art was another important expression of the common culture of the people.

There is rarely any art for art's sake, for, such a basis for art is considered flimsy. In India, art lives and moves and has its very being in religion. This indissoluble link between art and religion is emphasised through the medium of sculpture and painting.

"Buddhist art radiated a spirit of Other-Worldliness, or in the narrative art, based on the Jatakas and similar source materials, a naive aud charming naturalism, while Jain images suggested the immobility of death itself. Hindu images, on other hand, though probably the work of the same craftsman, were disturbingly vital in their effect. Intensely human in action, they were at the same time much more than human". The emergence of the Pauranic imagery early in the Gupta era finally determined iconography ; the craftsman merely selected from vast store-house of episodes, established the artistic conventions and popularized the forms of polytheism by endless repetition.

An intense artistic activity swept India, ushering in a new phase in India's cultural development. When, on the passing away of the Gupta power, local dynasties sprang into prominence India was seized by an incredible craze of temple building and innumerable temples were built all over the land. Many of these mediaeval temples are still nobly intact, frequented by devout Hindus today as they have been a thousand years ago.

In the seventh and eighth centuries Indian sculpture produced a large variety of masterpieces, all of them religious and subservient to architecture. During this period "Brahmanical gods and goddesses were imbued with amazing vitality and rhythmic movement. Though the modelling was done in simplified planes, the total effect acquired a vigour suggesting movement".

The best examples are the mighty caves of Ellora with the Kailasa temple, Karli, Elephanta and Mahabalipuram. At Elephanta, the gigantic figure of Trimurti carved in deep relief in the caves, is an outstanding example of human conception and its perfect execution. The monolithic rock shrines of Mahabalipuram near Madras have some most robust sculptures. In the mediaeval period, sculpture fell into ornate use, and was made to adorn pillars, friezes and brackets in temples. Gods and goddesses were carved with a number of heads to represent their multifarious aspects. In some cases art was based on erotic themes, because the artist was supposed to identify himself with nature in all her moods, to express the essential harmony of men with nature and the universe.

## PAINTING

Painting was a widely practised art in ancient India. It existed in the pre-historic caves of central India many thousand years ago. It is frequently referred to in early Buddhist and epic literature, and in the early Indian dramas portrait of a heroine is almost a stock device. Painting reached an almost bewildering height of perfection in the frescoes of Ajanta caves painted by Buddhist monks between second century B.C. and seventh century A. D. The subjects are taken from the Jataka stories, scenes from courts and domestic life, and the life of Buddha. The other glories are Ellora and Bagh in Malwa belonging to the same period. Time and vandalism, have ravaged much of their artistic wealth but what still remains is a breath-taking wonder which, according to Signor A. Cecconi, the greatest authority on Italian fresco painting, "will bear comparison with the best that Europe could produce down to the age of Michaelangelo".

In the Middle Ages, mural painting revived in south India where temples and palaces were decorated with elaborate paintings. In the sixteenth century, Rajput miniature painting of great excellence made its appearance, which, though sometimes secular, was mainly based on popular religion and was therefore universal in appeal. Almost simultaneously and under the patronage of the Imperial Moghuls developed the exquisite school of Moghul miniature painting which, unlike Hindu painting, was essentially a secular art. It presented a rich pageant of court scenes, war and hunting episodes and studies of birds and flowers combining Persian and Indian styles.

Aurangzeb's austere fanaticism gave a death-blow to Moghul painting. But painting survived in Rajasthan and in some remote valleys of western Himalayas, particularly in Kangra, where under the patronage of Raja Sansar Chand, most charming paintings were created till the end of the nineteenth century. The Kangra school represented the finest and the last phase of Rajput painting.

About fifty years ago Bengali artists brought about a revival of Indian painting, drawing upon the past traditions of India. Abanindranath Tagore and Havell were the pioneers of the movement. Contemporary

61

Indian art abounds in outstanding painters who use forms and motifs of various countries.

## MUSIC

Music, singing and drama form part of the Hindu devotional services. Hindu hymns and prayers have been chanted since the beginning of Aryan civilisation. The deeper spirit of religion shows itself more in music than in any other art because of the elevating influence of music over the soul. With the spread of the Bhakti cult in the Middle Ages the inner spirit of Hinduism found a vivid and beautiful expression in fervid religious songs of saints and mystics. The doctrine of Bhakti inculcated the highest spiritual union with the Divine through emotional yearning and passionate love for the Supreme Being expressed in devotional songs. A great many singers of India were saints and many saints singers. Jaydev Goswami's *Gita Gobinda* which eulogises Radha's impassionate look for Krishna is a masterpiece entirely in songs.

In Bengal, 'Kirtan' which is a special kind of song relating to the Krishna legend, has the most popular appeal. Again, in the highest technical compositions as well as in folk-music the glories of Lord Krishna and other gods are eulogised.

In the Middle Ages, music was not only a court speciality, but flourished in the villages in the folk-songs and love-songs of the people ; the song of the camel-drivers on their night journeys through the deserts ; the pipes of the village musicians playing at harvests and weddings ; the flutes played at dawn on roof of the bridegroom's house, and the songs of the peasant women tending their goats on the high Himalayan pastures. Indian deserts, mountains, her moon and the loneliness of the midday sun in the plains all lend themselves to poetry and song.

## DANCE

In India, dancing did not exist as an independent art. Together with music it formed an inseparable entity of aesthetic perfection for the worship of God. It was an integral part of Vedic rituals, and in later years it was the sacred duty of the *Devadasis* (vestal virgins attached to the temples) to worship the Lord by dancing before him. The tradition survives even to this day through Bharata Natyam, a highly perfected devotional dance of South India. The *Rash Lila* (Rasa Dance) where Lord Krishna played sweet music on his flute while the Gopikas danced and sang before him is described in the most soul-stirring manner in the Bhagabat Purana. The loveliest piece of bronze that comes from South India is that of *Nataraja*, Siva dancing.

The art of classical dance received a fresh stimulus with the commentary on Bharata's Natya Sastra by Abhinabha-guptacharya in the 10th century and Jaidev's *Gita Gobinda* supplied in with popular themes based on the life of Krishna.

Essentially devotional in character, Indian classical dance is a highly perfected art. The movement of eyes, neck and arms, grace and beauty of the poses, the tilt of the head, the control of limb and gesture, and the perfect sense for the music constitute a rhythmic whole ; in fact, the entire body pulsating with rhythm is used as a medium of passionate self-expression.

There are four major schools of dancing in India : the Bharat Natyam of Tanjore, the Kathakali of Malabar, the Kathak of northern India and the Manipuri of Assam. Rukmini Devi, Shanta, Ram Gopal and Mrinalini Sarabhai, to mention only a few, are the well known exponents of Bharat Natyam. Udai Shankar has imbibed and borrowd from all the traditions and evolved a technique of dancing which preserves the purity of the classical tradition. Some of the well known troupes like the National Theatre, the Chitra players and the students of Vishwa Bharati and the Kalakshetra have used the dance drama to interpret certain aspects of India's cultural tradition.

# CHAPTER VII

# INDIAN HANDICRAFTS

Pliny, the celebrated Roman writer, once raised a storm of protest against the extravagence of his fellow-countrymen who sent the equivalent of 5,000,000 dollars every year from Rome to India for purchase of silks, brocades, muslins and clothes of gold—a reluctant and yet eloquent tribute to the antiquity and excellence of Indian handicrafts.

Art was incidental to the lives of our forefathers, and to them it was often a method of offering devotion to the gods. Ancient visitors to India were invariably impressed by their exquisite artistry and uncommon beauty, and many, beginning from Megasthenes, spoke of them in eloquent terms.

Today, as in the past, Indian craftsmen are plying their ancient trades in brass, iron, ivory, gold, silver, wood-work and textiles, and it is impossible to give even a partial catalogue of the many specialities, for every State has some distinctive form of handicrafts to show. An instinctive feeling for beauty, infinite patience and accumulated experience of centuries enable them to master the intricacies of design, the mystery of the delicate craft of weaving gold into silk, carving ivory and wood, of matching ornaments with enamel and creating out of it all a fairy-like quality.

Textiles are among the oldest and best known of

Indian handicrafts. The fame of Banaras silks and brocades travelled throughout the world for centuries. "From the looms of Banaras", wrote Lord Macualay, "went forth the most delicate silks that adorn the halls of St. James and Petit Trianon". Today they are popular among the foreigners more than ever before. Patola silk of Gujrat, in which threads are dyed in various colours, before weaving, is one of the most difficult handicraft techniques practised in India. Mysore and Bangalore produce an exuberant variety of silks, georgettes and chiffons; the shawls of Kashmir are prized throughout the world for their delicate craftsmanship. Silk-weaving is also a growing cottage industry in Bombay, Tanjore, Manipur, Murshidabad and Jaipur.

Some of the finest cotton prints come from Sanganir, a village near Jaipur and from Tanjore in Madras. The richly decorated kerchiefs of Chamba in the Kangra valley form a special embroidery—their motifs sometimes duplicating the rich Rajput paintings, while the *phulkari* or the flower work embroidery of the Punjab is exquisite for its intricate stitch.

Mysore and Travancore are famous for ivory carvings; some fine pieces also come from Murshidabad in Bengal. The ivory idols of gods and goddesses are worked out with superb craftsmanship.

Kashmir leads in wood carvings while Mysore produces highly ornate sandalwood articles of everyday use.

Carpet-making reached high watermark in Northern India under the imperial patronage of the Moghuls. Mirzapore carpets are exquisite in colour and fabric. Of them wrote Abul Fazal : "His Majesty (Akbar) has given such encouragement to this manufacture that the carpets of Persia and Tartary are thought of no more."

At Agra and Fatehpur Sikri one can see stonecraft and sculpture reaching perfection per excellence. From there the visitor can carry with him something more concrete than the melody of the Taj by moonlight—a beautiful stone replica of the mausoleum itself or a collection of finely chiselled powder-boxes, dishes, trays and paper-weights.

The stone inlaying and mosaic work led to the dovelopment of the costly art of *pietra dura* which took root in Agra where it has been handed down from father to son with the traditional fidelity of the East. "The process consists of cutting thin slices of variously coloured precious stones to the exact shape of petal, leaf or other ornament. These are cemented into white, or black marble with such exquisite precision that even a microscope fails to reveal any joint in a rose composed of sixty fragments". The first specimen of this unique art apppears on the tomb of Itmad-ud-daula, father of Nur Jahan, at Agra.

Jewellery of gold and silver, patterned exquisitely and studded with diamonds, rubies and other precious stones is an ancient art in India and each State has its distinctive specialities to offer.

The jewellery of Jaipur and Delhi is renowned for artistry : but the loveliest piece comes from Jaipur—the enamelled jewellery which has hardly any parallel in India. The silver filigree work of Cuttack is as intricate as it is fascinating.

Tanjore copper and brass bowls and exquisitely shaped metal images make excellent souvenirs while the enamelled metalware of Banaras, Moradabad and Hyderabad of lovely design and infinite variety appeal to the eye and satisfy the aesthetic urge of connoisseurs and laymen alike.

# CHAPTER VIII

# HINTS FOR TOURISTS

## Entry Formalities for Foreign Tourists

A foreign tourist entering India should be in possession of a valid passport issued by his Government. He should also obtain a visa from the Indian representative abroad (or the British representative in countries where there are no Indian representatives). They also issue a Tourist Introduction Card which secures for the tourist many facilities during his stay in India. Commonwealth citizens are exempt from the visa requirement, provided their passports are valid for travel to India. Persons of non-Indian domicile in S. Africa are, however, required to obtain entry permits. Visas for India are, unless otherwise specified, valid for a single journey only.

All non-Commonwealth tourists arriving in India are required to get themselves registered at the port of arrival and obtain certificates of registration. They will be registered as "tourists" and will not be required to inform their movements to the police or the registration authorities during their stay in India. The period for which a 'tourist' is normally allowed to stay in India is three months.

The Government of India have placed no health restrictions on persons entering India by sea or air, except in regard to yellow fever. But in their own interest the tourists are advised to be protected against small-pox and cholera according in international requirements.

## Customs

Visitors to India will find Indian Customs officials courteous and helpful. Duty payable on most articles varies from 25 per cent to 75 per cent according to the article. Personal effects are allowed to enter free. These include a reasonable quantity of films ; two cameras (including one cine) ; two watches ; 200 cigarettes ; 50 cigars ; 1 lb. of tobacco and personal jewellery of a value not exceeding Rs. 2,500.

Visitors to India may carry home souvenirs from India for themselves or for friends. These are allowed to be exported without restriction. Visitors should, however, note that export of antiquities, including old curios, is strictly controlled under the Antiquities (Export Control) Act.

Arms, motor cycles, and radio sets are dutiable. But if the tourist does not want to pay the duty, these may be kept in bond with the Customs to be collected later.

## Travel Agents

The tourist will find it convenient to entrust the clearing and forwarding of baggages to travel agents. Their expert knowledge of customs regulations, routes, modes of transport and hotel arrangements enable the tourist to enjoy a very comfortable journey to and within India. Some of the overseas travel agencies are represented in the Indian Union ; Thomas Cook and American Express have their offices in the principal cities of India. Here is a list of the principal travel agents.

AMERICAN EXPRESS CO., INC.,
    264, Dadabhai Noroji Rd., Bombay ; Pollock House, Calcutta:
    60 Janpath, New Delhi.

BALMER LAWRIE & CO., LTD.,
    21, Netaji Subhas Road, Calcutta.

BHARAT TRAVEL SERVICE LTD.,
Vanguard House, 310/311 Linghi Chetty St., Madras 1.

THOS. COOK & SON,
Thos Dadabhai Naroji Rd., Bombay.

COX & KINGS (AGENTS) LTD., .
Mission Row Extn. Calcutta ; Lloyds Bank Building, Bombay.

FLY-WINGS LTD.,
1 Netaji Subhas Road, Calcutta.

GRINDLAYS BANK LTD.,
98 Mint Road Bombay ; 4, Chruch Lane, Calcutta.

INDIA TRAVEL SERVICE LTD.,
16, Old Customs House Road, Fort, Bombay· 1.

IYER & SON LTD.,
United India Buildings, Connaught Circus, New Delhi.

JEENA & CO.,
10, Veer Nariman Rd., Bombay; Gr. Eastern Hotel, Calcutta.

LEE & MUIRHEAD (INDIA) LTD.,
12, Rampart Row, Fort, Bombay.

MERCURY TRAVELS INDIA LTD.,
Grand Hotel Calcutta; Imperial Hotel, New Delhi.

NATIONAL TRAVEL AGENCY, (INDIA)
Mercantile Buildings, 9-10, Lall Bazar, Calcutta.

ORIENT EXPRESS TRAVEL SERVICE.
Janpath, New Delhi; Norton Buildings, Calcutta.

RAM MOHAN CO. LTD.,
362, Netaji Subhas Bose Rd. Madras.

TRADE-WINGS,
30, Rampart Row, Bombay; Old Court House St. Calcutta.

## Money

Tourists are allowed to bring into India any
amount of Indian or foreign currency notes and coins
except in the cases specified below :—Bank of England
notes up to £ 10 per head ; U.S. dollar notes up to $ 45
per head ; Australian notes up to the A£ 10 per head ;
Egyptian notes up to E£ 20 per head. Tourists can
bring any amount of money in travellers' cheques, or
Bank drafts subject to export limits in their own
countries.

Tourists have to make a declaration in the prescribed form to the Customs authorities and to get it

countersigned by them. Currency in excess of the prescribed limits can be deposited with the Customs and a receipt obtained. At the time of leaving India, tourist can take back the money on production of the receipt. It is unlawful to transact business except through an authorized dealer in foreign exchange.

The official rates of exchange are :

£ 1—Rs. 13.33        $ 1—Rs. 4.76

Buying and selling rates of the banks will, however, be a fraction less or more than the official rates.

## Indian Currency

The monetary unit is the Rupee (16 annas) which equals to approximately 21c in U.S. and 1s. 6d. in British currency. There are money changers at air ports and leading hotels. The Indian currency consists of the Reserve Bank of India notes in denominations of Rs. 100, 10, 5, 2 and Re. 1. Coins are : 1 pice, half anna (two pice), 1 anna, 2 annas, 4 annas, 8 annas, 1 rupee. Based on the average rate of exchange, the rupee equivalents are :

| Indian | British | American |
|---|---|---|
| 1 pice | 1 farthing | ...... |
| 4 pice-1 anna | 1 penny (approx) | ...... |
| 16 annas-1 rupee | 1s. 6d. | 21 cents |
| 13 rupees 6 annas | £ 1 sterling | ...... |
| 4 rupees 12 annas (approx.) | | 1 dollar |

India's new coinage scheme—The Naye Paisa—has come into force from April 1, 1957. Under this scheme, there will be seven new coins in use. These are :

| | |
|---|---|
| 1 Rupee...100 Naye Paise | 8 Annas...50 Naye Paise |
| 4 Annas....25 Naye Paise | 3 Annas...19 Naye Paise |
| 2 Annas....12 Naye Paise | 1 Anna... 6 Naye Paise |

½ Anna...3 Naye Paise

The rupee will remain the standard coin with no loss or gain in its value. The changeover from the old to the old and the new coins will be current. During this period payments can be made or accepted either in new or old coins or in both.

## Postal Information

Post offices are open throughout India on week days between 10 A.M. to 5 P. M; on Saturdays 10 A.M. to 1 P. M. Not much work is transacted on Sundays but at important places like Calcutta, Bombay, Madras, Delhi, Kanpur, Banaras, Sholapur, Ahmedabad, Hyderabad, Indore and Jaipur post offices are opon on Sundays also and do all transactions except Savings Bank and delivery. In Calcutta there are a number of night post offices including the one at Esplanade East.

## "Air Letter" Service

A light weight "Air letter" service is available for writing to all countries served by the air mail. The postage rates are 3 annas to Ceylon and Pakistan, 5 annas to Afghanistan and Burma, 6 annas to rest of Asia and to Europe, 8 annas to Africa and to Oceania (that is, Australia, New Zealand, Fiji, etc.) and 10 annas to North and South America.

## Telegram & Telephone

Telegrams are accepted at principal telegraph offices and main post offices on all days of the week at all hours. There is a net-work of inland and overseas telephone system throughout India and radio telephones in big cities.

## Liquor Permits

India is a temperate country where society and Government discourage wine drinking among Indians. Complete prohibition exists in Bombay and Madras States and in the city of Delhi. But there is no restriction for foreign tourists coming from countries where drinking is a matter of course and social behaviour. To such tourists are issued temporary Liquor Permits on production of which the tourists can obtain liquor from wine dealers and drink in their rooms. In other States the tourists can freely obtain drinks.

## Conveyance

Taxis are readily available at all principal cities and are the most popular transport. In India bus services are admirably organised all over the country. Besides the government bus services, there are very efficient private services from town to town and from region to region, even lining up those remote places not accessible by other means. At Delhi, Bombay and Calcutta and Banaras special tourist cars are available for sight-seeing through the Tourist Information Offices.

## Books & Literature

There is a vast range of books on India and Indian culture including guide books and tourist maps. These are available from the leading book-sellers, such as, Oxford Book & Stationery Co., Calcutta, New Delhi and Darjeeling ; Newmans and Thacker Spink & Co., Calcutta ; New Book Depot and E.D. Galgotia & Co., Connaught Place, New Delhi ; Taraporawalla Sons & Co., Popular Book Depot and New Book Co., Bombay.

## Information & Guides

In big cities and in most places of historic interest, educated guides are available through Government Tourist offices and travel agents. Their employment is advisable, as apart from their special knowledge a well-known guide has the *entree* to places which might be closed to the unescorted visitor. In addition, guide lecturers of the Archaeological Department are available at Ajanta, Ellora, Mandu, Sarnath and Nalanda.

Indians, as a rule, are a very hospitable and informal people, and a courteous request for information will meet with a ready response. Whether he is a polished city dweller or an unsophisticated villager, all are willing to help.

## Climate, Dress & Health Hints

The months from November to March are the most pleasant for travel in India. In some parts of Northern India, where the temperature falls between

72

40° to 50° in the evening, real winter clothing is necessary, and one has to be on guard against the risk of serious chills. It is said that more illness is contacted from chills in India than from the heat. Heavy winter clothing will be necessary if it is intended to visit any hill-station during the winter, Light suits or warm tropicals are sufficient for use in Calcutta and Bombay and throughout the South. During the summer months thin tropical or linen clothing may be used. It is also necessary then to be provided with solar hats and sun-glasses, as over exposure to the sun will result in severe burning and may often produce sun-stroke.

## Language

There is no language difficulty. Although as many as 250 dialects are spoken in India, English is the common language, spoken at its best by all educated people and also understood and spoken by hotel attendants, tourist guides, taxi-drivers and shopkeepers. Most of the leading newspapers and periodicals are published in English and so are the Government papers, railway and airline time-tables. French is spoken by many including some tourist-guides and shop attendants. Bar-tenders attached to the leading hotels of Calcutta, Delhi and Bombay speak many of the Continental languages.

## Hotels & Accommodation

In all the principal cities of India there are good hotels which provide good food and comfortable accommodation in Western style without dispensing with personalised service and traditional Indian hospitality. Daily charges in Calcutta, Delhi, Bombay and Madras vary from Rs. 16/- to Rs. 40/- per head while charges for de-luxe (airconditioned) suites in the big hotels of those cities range from Rs. 70/- to Rs. 100/- per day. Charges of other Western style hotels in different parts of India and Guest Houses and Circuit Houses in Rajasthan (also Western style) are still cheaper. In small towns and out-of-the-way places of tourist interest are the State Guest Houses, Dak Bungalows and Rest Houses where foreign tourists are given top priority. The bed-rooms in the Dak Bungalows have adjoining bath-rooms and are provided with reasonably good furniture and light. The keeper of the Dak Bungalow provides meals.

At many railway stations there are good retiring rooms for the use of upper class passengers on payment of prescribed charges. Arrangements for meals can be made through the keeper of the station restaurant. India is a land of plenty ; supplies of eggs, fowls, milk, fruits, vegetables and grains can be easily obtained at inconceivably cheaper price in any village of India. 'Tourist Introduction Card' issued by the Regional Tourist Officers will be useful for purposes of reservation in hotels, Dak Bungalows, Rest Houses and Railway Retiring Rooms.

## Travelling Servants

A travelling servant, though not an absolute necessity, is well worth the expense. He is at once a valet and an interpreter, and will be found useful in the interior. Registered servants are available from the leading travel agents, such as, Thomas Cook & Son, and American Express Co.

## Behaviour

"Anyone who has the good sense to realize that what is customary in one country is not necessarily customary in another will get off on the right foot. Here are a few examples. Do not expect an Indian woman to behave as a British or American woman. She has been brought up differently and is much more reserved. She will not thank you if you will try to make her acquaintance without a formal introduction. She may even misunderstand if, with the best of intentions in the world, you try to help her off a bus.

Do not be surprised if, when you are invited to an Indian house, there are no women present : it sometime happens that they do not meet casual visitors, especially males.

For the rest it is a matter of good taste. Do not use the word 'native' which in India is regarded as a term of contempt. Do not make the elementary mistake of thinking that an Indian is essentially different from yourself merely because his skin is of a different colour. (Remember that he was a civilised person when your own ancestors were living in caves and beating their mates with clubs). Be careful to obey instructions about entry into temples and mosques. Take your shoes off (where necessary) and do not trespass beyond prescribed limits.

Broadly speaking, the Indian is more sensitive than the Westerner ; his feelings are more quickly hurt and he responds more quickly to courtesy and generosity. An Indian, once he is your friend, is capable of self-sacrifice that is beyond the imagination of the West." (From *Introduction to India* by F.R. Moraes and Robert Stimson : Oxford University Press)

## Tourist Introduction Card

The Ministry of Transport (Tourist Traffic Branch) seeks to ensure reasonable amenities to foreign tourists and furnish them information and literature pertaining to travel in India. The Regional Tourist Officers at the major cities look to the convenience of the tourists. A Tourist Introduction Card is issued to all overseas visitors to enable them to secure prompt customs clearance, reservations on the railways and airlines, in hotels and Dak Bungalows and assistance during visits to museums, ancient monuments and other places of interest.

# CHAPTER IX

# TRANSPORT

## AIR SERVICE

The air services of India are admirably organised. To quote an experienced globe-trotter, "They can challenge comparison with the finest in the world for safety, for comfort and for civility". Using Skymasters, Vikings aad Dacotas, the Indian Airlines Corporation (owned and operated by the Government of India) operates regular schedules throughout the country forming a thorough net-work, complete and efficient; and in the words of the same foreign visitor "it is a delight to go to the air centres and find oneself treated as a valuable customer and not as a regrettable interruption to the more important affairs of life". Thanks to the IAC one can enjoy all the attractions of this vast country in a limited time by air using automobile or bus service for trips to the interior.

There are lounges and restaurants at all the main airports and the airlines provide hostess service and good cuisine during flight. Free transport between the aerodromes and principal hotels and *vice versa* is available almost everywhere.

There are several private companies and flying clubs who have machines available for internal flight. All flying is controlled by Civil Aviation Directorate.

# INDIAN RAILWAYS

India is a land of vast distances. From Bombay, where the fast mail trains steam away from the ships side at Ballard Pier, to Amritsar, where the bearded sturdy Sikh ably guards India's frontier, the distance is 1275 miles. Should the traveller fare east he will have to traverse 1341 miles before he arrives at Howrah Bridge which is his gateway to Calcutta, the largest city of India. Southward from the capital of India to Madras, and so to Dhanushkodi, the nearest point to Ceylon, is a distance of 1768 miles.

To cover such distances as these the Indian Railways have flung their net-work across the country. Its 34,200 miles of track are India's life-lines. The Indian railway system is the largest in Asia and the fourth largest in the world, exceeded only by the United States, the Soviet Union and Canada. In comfort and service it is second to none in the world.

## Tourist Facilities

Indian railways provides special facilities for tourists and the staff is instructed to look to their comforts. In addition to the comprehensive organisation maintained by the Railways, the recognised travel agents also are equipped to make the fullest travel arrangements for tourists, particularly on an inclusive cost basis, that is : Railway fares, conveyance, hotels sight-seeing, guides, etc.

Dining cars are attached to most of the mail and express trains. On trains on which there are no dining-cars, meals can be obtained at refreshment rooms at the more important stations where longer hauls are provided to enable passengers to take their meals. It is generally advisable to get the guard of the train to wire ahead that meals are required. Food is served in Western style both in dining-cars and refreshment rooms.

## Tourist Cars

For those to whom expense is not of primary

importance and who wish to be independent of hotels, comfortable tourist cars can be reserved. Popularly known as 'hotels on wheels', these cars are designed to provide the maximum space possible for the comfort of the tourists. The tourists can have their personal servants, private parlour and bedroom throughout the trip : meals are in the way in which they desire them and they can dictate the menu in the same way as they do in their homes.

There is accommodation for eight persons generally in a tourist car on the Broad Gauge system and for six only on the Metre Gauge. Coaches can be cut off at any place the tourists wish and they may stay as long as they like.

The cost per head for travel in these tourist cars and saloons works out at a little over 50% over the first class fare. For big parties special tourist trains are available at a little over double the first class fare. The railways concerned quote the final rates on request.

## Air-Conditioned Coaches

Air-conditioned coaches, luxuriously appointed, are available on Calcutta-Nagpur-Bombay, Calcutta-Allahabad-Bombay, Calcutta-Delhi-Kalka, Bombay-Delhi, Bombay-Amritsar, Calcutta-Amritsar, Bombay-Madras, Calcutta-Madras, Delhi-Madras. Bombay-Viramgam, Bombay-Ahmedabad and Delhi-Pathankot routes. Berths in air-conditioned coaches may be reserved up to one month in advance of the journey.

## First & Second Classes

First and second class passengers are provided with sleeping accommodation at night on payment of only as -/8/- extra per ticket. At all terminal stations and at important roadside stations berths may be reserved, in advance, for the night journey only. Beddings can be arranged, at a small charge, for passengers travelling by specified trains on the Calcutta-Delhi, Calcutta-Bombay and Delhi-Bombay routes. Each first and second class compartment is provided with a toilet. Third class passengers travelling long distances can also reserve sitting accommodation on certain mail and express trains on payment of an additional amount of as -/4/-. For the convenience of long-distance passengers special compartments are ear-marked on certain trains.

## Third Class

The introduction of Janata Express trains has made third class travel much more comfortable with better accommodation and facilities, and greater speed. Third class passengers can reserve their seats in advance for long-distance travel.

## Special Concessions in Fares

One important concession in fares allowed by the Indian Railways for the benefit of tourists, is for journey to the hill stations. Return tickets, valid for 3 months, are issued for First, Second, and Third classes at a concession of one and half single journey fares during the seven-month period—April 1 to October 31. Another attractive concession is for circular tours of 1,500 miles or over at three-fourths of tariff fares for passengers of all classes. There are also fixed itineraries with fixed charges which may be obtained from the railways concerned.

## Luggage

The free allowance for luggage is :

| | |
|---|---|
| Air-Conditioned and 1st Class ... | 60 Seers |
| 2nd Class ... ... | 40 Seers |
| Third Class ... ... | 25 Seers |

exclusive of bedding.

## Break of Journey

A passenger, irrespective of the class in which he travels, is permitted to break journey at any station *en route* at the rate of one day for every 100 miles or part of 100 miles, in addition to the time occupied by the journey, provided that he holds a ticket covering more than 200 miles of single journey. The first break of journey may not, however, be made until a distance of 150 miles has been travelled from the starting station.

# IMPORTANT MAIL & EXPRESS TRAINS

## Central Railway : Bombay (V. T.)

The following daily mail and express trains run from Victoria Terminus, Bombay, the terminus of the Central Railway.

Calcutta Mail : Bombay-Bhusaval-Nagpur-Howrah

Dehra Dun Exp. : Bombay (C) Ratlam-Mathura-Delhi-Saharanpur-Laksar-Hardwar-Dehra Dun

Punjab Mail : Bombay-Bhopal-Agra-Delhi-Bhatinda-Ferozepur

Pathankot Exp. : Bombay-Jhansi-Delhi-Amritsar-Pathankot

Poona Mail : Bombay-Poona-Hubli-Harihar-Bangalore

Madras Mail : Bombay-Poona-Raichur-Bangalore-Madras(C)

Kasi Exp. : Bombay-Bhusaval-Khandwa-Itarsi-Allahabad-Kasi.

## Western Railway : Bombay (Cent.)

The following mail trains run from Bombay Central station, the terminus of the Western Railway.

Frontier Mail : Bombay (C.)-Baroda-Ratlam-Delhi-Amritsar

Gujarat Mail : Bombay (C.)-Baroda-Ahmedabad

Saurastra Mail : Bombay (C)-Baroda-Ahmedabad-Viramgam

## Eastern Railway : Calcutta

The following mail trains run from Howrah, the terminus of the Eastern Railway :

Amritsar Mail : Howrah-Patna-Banaras-Lucknow-Amritsar

Delhi Mail : Howrah-Allahabad-Delhi-Ambala-Kalka

Doon Exp. : Howrah-Banaras-Lucknow-Hardwar-Dehra Dun

Bombay Mail : Howrah-Allahabad-Itarsi-Bombay

Toofan Exp. : Howrah-Gaya--Tundla-Agra-Mathura-Delhi

Janata Exp. : Howrah-Patna-Allahabad-Delhi

## South-Eastern Railway : Calcutta

The following mail trains run daily from Howrah, the terminus of the South-Eastern Railway.

Bombay Mail : Howrah-Nagpur-Bhusawal-Bombay (V.T.)
Madras Mail: Howrah-Cuttack-Waltair-Bezwada-Madras (C)
Puri Exp. : Howrah-Cuttack-Khurda Road-Puri
Janata Exp. : Howrah-Cuttack-Waltair-Bezwada-Madras.

## Southern Railway : Madras

The two terminal stations of the Southern Railway are the Madras Central station and Egmore station ; the mail and express trains that run from these stations are the following:

Nilgiri Exp. : Madras Central-Mettupalayam
(change)-Ootacamund
Trivandrum Exp. : Madras Egmore-Chingleput-Tiruchira-
pally-Kodaikanal-Madurai-Quilon-Trivandrum
Indo-Ceylon Exp. : Madras-Kombakonam-Tanjore-Dhanus-
kodi

## Northern Railway : Delhi

Delhi is the headquarters station of the Northern Railway. The following trains are important:

Grand T. Exp. : Delhi-Nagpur-Ballarshah-Bezwada-Madras
Kashmir Mail : Delhi-Kurukshetra-Amritsar-Pathankot
Janata Exp .: Delhi-Nagpur-Bezwada-Madras
Mussoorie Exp. : Delhi-Saharanpur-Dehra Dun (Bus for
Mussoorie)
Bikaner Mail : Delhi-Rewari-Loharu-Sadulpur-Bikaner

## North-Eastern Railway : Gorakhpur

Gorakhpur (Uttar Pradesh) is the headquarters of the N. E. R. The following are the important express trains:

Agra Exp. : Katihar-Gorakhpur-Lucknow-Kanpur-Kasganj-
Mathura-Agra Fort
Kumayun Exp. : Agra-Mathura-Bareilly-Bhojeepura-
Kathgodam
Nainital Exp. : Lucknow-Bareilly-Kathgodam (Bus for
Nainital)

# SOME DISTANCES BY RAIL

| FROM | TO | | | |
|---|---|---|---|---|
| | Calcutta | Bombay | Delhi | Madras |
| AGRA | 786 | 835 | 122 | 1239 |
| AHMEDABAD | 1328 | 306 | 540 | 1100 |
| ALLAHABAD | 505 | 845 | 391 | 1251 |
| AURANGABAD | 1133 | 233 | 566 | 801 |
| BANGALORE | 1254 | 695 | 1446 | 222 |
| BANARAS | 422 | 942 | 473 | 1335 |
| BOMBAY | 1223 | — | 861 | 794 |
| CALCUTTA | — | 1223 | 895 | 1032 |
| DARJEELING | 416 | 1598 | 966 | 1448 |
| DELHI | 895 | 957 | — | 1361 |
| DIBRUGARH | 979 | 2111 | 1529 | 2011 |
| GAYA | 285 | 1057 | 611 | 1251 |
| GWALIOR | 801 | 763 | 195 | 1167 |
| HYDERABAD | 987 | 401 | 1044 | 491 |
| JAIPUR | 933 | 720 | 191 | 1552 |
| JABALPORE | 725 | 616 | 572 | 1021 |
| LUCKNOW | 606 | 885 | 303 | 1376 |
| MADRAS | 1032 | 794 | 1361 | — |
| MYSORE | 1339 | 781 | 1529 | 308 |
| MADURAI | 1337 | 1099 | 1706 | 308 |
| MATHURA | 819 | 868 | 90 | 1272 |
| NAGPUR | 703 | 520 | 679 | 682 |
| OOTACAMUND | 1448 | 1125 | 2259 | 908 |
| PATHANKOT | 1196 | 1302 | 301 | 1706 |
| POONA | 1276 | 119 | 989 | 675 |
| PURI | 310 | 1309 | 1460 | 776 |
| SIMLA | 1335 | 1180 | 440 | 1801 |
| TIRUCHIRAPALLY | 1241 | 1003 | 1610 | 249 |
| TRIVANDRUM | 1544 | 1306 | 1913 | 779 |

For distances of 500 miles or more, average speeds are 45 m.p.h. for mail and 40 miles for express trains.

# ABBREVIATIONS USED

| | | |
|---|---|---|
| Accom. | | Accommodation |
| Com. | | Communication |
| C. H. | ... | Circuit House |
| B. S. | ... | Bus Service |
| I. A. S. | ... | Indian Airlines Corporation |
| Jn. | ... | Junction |
| m. | ... | Miles |
| D. B. | ... | Dak Bungalow |
| R. H. | ... | Rest House |
| R. | ... | Railway |
| E. R. | ... | Eastern Railway |
| N. R. | ... | Northern Railway |
| N. E. R. | ... | North Eastern Railway |
| W. R. | ... | Western Railway |
| C. R. | ... | Central Railway |
| S. R. | ... | Southern Railway |
| S. E. R. | ... | South-Eastern Railway |

# GLOSSARY OF INDIAN TERMS

Chattri, structure erected in honour of a high personage
Darwaza, high gateway
Dharamsala, place of free accommodation
Ekka, cart drawn by one pony
Ghari, horse carriage
Ghat, bathing place on riverside ; range of hills
Johar, self-sacrifice on fire practised by Rajput women
Khansama, a butler, a cook, a table servant
Lingam, a stone symbol of Siva
Math, monastery
Mela, a fair
Sangam, confluence of rivers
Stupa, tower containing holy relics
Vihara, Buddhist monastery
Chaitya, Buddhist temple

## PART TWO

# CHAPTER I

# EASTERN INDIA

\* \* \* \* \* \* \* \* \* \* \* \* \* \* \* \* \* \* \* \* \* \* \* \* \* \* \* \* \* \* \* \*

*Land of mighty rivers, of most fertile stretches yielding great crops of rice, wheat, yellow mustard, tea and a score of other crops, interspersed with groves of mango and bamboo trees and cocoanut and palm, and blessed with all the riches that Nature and human endeavour could combinedly provide, Eastern India is the centre of agricultural, mineral, industrial and cultural possessions of India.*

*The two great life-giving streams—the Ganges and the Brahmaputra—sustained all the year round by the Himalayan snows, wind their majestic current through the centre of the immense level which swarms with life while over its eastern fringe rise the great snowy heights of the majestic Himalayas as if to shut it behind a gigantic wall. Further south is Calcutta, the great commercial and cultural centre of India, which dwarfs the largest conception of Lancashire.*

\* \* \* \* \* \* \* \* \* \* \* \* \* \* \* \* \* \* \* \* \* \* \* \* \* \* \* \* \* \* \* \*

## CALCUTTA

**History :** Standing on a huge cake of land along the Ganges delta is the great city of Calcutta, the metropolis of India's culture, politics and industry. A city of great variety, it satisfies so many tastes. Her great academies of culture, priceless galleries of art and architecture, archives of a rich literature, theatre and music, lively festivals and colourful customs and last but not least her giant industry and commerce have earned for her the proud term the 'Jewel of India' to whom the entire country turns in homage.

Since Job Charnock, the British merchant adventurer, sailed up the river and founded the city in 1690, Calcutta progressed at a romantic speed. Increasing foreign trade, influx of traders, foreigners, missionaries, and scholars and above all, the military and political achievements of the British rulers, who made Calcutta their capital, evolved the city at the end of the 18th century into the most characteristically Western of all Eastern cities. So it was that in the middle of the 19th century Calcutta was not only the greatest city in India but one of the greatest in the world.

Calcutta is a city of immensities. Wharves fitted with modern contrivances to facilitate the loading and unloading of vessels hum with activity. The din of traffic and huge workshops turning out engineering products of every description adds to the clangour and bustle ; and in spite of the shifting of the capital to Delhi, Calcutta continues to be the premier city of India, "the London of the East". Its friendly and hospitable people, varied charms and startling contrasts—fabulous luxury and abominable misery, high intellect and ignorance abounding, magnificent palaces and stinking slums—all these are objects of mystery and permanent interest to all.

In the economic and industrial fields the city's leadership is striking. Even after the partition, West Bengal is the largest industrial area of India and contains 23% of the factories registered in the Indian Union. Extending over an area of 45 miles along both sides of the river Hooghly there are 104 giant jute mills employing over 2,10,000 persons and producing goods valued at over Rs. 120 crore, 467 sugar mills, 377 rice mills, 17 iron and sheet mills, 32 cotton mills, 68 medical and chemical works and a thousand other industries providing employment to well over one-fourth of the country's entire industrial labour.

Vast quantities of tea from the gardens of Darjeeling and Assam and as much as 15.491 million tons of coal of Bihar and Bengal are yearly carried from the mines which are managed by companies having their offices in Calcutta.

Equipped with the most modern machinery, the Port of Calcutta, one of the world's largest, has a warehouse area of 60 lakh sq. ft. and everyday accommodates a colourful variety of ships that the East and the West can show. All this trade is controlled by the Commissioner for the Port of Calcutta, who earned a profit of Rs. 36.89 lakh during 1952-53 alone. 1,503 vessels entering the port totalled 1,873,891 gross tons in 1952-53, while the total imports of goods were nearly 3,319,018 tons, and the exports were 6,354,058 tons.

## Places of Interest in and around Calcutta

Calcutta is like London in that it is a great port and that it can provide such a wealth of interest, so many beautiful, impressive and curious sights, so many diversions, occupations, entertainments and pursuits, that to be in Calcutta might be considered not only a privilege but almost a profession.

**Government House :** At the northern end of the Maidan, near Esplanade, stands the stately Government House, the residence of the State Governor and the venue of many social and cultural functions. The building abounds with a number of famous paintings, busts and objects of historic interest.

**Dalhousie Square :** From the Government House only a few steps northward, and one is in the midst of frenzied crowd, almost hysterical, which is the business community of the city. This is called Dalhousie square where imposing mercantile buildings and Government houses, standing close to each other around a fine tank, shape the economic and political pattern of the country. Looking at the seething malestorm of city's business life and the endless flow of traffic it was here that a British Viceroy once exclaimed : "Here I feel the pulse of human life".

**Chowringhee :** The scene then shifts to the famous Chowringhee, the beautiful wide avenue flanked on one side by fashionable shops, hotels, cinemas, restaurants and clubs and on the other by the green meadows of the Maidan, most wonderful of open spaces. At the back of Chowringhee is New Market, the most fashionable and systematised shopping centre in the East.

**Ochterlony Monument :** On the Maidan, opposite the Grand Hotel, rises the Ochterlony Monument, the city's outstanding landmark commanding a splendid view of the city and its environs. 165 ft. in height, the monument was erected in 1828 to commemorate Major-General Sir David Ochterlony's victory in Nepal. The visitor can ascend the top with the formal permission of the Commissioner of Police.

**Fort William :** Occupying a strategic position on the Maidan on the one side and river on the other is the bomb-proof, underground fort—Fort William—considered one of the finest of its type in the world. It has six gates and is capable of accommodating 10,000 men. Inside it, there are markets, cinemas, swimming pool, firing range, parade and football grounds, church, post and telegraph office and a military prison. The tourist can visit the Fort by permission.

**Victoria Memorial :** Standing majestically on the south end of the Maidan is the Victoria Memorial, the marble monument erected to the memory of the great sovereign whose name it bears. Built by Lord Curzon in 1921 at a cost of Rs. 76 lakh as a replica of the famous Taj Mahal at Agra, the Memorial is regarded as one of the great buildings of the modern world and is the repository of a priceless collection of pictures, statues and historical documents and other objects of art and interest illustrative of Indian history in general and the Victorian era in particular. The spacious grounds around the building are well laid out with exquisite flower beds, wide lawns and gleaming stretches of water, which all make it one of Calcutta's pre-eminent show-place.

**Indian Museum :** The magnificent building with a frontage of over 300 ft. along the Chowringhee Road is the Indian Museum, one of the largest museums of the world. A veritable treasure-house of knowledge, the Museum contains rare collections, illustrative of Indian art and archaeology, natural history, coins and manuscripts, jewels, busts, engraving and other objects of absorbing interest.

**The Zoo :** To the south of the Race Course lies the famous Zoo, one of the world's largest, which maintains rare specimens of animals, birds and reptiles collected from all parts of the world. There is a restaurant which serves light refreshments in Western style (daily open between sun rise and sun set). Not far from the Zoo stands the **Belvedere Palace,** a historic building which now accommodates the National Library, the largest repository of books and rare manuscripts in the East. To the south of Belvedere are the **Agri-Hoticultural Gardens** which present a charming picture in the flovering season. Flower shows are annual events.

**Howrah Bridge :** The third largest cantilever bridge in the world, the Howrah Bridge was completed in the year 1943 at a cost of Rs. 32,200,060. It is the only road link between Calcutta and Howrah, India's busiest and biggest railway terminus. The bridge is worth a visit.

**Botanical Garden :** On the west bank of the Hooghly and approximately three miles south of the Howrah Bridge is situated the extensive Botanical Garden. It is more pleasant to reach the place by steamer from Chandpal Ghat. It has an area of 272 acres and a river frontage of about a mile. The Garden with its scenic

beauty, delightfully cool river breeze and different specimens of plant life, is a welcome retreat to the citizens of
Calcutta from the noise and bustle of city life. No one
has better described the beauties of the garden than the
poet Bishop Heber who saw it over a century ago. Said
he: "It is not only a curious but picturesque and most
beautiful scene which perfectly answers Milton's idea of
Paradise, except that it is on a dead flat instead of on a hill,
than anything I ever saw". There is a Herbarium and a
rich Botanic library in the garden.

**Jain Temple :** The Jain Temple, popularly
known as Parashnath Mandir, is situated at Budreedas
Temple St. in Manicktala at the eastern end of the city.
No visit to Calcutta is complete without a pilgrimage
to this holy sanctuary which for architectural abandon and
sublime tranquillity is unsurpassed in the city. Built in
1867 by Rai Budree Das Bahadur, Mookim and Court
Jeweller to the Viceroy, the temple stands on a fascinating
fairy-like garden and bewilders the eye with fantastic
beauty and extravagant sparkle of kaleidoscopic light.
Within the sanctuary, directly under the spire, is the altar
set with diamonds, rubies and other precious stones on
which reposes Sitalnathji, to whom the temple is dedicated, in serene calm and constantly garlanded with rich
fragrant roses.

**Marble Palace :** Situated at 50 Muktaram Babu
Street in Central Calcutta, the Marble Palace is the
residence of the famous Mullick family whose proverbial
charities have earned for them immortal fame. But the
Palace is more famous for its priceless treasures of art,
statues, pictures and oil paintings. Among the paintings
are two by Rubens—"The martyrdom of St. Sebastian"
and "Marriage of St. Catherine"—which deserve special
attention. The owner refused an offer of £ 15,000 for the
last named painting.

**Kalighat Temple :** About one and half a mile
south of the Victoria Memorial, in the midst of a congested Indian residential quarter stands the Kalighat
Temple built in 1809 in mediaeval Bengali architectural

style. Kali is the patron goddess of the Saktas and the Tantric Hindus, and in Calcutta she is worshipped as the presiding deity. A little over a mile to the south of the Kali temple lies the **Dhakuria Lake** adorned with tiny islands joined by a suspension bridge to the mainland. It has an idyllic setting with swaying palm trees, a lovely children's park and numerous open lawns all of which combine to make it an ideal place for restful relaxation. On the eastern shore of the Lake is the **Buddhist Temple** built by the Japanese Buddhists and now maintained by their Indian co-religionists. The chime of a big bell in evening coupled with the chanting of hymns provides a mystical atmosphere conducive to meditation.

**Kali Temple of Dakshineswar :** Above the Bally Bridge, on the east bank of the river, 7 m. from Calcutta, is situated the Dakshineswar temple which is a great place of pilgrimage of the Hindus. It was here that Sri Ramkrishna dedicated himself to meditation and attained *Moksha* for the good of humanity.

**Belur Math :** On the west bank of the river Hooghly, across the Bally Bridge, stands the magnificent Hindu monastery—the Belur Math—which was built by the donation of an American lady in honour of Sri Ramkrishna and his notable disciple Swami Vivekananda, who earned immortal fame at the Parliament of Religions held at Chicago. The temple at once represents a church, a mosque and a temple when viewed from different angles. This is the headquarters of the Ramkrishna Mission, India's greatest philanthropic organisation.

**Nakhoda Mosque :** The largest Mohammedan mosque in Calcutta is the Nakhoda Mosque, a stately prayer house of distinctive oriental design capable of accommodating 10,000 worshippers at a time. Its majestic dome and two lofty minarets, each 151 ft. high, add to the grandeur of the 'City of Palaces.'

Other places of interest are : the Asiatic Society,

the greatest centre for Oriental study at Park Street;
Calcutta University at College Street; Science College
and Bose Institute at Upper Circular Road; Mahajati
Sadan, founded by Netaji Subhas Bose, on Chittaranjan
Avenue; the new Mint House at Behala and, of course,
the Tagore House at Jorasanko.

## Excursions from Calcutta

**Diamond Harbour :** 30 miles to the south of
Calcutta is Diamond Harbour where the river Ganga
lends herself to a panoramic expansion before meeting
the Bay of Bengal another 30 miles ahead. Noted for
scenic beauty, it is a favourite place for sightseeing and
picnic. It is accessible by bus or by train from
Sealdah. Food and drink should be carried along as there
is no good restaurant there.

**Dum Dum :** Seven miles from Calcutta is Dum
Dum, well known for its great air port. Dum Dum was
once the favourite country residence of Clive and his
old house can be seen on the west side of the Dum Dum
road (4 miles) in a neglected large compound.

**Barrackpore :** About 14 miles from Calcutta is
Barrackpore where the Gandhi Ghat on the Ganga
has become a veritable place of pilgrimage. It attracts
a large crowd of admirers on the birth and death
anniversaries of Mahatma Gandhi. The Ghat is of
considerable architectural interest as well. The other
object of interest is the Government House which is
picturesquely situated on an extensive garden on the
river-bank, the greater portion of which is open to the
public. Barrackpore can be reached either by road or by
steamer from the Strand Road ghat.

**Chinsura :** 28 miles by road or rail is Chinsura, headquarters of the Commissioner of the Burdwan Division.
It was an old Dutch settlement and got in exchange
for Sumatra by the British in 1824. The fort and the
Government House were demolished and English barracks constructed in their place. The visitor can see the

quaint old Dutch church built in 1767 and another older church dating from 1695.

**Bandel Church :** Two miles further north is Hooghly which contains the Imambara, an imposing edifice built in honour of Mohamed Mahsin who gave away his vast fortune for charities and educational advancement. About a mile to the north of the Imambara is the noted Bandel Church (Roman Catholic) on the river bank which is the oldest place of Christian worship in Bengal (1599 A.D.) In 1629, Emperor Shah Jahan's wrath fell on the Portuguese community of Bandel, the fortification and the entire establishment were demolished and over a thousand captives—men, women and children—including the Chief Priest were carried to Agra where the Emperor ordered a monstrous persecution of the Christians. At last the Emperor was impressed by the religious merit of the Prior and granted him full liberty to return to Bandel and preach the Christian faith throughout the kingdom. The Emperor also made a gift of 777 bighas of land in the village of Bandel surrounding the monastery and gave power to administer justice within that area. The monastery today is a solemn place of worship and attracts a large number of worshippers and sightseers.

### Cruises and the Hooghly

The visitor to Calcutta must not miss the pleasure of an excursion to its great and historic river. The most refreshing trips are: to Botanical Gardens, Matiaburuz and Rajgunge from Chandpal Ghat. There are regular steamer services to many places up and down the river. There are services to Uttarpara and Bally, the site of the Wellingdon Bridge. The steamer service is almost half-hourly practically the whole day.

\*     \*     \*     \*     \*

COMM : Calcutta (Howrah) is the terminus of the Eastern Railway, and the South-Eastern Railway as well. Numerous mail and express trains directly connect the city with almost all the cities and towns of India. The other railway station of the city is Sealdah, the gateway to East Pakistan. Trains for Darjeeling and Assam, India's easternmost State start from here. From Dum Dum, seven miles east of the city, the Indian Airlines Corporation operates a network of air services throughout India while about a dozen international airlines operate overseas air services directly linking every important part of the world.

CONVEYANCE : Calcutta provides the cheapest, quickest and the most comfortable transport in the East. Taxies are numerous and the best mode of transport. In addition, the city's trams and buses are remarkable for comfort and efficiency. Conveyances are plentiful and cheap. The Regional Tourist Officer provides special tourist cars for the tourists.

SHOPPING : New Market is the fashionable shopping centre. The other centres are College Street Market and Burrabazar. Prices are more or less fixed. Shops are closed after 8.45 P.M.

# CALCUTTA : GENERAL INFORMATION

## HOTELS (Western Style)

Grand Hotel
  Chowringhee Rd.
Great Eastern Hotel
  Old Court House St.
Spences Hotel
  Wellesley Place
Continental Hotel
  12 Chowringhee Rd.
Russel Hotel
  Russel Street.

### Indian & Euro. style

Asian Hotel.
  Princep St.
Broadway Hotel
  Mission Row, Extn.
Hotel Minerva,
  Mission Row Extn.
Wedgewood Hotel
  Sudder Street.

### Indian style

Ideal Home (Bengal style)
  63/2A Mirzapore St.
Tower Hotel (B.S.)
  Sealdah
Hotel Royal (B S.)
  47 Harrison Rd.
Kamala Vilas (Madrasi)
  Rashbehari Avenue.
Maharastra Bhawan (Gujarati)
  69 Kansaripara Rd.
New Central Hotel
  90 Chittaranjan Avenue.

## NEWSPAPERS (English)

"The Statesman"
"Amrita Bazar Patrika"
"Hindustan Standard"

## AIR OFFICES

B. O. A. C.
  41 Chowringhee
K. L. M.
  7 Chowringhee.
Pan-American
  42 Chowringhee.

Air France
  41 Chowringhee
Air-India International
  Great Eastern Hotel

## INFORMATION CENTRES

Regional Tourist Office
  13 Old Court House St.
British Information Service,
  1 Harrington Street.
U.S.I.S.
  7 Chowringhee Road.

## BOOKSELLERS

Newmans
  Great Eastern Hotel
Oxford Book & Staty. Co.,
  17, Park Street,
Thacker Spink
  Esplanade East.

## ART DEALERS

Curio House,
  G. Eastern Hotel,
Hotchand Motumal
  New Market,
Kashmir Art Emporium
  12 Chowringhee Road,
Oriental Art Palace
  Great Eastern Hotel
Punwani & Son.
  New Market.

## RESTAURANTS

Firpos,
  Chowringhee Rd.
Ferrazinis (Tea Room)
  Lindsay St.
C Trinka
  Park Street,
Lighthouse Brasserie
  Lighthouse Cinema
Kwality
  Park St.

# SANTINIKETAN

Vishwa-Bharati which is known throughout the world as the centre of India's cultural renaissance and a great seat of international fellowship grew out of the Santiniketan Ashram founded by the Poet's father, Maharshi Devendranath Tagore, in 1863. The Ashrama was meant to be a retreat where the seekers of Truth might come and meditate on the mystery of the Absolute in peace and seclusion.

Fifty-six years ago, in 1901 the Poet, realizing the unsuitability of the educational system prevailing in the country under the British, founded at Santiniketan the Brahmacharya Ashrama with only five boys. In twenty years time, the Ashrama grew into an international university, known throughout the country and abroad as ths Vishwa-Bharati, where the whole world meets in a single nest. The Poet wanted to provide a seat of culture which would not only focus the entire cultural heritage of the East but also be a meeting place of all the cultures of the world. "The fuller idea of Vishwa-Bharati", said he, "included the thought of the complete meeting of the East and West in a common fellowship of learning and common spiritual striving after the unity of human race". To this seat of learning were drawn such scholars of international repute as Sylvain Levi, Sten Konow, Winternitz, Lesny, Formici, Germanus, Aga Poure Davoud and others, as well as students from many countries, particularly from China, Japan and Indonesia. Men of goodwill like C. F. Andrews, William Pearson and Leonard Elmhirst gave their services to the institution as enthusiastic workers. By an Act of Parliament, the Vishwa-Bharati was constituted into a Central University in May 1951.

## Places of Interest

**Udayan** : the Poet's mud-hut where he wrote many famous books is now in ruins. **Uttarayan ;** the residence of the Poet, which now contains the office of the Univer-

and the Poet's personal belongings, his manuscripts, paintings, books and rare art collections in the first flour; **Kalabhaban :** Art academy where the great master Nandalal Bose gives lessons in Painting and Sculpture; **Chatimlata :** the secluded prayer-place in the mango-groove ; **Sangit Bhaban :** the academy for Indian Dancing and Music ; **Cheena Bhaban :** the centre of Chinese culture. A mile and a half to the south is **Sreeniketan** which accommodates the cottage industries section of the Vishwa-Bharati, the farm and other agricultural and allied institutes.

*     *     *

COMM. 91 miles from Calcutta to the north is Bolepur railway station, reached in 4 hours from Calcutta. From Bolepur, Santiniketan is only 2½ miles to the west approached by a fine road. Cycle rickshaws and Vishwa-Bharati transport buses carry visitors to Santiniketan.

ACCOM. There is no good hotel ; but the Vishwa-Bharati Guest House has excellent arrangements for visitors. Charges Rs. 4 per head (Rs. 6/- for European food). For advance booking, application has to be made to the Manager, New Guest House, Santiniketan. There are Railway Retiring Rooms at Bolepur Station. Cycle Rickshaws are the usual transport.

# DARJEELING

Darjeeling, the "Paradise of Hill Resorts" needs no introduction to the discerning tourist. Nestling on the south-eastern flanks of the mighty Himalayas (7,000 ft.), this queen of hill stations is just the spot where a visitor may see his dreams come true and where nature in all her beauty simply baffles description. No other spot in the world unfolds to the visitor a more sweeping panorama of mountain beauty culminating in the 28,146 ft. high Kanchanjunga and Everest, the world's highest peak, glittering white walls of perpetual snow painted by the sun at dawn and glowing under the moon at night. To the globetrotter acquainted with far-famed Alpine beauties, Darjeeling is a thrilling experience and is held by many of them as the most beautiful hill station in the world before which Alpine scenes pale into mere insignificance.

The glorious sight achieves an unrivalled scenic splendour at sun-rise when the crimson sun as it leaps above the horizon throws a flood of brilliant colours over the peaks, providing a unique feast for the eyes and the senses which once enjoyed remains a treasured memory for a life-time. The phenomenon is best seen from the Tiger Hill ( 7 m. from Darjeeling) on a clear morning.

Besides the spell of the mystic Himalayas, Darjeeling has other attractions. With its residences picturesquely balanced on the spur of hills the city itself is set in the midst of wondrous Nature. Meadows of wild flowers, pine-clad slopes with shady nooks and walks, glistening waterfalls, charming lakes and surging gorges make a wonderful setting for an invigorating holiday the like of which you have never experienced before. There is a bewildering variety of hill-folk ; at folk evenings a picturesque assortment of hill tribes display their own colourful dances and shows.

Climatically, the best seasons in Darjeeling are from mid-March to mid-June and then again from mid-September to November. The climate is always exhilarating and delightfully cool. The temperature averages 2° above that of London all the year round ; that is, it neither exceeds 75° in summer nor falls below 35° in winter. Warm clothes are necessary throughout the year. In winter months heavy warm clothes must be taken.

**Places of Interest**

There are many objects of absorbing interest in and around Darjeeling, and it is for the visitor to make his choice and enjoy his stay to its best. The Lloyd Botanical Garden with its wonderful flower beds is an attraction. Those interested in Natural History will find much for study at the Natural

History Museum. Then there are Raj Bhawan on Birch
Hill ridge and 'Step Aside', the historic house where
Deshabandhu Chittaranjan Das, the immortal fighter for
freedom, breathed his last. 'Observatory Hill' above the
Chowrasta is a centre of attraction, for it affords an excellent view of the giant twin peaks of Kanchanjunga covered with perpetual snow. Birch Hill Park with its wooded
hills and shady nooks and walks is an ideal place for
horse-riding and picnics, and so is Senchal Lake, 6 miles
from Darjeeling. The colourful Buddhist monasteries at
Bhutia Busty and at Ghoom (4 miles) are attractions. The
image of the Maitreya Buddha which adorns the shrine
at Ghoom was made at a huge cost and it is said
that inside its base are kept precious stones, diamonds
and gold of fabulous value along with sixteen volumes
of sacred Buddhist scriptures. Spectacular Lama
dances and other peculiar observances provide ample
food for the eyes and the senses. To the excursion-
ist the other attraction is Lebong Race Course, 2½
miles north of Darjeeling, which is said to be the world's
smallest.

### Excursions

Darjeeling is the excursionists' paradise. A trip to
**Tiger Hill for viewing the sun-rise** on Kanchanjunga
is bound to be a memorable event. One must leave
Darjeeling at 4. a. m. by car or pony to be at the top
of the hill in time for the wonderful view.

For the sturdy excursionists facilities exist for spen-
ding a few days on treks to more magnificent
theatres of Nature's beauty at higher altitudes. The
most enjoyable trek is the one to **Phalut** (12,000 ft.)
which unfolds a gorgeous mountain beauty which
makes one gasp in wonder and delight. "The calm and
serene atmosphere of the surroundings, the lovely view
of the superb panorama and above all the magnificent
view of the sun-rise and of the Everest group of
mountain peaks are things never to be forgotten".
Short trips by car or bus may also be made to Ran-
garoon, Rambi, Takdah, Mungpoo, Kalimpong (32 m.)

and Gangtok (60 m.), the capital of Sikkim. There are regular bus services to these places.

COMM. 416 m. from Calcutta, Darjeeling is reached in 26 hours by rail. By air it is 3 hours from Dum Dum. From Bagdogra, Darjeeling's airport (8 m. below Siliguri and 59 m. from Darjeeling) IAC transport buses maintain a corresponding service to Darjeeling. In addition, private bus services are available at the airport.

Train journey from Calcutta is rather tiresome. Leaving Sealdah the train reaches Sakrigali Ghat where the train is changed for the steamer to Monihari Ghat whence an overnight journey by metre gauge brings one to Siliguri (365 miles from Calcutta). The 51-mile journey (5½ hours) by toy railway from Siliguri to Darjeeling affords the crowning beauty and thrill of the visit. The toy railway spirals upwards for 51 miles through some of the most fascinating sights of the world, doing sharp bends and precipices and affording splendid views at every turn. The actual ascent starts from the railway station Sukna, 7 miles from Siliguri and continues through a wonderful country till suddenly the mighty Kanchanjunga leaps into view at Kurseong, 32 m. from Siliguri. From Kurseong to Darjeeling is 19 miles uphill journey through entrancing sights.

For those who are in a hurry there are cars and buses at Siliguri which cover the distance in 3 hours. (Bus fare : Rs. 5/-)

ACCOM. High class Western style hotels of the town are : Mount Everest, Windmere and Bellevue. They provide superb cuisine in European style. Other good Indo-European style hotels include Central Hotel, Swiss Hotel, New Elgin Hotel and Pliva's Confectionery and Restaurant. Good middle class hotels are : Lowis Jubilee Sanatorium, Hindu Boarding and Snow View Hotel. For the orthodox Hindus there is the Mohanlal & Shewanlal Dharamsala in Judges Bazar.

CONVEYANCE : Taxis are not allowed to ply in the station, but they are available for sight-seeing outside. For trekking or riding ponies can be hired. Regular bus services connect the neighbouring towns through many entrancing sights.

# KALIMPONG

32 m. from Darjeeling lies Kalimpong (4,500 ft.), an all-the-year-round hill station with a milder climate and lovely surroundings. Picturesquely situated on the spur of a hill, it has a peculiar charm of its own and

affords beautiful walks and drives, excursions and fishing. In the background there are the snow-clad Himalayan peaks which afford a mystic setting for an invigorating holiday.

Scenic beauties aside, Kalimpong has considerable commercial importance. The trade route to Lhasa starts from here ; and huge quantities of wool and other commodities are brought to Kalimpong from Sikkim, Tibet, Bhutan and Nepal. A road runs to Gangtok (42 m.), capital of Sikkim. Kalimpong is noted for its excellent educational institutions and institutes for arts and crafts. St. Andrew's Colonial Homes, Kalimpong Arts & Crafts, the Tibetan Monastery and Bhutia Durbar House have much to interest the visitors.

\*　　\*　　\*　　\*　　\*

COMM. Kalimpong is reached by motor from Siliguri (42 m.) and Darjeeling (32 m). Buses and taxies ply from Bagdogra air port to Kalimpong (48 m.)

ACCOM. The only hotel that caters in European style is the Himalayan Hotel, 1 mile south of the town. Middle class hotels include Hindustan, Tripti and Tripathi hotels in the bazar and Hotel Hill View near Himalaya Hotel. There is a Works & Building Dept. Inspection Bungalow where visitors can stay with permission from the Executive Engineer, Darjeeling. Taxies are available for sight-seeing in and around the town.

## GAUHATI

Five miles from Pandu is Gauhati, the 'temple town of Assam', which stands on the bank of the Brahmaputra which here presents a panoramic view with wooded banks and tiny islands. · On an island in the middle of the river is the temple of Umananda, which is a dream in rock and foliage, while the celebrated temple of Kamakshya on the Nilachal Hill is 2 miles below the town, centrally between Gauhati and Pandu. The shrine (Kali) is regarded as very sacred and draws thousands of pilgrims from all parts of India. The surrounding panorama from the flat-topped Kamakshya hill is superb.

Being the central town of Assam, Gauhati has

good commerce, a number of colleges, a university and a museum. From Pandu the Assam section of the N. E. R. runs past Gauhati eastward to Lamding from where it spreads a net-work to connect the chief towns of upper and lower Assam. A fine, picturesque metalled road connects Gauhati with Shillong (63 m.) and further south with Cherrapunji, while the all-weather Assam Trunk Road runs straight to Dibrugarh (Gauhati-Nowgong-Jorhat-Sibsagar-Dibrugarh) and thence to Saikona for the north-east frontier town of Sadiya. Motor transport is highly developed in Assam and buses takes one from anywhere to everywhere.

\*   \*   \*   \*   \*

COMM. From Calcutta to Gauhati is 351 miles by air and is covered in less than 3 hours : whereas it is 650 miles by Assam Rail Link (Sealdah-Sakrigali-Siligiri-Amingaon-Pandu-Gauhati) involving ferry crossing at two places (Sakrigali Ghat and Amingaon) and a tedious journey of about two days. It is advisable to undertake the journey by air. (Air fare ; Rs. 70/-, Rail fare : Second class Rs. 32/8/-. Third Rs. 18/8/-).

ACCOM : There are a few middle class hotels such as, Grand Hotel, Paradise, Punjab and Kamakshya Hotel (Rs. 3/- to Rs. 5/- per day)—all in the Fancy bazar. There are Rly. Retiring Rooms at the station. The Strand Hotel (Rs. 12/- per day) is the best. The palatial Circuit House (no rent) accommodates government Officers. From its lawns one gets a splendid view of the river.

# SHILLONG

Set amid a most beautiful meadow of wild flowers and pine-clad slopes in the heart of the Khasi and Jaintia hills, Shillong (4,921 ft.), the capital of Assam State, is the leading hill station in Eastern India.

It has a most bracing and equable climate. The temperature in the height of summer hardly reaches 75° nor falls below 38° in winter. With its wooden houses picturesquely wedged and balanced on rolling hills Shillong is a well-planned State capital where delightful walks, folk dances, racing, golfing and many excursions make for a pleasant holiday resort where thousands flock during summer every year.

To the anthropologist Shillong is of absorbing interest. The hills of Assam are inhabited by tribal people of bewildering variety of which the Lushai and the Nagas, once fierce head-hunters, are as notorious as their ways are curious. The Khasis, who dwell in the environs of Shillong, are an interesting people. Their colourful dance is seen at its best at the village of Nong Krem, only 13 miles from Shillong and accessible by motor. Dance festivals at Nong Krem are usually held during June.

Of the many interesting sight and scenes, the water-falls of Shillong occupy the pride of place. Beadon and Bishop waterfalls (3 m.) afford thrilling sights at sunset—a riot of colour and beauty for the eyes to feast on. Ward Lake near Government House is a popular beauty spot of the town. A visit to the Shillong Peak (7,000 ft.), the highest point in the district, will be amply compensated. There is a bus service. Then there are Gunner's Falls, Elephanta Falls (7 m.) and the weekly Burra Bazar where the hill tribes from the distant parts flock with their curios and strange commodities for sale.

## Excursions

34 m. from Shillong, along a picturesque road, is the charming **Cherapunji** (4,500 ft.) situated on a small plateau commanding a magnificent view of the surrounding cliffs and of the luxuriantly wooded plains to the south. Chera is famous as the wettest place in the world—average rainfall being 426 inches. But all records were broken in 1861 when about 903 inches fell, of which 365 inches fell in July alone.

In spite of its heavy rainfall, Chera was once a small but gay European station ; and the jail, court-room and various other houses built of solid masonry can still be seen. There is a Circuit House (Khansama prepares Western style food) commanding a wonderful scenery. There is a regular bus service from Shillong.

COMM. Shillong is easily reached in a day by air from Calcutta to Gauhati and thence 63 miles by motor (4 hrs. journey) running through rolling grassy downs along a most picturesque road. (Bus fare from Gauhati : 1st. class—18/12/- ; 2nd 11/8/- ; Inter—5/13/- ; and third 3/2/-). The Assam Rail link provides connection to Gauhati whence the journey is to be again made by bus as detailed above.

ACCOM. Good European style hotels are : Pinewood Hotel, near Government House, and Peak Hotel, near Secretariat.

Government Officers and distinguished guests can stay at the M.L.A's hotel (rent Rs. 6/- per day) and at the Circuit House (rent Rs. 2/- per day).

Cheaper hotels are : Pine View Hotel, Hill Top Hotel, Happy Lodge Sunny Hotel—all in the bazar (Rs. 3/- to 5/- per day).

CONVEYANCE : Taxis are cheap and readily available. There is a city bus service.

# MANIPUR

From Manipur Road (Dimapur) railway station, on the Lamding-Tinsukia section, a fine motor road runs through the State of Manipur to its capital, Imphal, via Kohima. There is a regular Rail-cum-Bus service and the distance of 136 miles is covered in 8½ hours. At the outest the road ascends to 6700 ft. and then descends to the valley which is level for 15 miles. There are a number of well-furnished Dak Bungalows at convenient points on the way from which excursions can be made to the interior of the Naga Hills. Supplies may be taken either from Kohima, or Manipur Road where there are a D.B. and stores.

# KOHIMA

46 m. from Manipur Road is Kohima, the adminis- trative centre which gives access to the entire Naga Hill region. "Each year during the spring festival, tiny villages nestling among the Naga Hill resound with the beating of drums and the singing of traditional tribal chants. Decked in full war-paints, Naga menfolk run through a rich repertory of dances, mostly tribal in

character.   Slender Naga maidens, liberally adorned with bead necklaces, brass bangles, and amulets, dance before the Naga chief's house, swaying hand in hand for hours on end to the accompaniment of charming melodies."

\*　　　\*　　　\*　　　\*　　　\*

ACCOM.　There is an Inspection Bungalow at Kohima ; and cars, petrol and other facilities are available for trips to the interior of the Naga Hills.

# IMPHAL

Imphal, the capital of Manipur, lies in a picturesque valley, 60 miles long and 30 miles wide and is 2,600 ft. above sea level.  The valley is surrounded by lovely wooded hills and abounds in lakes which afford magnificent duck shooting in winter. But the people of Manipur are even more colourful than their beautiful land. Much has been written on the folk dance and charm of Manipur and the religious dance of the Nagas. The connoisseurs of art, the anthropologists and those who love beauty in any form will find many things of absorbing interest in Manipur.  Handloom products of Manipur are excellent.

\*　　　\*　　　\*　　　\*　　　\*

ACCOM.  The Peak Hotel, Imphal, run in European style, offers good accommodation and food.  There are also a few cheaper hotels.  There is a State Dak Bungalow at Imphal where visitors can stay with permission from the Deputy Commissioner. Rickshaws, cars and buses are usual transport.

COMM.  Bus fares  from Manipur Road to Imphal (136 m.) are, Second class—Rs. 5/-.  Third class—Rs. 4/8/-.  There is a regular air service to Imphal from Calcutta (single fare : Rs. 95/-).

# KAZIRANGA GAME SANCTUARY

Seventy-five miles from  Gauhati  by bus is Nowgong.  From there another bus takes one to Jorhat (115 miles) through Kohara (56 miles) which is the base for journey to the  Kaziranga Game Sanctuary. Tourist Lodge at Koharu offers good food and accommodation at scheduled rates.  District Forest Officer,

Jorhat can arrange for interior transport and shooting facilities on previous intimation. There are Inspection Bungalows at Baguri (with Khansama and all arrangements) and at Kaziranga (no Khansama), to occupy which permission may be obtained from the D.F.O., Jorhat.

Kaziranga is far-famed for big game shooting. Tiger, bison, wild buffaloes and the one-horned rhinoceros, which is not found anywhere else in India, are found in plenty. Elephants are strictly protected.

## PARASNATH

196 miles from Howrah, between Dhanbad and Hazaribagh, is Parasnath station from where the Parasnath Mountain temple is 18 miles to the north-east approached by a fine motor road up to Madhuban at the foot (13 miles). From Madhuban to the summit (4500 ft.) is about 5½ miles up-hill journey (occupying 2½ hrs.) by foot or dandies, through fine forest scenery. To reach the point two lower ranges have to be crossed and these consist of thick forests well stocked with game. Tigers and leopards roam over the hills. Deer is plentiful. On the summit there are 24 temples headed by that of Parasnathji.

The far-famed temple, the eastern metropolis of Jain worship, commands a splendid view of forest glades and the undulating plains of the Damodar valley below. The shrine contains the sculptured feet of Parasnath and some figures of Buddha. According to a Jain legend, Parasnath, the 23rd. Tirathankar of the Jains, was born in Banaras, lived 100 years and attained Nirvana on this mountain. The shrine attracts thousands of devotees every year.

Madhuban, (1320 ft.), is the local headquarters of the Digambara and Setambara sects of the Jains.

ACCOM. The convenient base for trip to the summit is the Nemighat D. B. (on G. T. Road) close to the mountain and 3 m.

from Parasnath station. Further ahead is the Dumri D. B. which is a favourite resort for motorists from Calcutta and northern India. Between them is Isri, a village which contains two Jain Dharamsalas. There is another D. B. on the summit (without servant and provision) where visitors can stay with previous permission of the Dy. Commissioner, Hazaribagh. Ekkas are the only mode of transport. Having done Parasnath, the motorist has the choice of two roads, one to Giridhi which branches off to the right from Dumri and the other to Hazaribagh to the left from Bagdoar, both on the G. T. Road.

# HAZARIBAGH

215 m. from Calcutta and 77 m. from Gaya is Hazaribagh Road station, on the Howrah-Moghulsarai Grand Chord line. From the station to Hazaribagh, a fine sanatorium at a height of 2000 ft., is 41 miles to the west reached by a Rail-cum-bus service.

Situated in the midst of an undulating plateau surrounded by forests which abound in game of all kinds and quaint little villages of aborigines' Hazaribagh is noted for its picturesque jungle scenery and the exciting games it affords. The three lakes situated at the centre of the town greatly add to the charm of Hazaribagh, which is a favourite Pooja rendezvous for motorists from all parts.

ACCOM. Besides District Board and P. W. D. Dak Bungalows, there are a number of good middle class hotels and boarding houses some of which cater in Indo-European style.

CONVEYANCE. Taxis, rickshaws and cycle-rickshaws are available. A fine metalled road connects Hazaribagh with Ranchi (50 m.) and with Gaya via G. T. Road. There is a regular bus service between Gaya and Ranchi via G. T. Road and Hazaribagh.

# DAMODAR VALLEY

On the basin of the river Damodar covering almost the whole district of Hazaribagh, parts of Ranchi, Santal Parganas and Manbhum and involving an area of about 1000 square miles, the Damodar Valley Project, the most spectacular of India's development schemes, is fast setting up a new civilisation, a pattern of industrial well-being only seen in the great Tennesee Valley of U.S.A.

The eight dams and one barrage across the turbulent Damodar will not only irrigate a million parched acres and build huge reservoirs for cultivating fish but the million kilowatts of hydro-electricity derived from power plant of the barrage will electrify an area of 53,000 square miles, supply power to the existing industries and new ones and electrify a vast railway system. The biggest of them, the Tilaya Dam was completed in September 1952 and this along with others, when complete. will store water to the extent of 4,500,000 acre feet of which Tilaya alone now stores 3,20,000 acre feet. The dams will finally banish the scourage of frequent floods from the Damodar basin and produce at least 26,000 tons of additional food in the areas brought under irrigation and give new life to this erst-while valley of tears. The 150,000 thermal power plant at Bokharo which was opened in November, 1953, will supply power to Jamshedpur, Burnpur, the Kharagpur Railway Workshop, to the rural areas, coalfields and industries of Bihar and Bengal. These installations, when complete, will certainly usher in industrial and agricultural prosperity of inconceivable proportions.

\*　　\*　　\*　　\*　　\*　　\*

COMM. Bokharo lies to the east of Dhanbad and can be reached either from Dhanbad or, Gomo by the Barkakhana line, while Tilaya in the Hazaribagh district, in the interior, can be reached from Kodarma by bus. The regular bus service from Hazaribagh to Ranchi passes through much of the Project area.

## RANCHI

The celebrated hill station of Bihar noted for its lovely scenery, fine dry climate and motor roads, Ranchi lies at the heart of the Chota Nagpur hills at a height of 2200 ft. above sea level. Its pleasant climate, tree-lined broad avenues and picturesque environs, which provide good excursions, game and picnic spots, are well known and thousands of holiday seekers come to Ranchi in hot as well as in cold weather.

Ranchi is truly "the motorist's Paradise". A network of fine metalled roads spread in all directions connecting it with Hazaribagh, Gaya, Purulia, (96 m.) Dhanbad, Jamshedpur, Calcutta, Lohardanga (46 m.) and Daltonganj besides many other subsidiaries which connect the town with other places through pleasing scenes and wooded hill sides. Bus services are many and take the visitor almost anywhere.

At Kanke, 6 miles from the town, is the Indian Mental Hospital, the largest of its kind in India. At Namkam (4 m) is the Lac Research Institute, one of the largest scientific institutes of India. Itki Tubercolosis Sanatorium lies at a distance of 18 m. on the Lohardanga Railway section. The Hundru Waterfalls (24 m.) is an attraction and is reached by a fine road. The other beautiful fall is at Jonha (5 m.) at the head of which is the temple of Jagannath which is a place of pilgrimage. A few miles from Ranchi is the reserved forest of Horhap where leopards, bears and jungle-fowl abound and occasionally a tiger prowls. 42 m. from Ranchi, on the road to Chaibasa, are the Hirni Falls. Further ahead the road passes through dense reserve forests which are the homes of tiger, bison and wild elephants.

96 m. west of Ranchi is **Naterhat** (3700 ft.), queen of beauty spots in Chotanagpur. It is connected with Ranchi by metalled road, except for the 13 m. of the Ghat portion. There are four furnished Inspection Bungalows where the visitors can stay. Somewhat like the Tiger Hill point in Darjeeling, a view of the sun-rise from Naterhat is a feast for the eyes.

\*   \*   \*   \*   \*

COMM. 251 m. from Calcutta, Ranchi is reached on a comfortable overnight journey via Tatanagar to Muri from where the narrow gauge railway runs to Ranchi. From the east it is approached from Gomoh via Barkhakhana to Muri. A regular bus service connects Ranch with Gaya via Hazaribagh. Bihar Government's buses ply dai y between Patna and Ranchi.

ACCOM. There is a number of good hotels in the town of which the Eastern Railway Hotel caters in high European style. Grand and Hill View are good middle class hotels. There are several others. Transport consists of rickshaws, cars and buses.

# GAYA

292 m. from Calcutta, on the Howrah-Moghalsarai Grand Chord line, is Gaya, a place of pilgrimage of Hindus, second only to Banaras in sanctity. Here every Hindu owes a duty to his forefathers, and that is the offering of *pindas* (funeral cakes) for the peace of their departed souls. Here come from all parts of India Hindus in their thousands to offer *pindas* and perform the Sradh ceremony which relieve the departed spirits from all earthly bondage and translate them to heaven.

The pilgrim has, first, to bathe in the sacred stream Phalgu and then offer *pindas* at the galleried ghats of the river and again at the Vishnupada temple and the *Akshya Bat*. Eight miles to the north is Pretsila Hill wher *pindas* are offered to the departed spirits of those who died abnormal deaths.

The centre of pilgrimage is the Vishnupada temple, which stands in a congested part of the old town, half a mile away from the river bank. The temple was built by Rani Ahalya Bai of Indore in 1707. Within its sanctum and in an octagonal silver basin inserted into the pavement is the Vishnupada (foot-prints of Vishnu) which receives constant offerings of *pindas* and prayers at all hours of the day. At one corner of the temple enclosure is the *Akshya Bat* (immortal Baniyan tree) at which the pilgrims make their final offerings of *pindas* and conclude the pilgrimage.

Half a mile to the west of Vishnupada, at the foot of the Brahmajuni Hill, is the original *Akshya Bat* which is yet another sacred spot; and a little to the west of it is the Brahmajuni Hill which is ascended by a flight of about thousand stone steps. There is a temple at the top from which the visitors get a good view of Gaya and its environs. To the south the spire of the Buddha-Gaya temple is seen peeping over the tree-tops.

*　　*　　*　　*　　*

ACCOM. There is no good hotel. A luxurious Circuit House caters for the discriminating visitors (permission from Dt. Magistrate). One can stay at the District Board D.B. (4 rooms) with permission from Dt. Engineer, Dt. Board, Gaya, or at the Railway Retiring rooms. There are a few middle class cheap hotels, two near the station and another at the Chowk, but they cannot be recommended. There is a Buddhist Rest House. Middle class pilgrims should make it a point to stay at the Bharat Sevasram Sangha (1 m. from the station to the north-west) which provides accommodation, food, advice and registered priests for performing the rites according to ones means. The Sangha provides family-suites for family parties. They do not charge anything for accommodation or food, but it is customary to contribute one's mite to the Sangha fund.

CONVEYANCE: Taxies are rare. Horse-carriages and cycle rickshaws are popular transport. The trip to Buddha-Gaya is made by cycle-rickshaws or horse carriages.

# BUDDHA-GAYA

Seven miles south of Gaya is Buddha-Gaya, the holiest of all the holy places of the Buddhists, for it is the scene where Siddhartha Gautama attained 'Supreme Enlightenment' twenty-five centuries ago. Here under a pipul-tree he sat in a long meditation and attained Buddhahood for the good of humanity. This tree afterwards known as Bodhi-tree, became the centre of worship from the earliest period of Buddhism. Emperor Ashoka erected a temple near it in honour of his Master, and when the stone pavement of the present temple was dug up, foundations of an older structure were found which are believed to be the remnants of the Asokan temple. The present temple, a pyramid-like building, dates from the 11th century, and resembles the temple seen by Hiuen Tsang in 635 A.D.

Access to the shrine is gained through the eastern gate. On the altar reposes a large gilded image of Buddha which is worshipped also by the Hindus as an incarnation of Vishnu. Much of the stone railing round the temple, believed to be Asoka's, has been restored. The pillars are adorned with carving of various types. At the back of the temple is the pipal-tree, the lineal descendant of the sacred Bodhi-tree, and under the tree is a red sandstone slab, the *Vajrasana*, marking the spot where the Lord sat in meditation. There are a number of stupas in the courtyard round the temple.

To the west is a small double-storied Tibetan temple with a huge standing figure of Buddha surrounded by a large number of Tibetan Buddha images and pictures. Two huge oil lamps with immense quantities of oil at the base burn throughout the day and night. Managed by Tibetans, the temple abounds in many unusual objects of interest. To the south of the Great temple is the Buddha kund filled with lotus. In it Buddha bathed.

The temple is managed jointly by the Buddhists and Hindus. Happily, the Mahabodhi Society predominates and to them goes the credit for reviving the place to somewhat like its former glory. The Buddhist monks will be found most kind and helpful.

The P. W. D. guide on duty undertakes to show the visitor round the temple and furnishes other information.

\* \* \* \* \*

ACCOM. There is a well furnished P. W. D. Dak Bungalow close to the temple where visitors can stay with the permission of Executive Engineer, P.W.D., Gaya. This is fited with electricity and tap water. There is another commodious rest house built by the Birlas. For Buddhist pilgrims there is the spacious Mahabodhi Rest House. There is a fourth rest house attached to the Tibetan temple. Light refreshments are available in the nearby bazaar.

CONVEYANCE. From Gaya the trip to Buddha Gaya is made by horse-carriage or cycle rickshaw; both are cheap. Government operates a bus service between Gaya and Buddha-Gaya.

# PATNA

More is known of Magadha than of any other part of ancient India, for the most glorious part of our ancient history centres round the great saints and mighty kings of Magadha. It witnessed the birth of the two great faiths—Jainism and Buddhism. Here was born Mahavira. Here wandered Buddha in search of truth and here he attained 'Enlightenment'. Udaya, son of king Ajatasatru of Rajgir. built a fort at Patali at the end of the 6th. century B. C. This grew into the magnificent city of Pataliputra during the reign of Chandragupta, the founder of the first Indian empire, and his successor, Emperor Ashoka the Great. Near Rajgir, the oldest city of Magadha, where Buddha stayed for a number of years, grew in later times the great University of Nalanda which attracted students from all parts of India, South-East Asia and China.

331 miles from Calcutta and 564 miles from Delhi, on the Eastern Railway main line, Patna the capital of Bihar is a fine city which spreads eight miles along the river Ganges. In Bankipore, the western extremity of the sprawling city, are Government House, the Secretariat, the Museum, the High Court, the University, the Khuda Bux Oriental Library and many other public buildings, fine parks and garden houses.

At one corner of the Bankipore maidan is the Gola Ghar, a huge bee-hive-shaped structure, 90 ft. high and 426 ft. at the base, of which there is hardly any parallel in the world as a wonderful whispering gallery. The faintest whisper at one end is heard most distinctly at the other. The top is ascended by steps from outside. Jang Bahadur of Nepal once rode a pony up the steps. From the top one gets a splendid view of the city—new and old with the river Ganga flowing around it for miles.

The Khudabux Oriental Library is a great centre of Islamic culture which contains a rare collection of Arabic and Persian manuscripts and the only volumes saved from the sack of the Moorish University of Cordova.

Patna is the birth place of Guru Gobind Singh, the last and the most famous of the Sikh Gurus who turned

112

Sikhism into a militant nationalism. In the old city, not far from Patna Ghat, is the Har Mandir Takhat, the Sikh Gurudwara, built by Ranjit Singh around the room in which the Guru was born and reared. The temple, which is one of the four sacred places of the Sikhs, preserves the Guru's cradle and shoes. Padrikihaveli or the old Roman Catholic Church (1775), also in the old city, bears mute witness to the priestly sufferings for the Christian good of mankind. Nearby is the cemetery which contains an obelisk dedicated to the memory of the 200 English captives murdered at the instigation of Mir Kasim in 1763. The massacre was later avenged by Major Adams.

The old buildings of the Gulzaribagh Opium Factory surrounded by high walls may be seen by the river side. This was an old citadel of the East India Company from where the British earned fabulous profits by opium trade with China. The buildings now accommodate the Government Press.

The ruins of ancient Pataliputra including the remains of Emperor Asoka's Palace and pillared halls, mentioned by Megasthenes, and many other Asokan relics can be seen in an excavated ground in the Kumhrar village, beside the railway line, between Patna Jnc. and Patna city station. Kumhrar is about four miles from the city and can be reached by cycle-rickshaw or taxi. Antiquities from Kumrahar and Bulandibagh including a fine collection of Maurayan and post-Maurayan stone sculptures are housed in the Patna Museum. There can also be seen the famous Didarganj Yakshi which marks the high water mark of Maurayan sculpture.

\*          \*          \*

ACCOM. There are several good hotels in the city. The Grand Hotel at Fraser Road caters in European style. Besides, there is a spacious Circuit House (permission from District Engineer, Patna) and a District Board Dak Bungalow. Good Indian style hotels are : Princes Hotel and Marwari Hotel, Fraser Road, and Agarwal Hotel, near the Station.

CONVEYANCE. Internal transport consists of taxis,

cycle rickshaws and ekkas. Government transport buses operate daily service between Patna and Ranchi via Hazaribagh and between Patna and Rajgir via Nalanda (61 miles). The city is connected with Gaya by the Patna-Gaya railway (86 miles). Patna is also connected by air.

# RAJGIR

28 miles south-east of Patna and 310 miles from Calcutta is Bakhtiyarpur station on the main line of the Eastern Railway. From Bakhtiyarpur a narrow gauge line proceeds south-west through Bihar Sareef and termintes at the hill-girt town of Rajgir (33 miles), which has been immortalized in the sacred Buddhist texts as the capital of the great king Bimbisara and the favourite resort of the Buddha. Surrounded by tree-clad hills and primitive forests, Rajgir today presents a charming and restful atmosphere charged with a spiritual calm. The hills around are filled with Buddhist and Jain remains, forts and other monuments of a remote past.

It was an important centre of Buddhism and Buddha himself passed many years of his life at this place. It was the scene of many sermons and numerous important events in the Master's life. The Gridhrakuta hill, 4 miles from the Kund, was his favourite abode. Mahavira, the last of the Jain Tirthankaras, passed 14 years of his life at Rajgir, which is a place of pilgrimage for Buddhist and Jains as it is for Hindus and Muslims.

Rajgir attracts not only antiquarians and pilgrims ; the sick and the infirm find in its picturesque meadows the most suitable setting for a real rest. It draws quite a number of visitors during October-March when the climate is salubrious and bathing in the hot spring most refreshing and helpful to those suffering from arthritic pains. About a mile south of the station, at the foot of the Vebhara hill, is the famous Satadhara group of hot springs which attracts people from far and near.

Other objects of interest include : the remains of the

'New Fort' built by king Ajatasatru, in front of the Buddhist Dharamsala ; the site of Veluvana, now an open ground between the Inspection Bungalow and the Kund ; the Jain and Siva temples at the top of the Vebhara hill, reached by a long flight of stone steps ; and the Saptapanni Cave (now in ruins), where the first Buddhist Council was held shortly after the death of the Buddha. A picturesque road between the hills leads to the Gridhrakuta hill, where the Buddha lived for sometime after his Renunciation and again after his Enlightenment.

\*     \*     \*

ACCOM. Accommodation is no problem. The District Board Rest House and the Inspection Bungalow (permission from District Engineer, Patna) provide food and accommodation. There are a number of Dharamsalas. Family suites are available at moderate rents.

CONVEYANCE. Bihar Government operates a regular bus service between Rajgir and Patna via Nalanda (61 m.). Local Transport consists of ekkas and rickshaws.

## NALANDA

Seven miles to the north of Rajgir lie the remains of the ancient University of Nalanda which sprang into great fame at the time of Kumara Gupta in the beginning of the 5th century A.D. and was reputed to be the highest centre of post-graduate study then available in all Asia. It attracted the best of scholars from China, Japan, Korea, Mongolia, Tibet and Ceylon. Even in those days of hazardous travel a continuous stream of foreign scholars came to Nalanda to complete the higher investigations upon which they had been engaged at home. The highest academic honour of the time was a fellowship of Nalanda, and on those who stole the name of 'Nalanda brother' were treated with respect throughout the East. Hiuen Tsang, the celebrated Chinese pilgrim, studied here for five years along with 10,000 residential students and monks.

Of the great Indian scholars that Nalanda pro-

duced, the names of Shilabhadra, the Chancellor, Dharmapala, the previous Chancellor, Arya Deva, a famous pu-
pil of the great chemist Nagarjuna—to mention only a
few—are even today a source of great inspiration. Nalanda
produced many other great Mahayana scholars who helped to spread the thought of India to foreign countries.

Nalanda, with its high academies of advanced
studies and allied institutes of arts and crafts, flourished
as a great centre of Buddhist culture for 700 years till it
was destroyed in 1205 A.D. by the advancing Maho-
madan hordes of marauders. The 'Tabakat-i-Nasiri'
describes how Muhammad Khilji mistook the University
for a fort, took possession of it, set fire to the library
and killed the residents.

Archaeological excavations have unearthed a fairly
large portion of the University buildings, monasteries
and temples. A local museum houses an interesting
collection of sculptures—mostly images of Buddha and
Bodhisattvas—dating from the 5th century A.D.

Close to the ancient buildings is the new building
of the Nalanda Institute, a centre of post graduate studies
in Pali and Buddhology which is staffed by scholars from
India, France, Japan and Tibet. The Institute was inau-
gurated by President Rajendra Prasad in 1951.

*     *     *

COMM. Nalanda (Baragaon) can be reached either from
Bihar Sareef or Nalanda station by country conveyance. From
Rajgir it is more easy to travel by the Government bus that runs
between Patna and Rajgir via Nalanda.

ACCOM. There is an Insp. Bungalow at Nalanda attached
to the Museum where visitors can stay by arrangement with
the curator. In addition, there are Dharamsalas and rest houses
for Buddhists.

# BHUBANESWAR

On the east coast, between the fertile plains of Bengal and those of the Deccan, lies the State of Orissa re-

116

plete with a glorious past. In ancient Orissa and Kalinga (Ganjam) ruled a long line of great kings as far back as 300 B.C. It came into great limelight during the reign of Kharavela in the 2nd. century B.C. The Oriya kings had a great passion for creative works and many of them founded immense temples and monuments which we now look at with awe and wonder. Between the 7th, and the 13th. century, however, the Oriya genius for stone carving and image making reached the zenith of its glory, and thousands of immense temples and monuments were built all over the land. But the Muslim iconoclastic bigotry of the later centuries succeeded in erasing most of these priceless works of art, and the few great monuments that have survived at Bhubaneswar, Puri and Konarak to-day bear evidence to the height of glory that Oriya artistic skill once achieved.

Of the 7,000 beautiful temples that once stood around the sacred lake of Bhubaneshwar about 500 still remain in decay exhibiting every variety of Oriyan architecture. The finest of them are the Great Lingaraj temple, the Rajarani temple, the Mukteswar temple and the Parsurameswar temple. Bhubaneswar is thus aptly called the 'Temple city of Siva', only next to Banaras in number.

The **Great Lingaraj**. Bhubaneswar's main shrine, is the finest and most majestic of all Oryan temples. It is one of the greatest monuments in all India, decidedly finer than the temple of Tanjore. "The Great Temple", says Fergusson, "is perhaps the finest example of a purely Hindu temple in India". The temple was built by king Lelat Indra Singh Kesari of the famous Kasari dynasty of Orissa about 617 A.D. and originally consisted of only a vimana and porch ; the Nat and Bhog mandirs being later additions (1090-1104).

The presiding deity, Tribhubaneswar or Lingaraj Mahadeb, is represented by a block of granite 8 feet in diameter, and 9 feet in height, with three shadings,

117

indicative of Brahma the Creator, Vishnu the Preserver, and Siva the Destroyer. The Great Temple dominates the landscape for miles and, like a magnet, draws towards it every stream of life that flows into the town; for the traffic that courses towards Bhubaneswar is attracted thither by the Great Lingaraj.

The Lingaraj temple is a world of its own, with its sixtyfour secondary temples clustered round the central pile. Of them Parvati's temple takes pride of place, and indeed, "were it not located beneath the shadow of Lingaraj, the goddess' abode would rank as a structural entity of supreme grandeur".

The Lingaraj is the only one of Bhubaneswar's important sanctuaries that non-Hindus may not enter. A special platform was erected just outside the surrounding walls for the archaeologist Viceroy, Lord Curzon. This vantage point still exists, and is the best place from which to glimpse Lingaraj's many-fold wonders.

**Vindusagar** : The Lingaraj rises on the southern shore of the Vindusagar tank, the largest in Bhubaneswar (measuring 1,300 by 700 ft.) which is supposed to have been originally filled with water brought from every sacred stream in India. The tank is considered very sacred and is greatly prized by pilgrims.

**Kedar-Gauri** : Half a mile north-east of Lingaraj is Kedar-Gauri Kand, the inevitable resort of residents and visitors alike. The temple of Kedar stands beside a well, the water of which is a sure remedy for intestinal ailments. The rush for the precious water is very great. Its shady and quiet surroundings and the adjoining small tank, which affords healthy baths, have made it the most favourite spot in the town.

**Mukteswar Temple** : A hundred yards to the north of Kedar-Gauri Kund stands the Mukteswar temple which, though the smallest (65 ft.), displays the finest sculpture of all. "The subjects reproduced are life-like and imaginatively carved, in a style that is vigorous and expressive of action. A woman is riding on a rearing elephant ; girls are dancing and playing on musical instruments ; a hermit who is nothing but skin and bones is teaching the way of life ; cobras writhe about and lift their heads with spread hoods and darting tongues ; and lions engage in a deadly fight". The *torana*, in front, contains elaborate carvings worthy of minutest study.

**Raja-Rani Temple :** A quarter mile to the east of Mukteswar, in the midst of a broad expanse of rice-fields, stands the temple of Rajarani (c.1100 A.D.) aptly called "a poem in stone". Of it Fergusson says : "The plan is arranged as to give great variety and play of light and shade, and, as the details are of the most exquisite beauty it is one of the gems of Oriyan architecture." On account of its secluded situation it has been suggested that Rajarani was designed by one of the kings of Orissa as a pleasure resort, rather than as a prayer retreat. Many statuettes of the Rajarani temple have fallen victims to conscienceless collectors who fliched them from their pedastals. However, sufficient remain intact to captivate the visitor by their natural-ness and grace. Here the Oriyan sculpture reached its zenith ; and one of the most attractive figurine is of a girl whose smile is well-nigh as haunting as that of Mona Lisa herself. "The Rajarani is not a temple over which to hurry, with one eye on the wonder walls and the other on a watch, for every figurine is deserving the minute and measured examination that is the birth-right of a masterpiece." Every inch of its exterior is covered with the most exquisite carvings and statuettes in buff sandstone which largely resembles the Khandariya Mahadev temple at Khajuraho.

**Parasurameswara :** About 200 yards west of Mukteswar stands the Parasurameswara temple, (750 A. D.) which Fergusson considers to be the oldest temple in Bhubaneswar with a "delicacy seldom sur-passed."

On the eastern shore of Vindusagar tank stands the imposing sanctuary of Ananta Vasudeva which is the only temple in Bhubaneswar dedicated to Vishnu. The last of the "Big Six" temples of Bhubaneswar is that of Brahmeswar (1075 A.D) which is one of the front rank temples.

Bhubaneswar's temples are just so many chapters in the story of Siva's domination over this "Metropolis of temples". Travellers who can afford the time will find it worth their while to spend three or four days at Bhubaneswar ; for besides the temples mentioned above, there are many other sanctuaries amongst the five hundred in and around Bhubaneswar that are rich in archaeological interest. Moreover, there are the ancient caves of Udaigiri and Khandagiri Hills (6 m. to the west) and Asokan rock edicts at Daulia near the ancient capital town of Sisupalgarh (4 m. to the south-east) where considerable time must be given in order to comprehend their great historical importance.

## Excursions

**Sisupalgarh and Daulia Rock Edicts :** Four miles to the south-east of Bhubaneswar, beside the Puri Road, lies the famous Daulia rock on which are inscribed the best-preserved edicts of Emperor Asoka. The edicts (mainly teaching the way of life) are inscribed on a huge projecting boulder on which stands a colossal figure of an elephant. Alighting from the cycle rickshaw or bus a little beyond Sisupalgarh, one has to walk a mile through open fields to reach the edicts.

2 m. from Bhubaneswar, on the way to the Rock Edicts and along the Puri Road, are the excavated ruins of the fortress city of Sisupalgarh which was probably the seat of the Jain Emperor Kheravela who ruled in the 2nd century B.C. and who inscribed an account of his rule on the caves of Udaigiri. The layout suggests that the people of ancient Orissa were well-versed in town planning and in the science of defence.

**Udaigiri and Khandagiri Hill Caves :** Six miles west of Bhubaneswar, on the hills of Udaigiri and Khandagiri are a number of caves which were once occupied by Jain monks and which contain remarkable carvings dating back to the 2nd. century B.C. Udaigiri and Khanadgiri are two separate rocks, close to each other, and altogether there are sixty-four caves in the two hills. In "The Cave Temples of India", Fergusson and Burgess declared that the "picturesqueness of their forms, the richness of their sculptures and architectural details, combined with their acknowledged antiquity" render the Udaigiri caves amongst the most important in India.

The Hathi Gumpha or Elephant Cave at Udaigiri bears an inscription which records year by year the achievements of Emperor Kheravela (150 B.C) in the first 14 years of his reign. From the architectural point of view the Rani Gumpha or Queen's Palace and the Ganesha Gumpha (both in Udaigiri) are the most interesting of all. The Queen's Palace is tuked away in a hillside glen suggestive of the Ajanta Cave gorge and it is said that it was inhabited about the seventh century A.D. by Lalendra Kesari's queen.

It is only a few minutes walk from Udaigiri to Khandagiri which is as attractive as its neighbour Udaigiri. The Ananta Cave is Khandagiri's special pride. Satghara Cave is also interesting for the figures of Jain Tirthankars depicted on the walls of the ante-chamber. The sacred hill is encircled by a belt of woodland ; bright green fields stretch away to the south ; on the north-east the new capital city of Bhubaneswar spreads like a picture on the slope of a wooded ridge, while from the east the Great Lingaraj summons the countryside to give homage to the great god Siva. Seen from the terrace of the new Jain temple on the summit, the scenery is enchanting.

The Caves can be reached from the Lingaraj temple gate by a bus (charge Re. 1/- both ways) which passes through the heart of the new capital which is situated in front of the railway station, to the west. From the New Capital the caves are only three miles to the west and reached by cycle rickshaws. Taxis are rare. For those who like to stay longer, there is a well-equipped Rest House at Khandagiri (with cook). Permission may be obtained from the Sub-divisional Officer, Khurda. There is also a Jain Dharamsala.

\*        \*        \*

COMM. 272 m. from Calcutta and 20 m. from Cuttack, Bhubaneswar is on the Calcutta-Madras main line of the S.E. Rly. and is reached in 9 hours from Calcutta. It is also reached by air from Calcutta and Madras. There is a regular bus service between Cuttack and Bhubaneswar and Bhubaneswar and Puri (38 m.). The Great Temple is about 2 m. from the station to the south. Cycle rickshaws are usual transport. Small planes for trip to Konarak may be hired from the Orissa Flying Club, Bhubaneswar. Charges; Rs. 50/- for a single-seater and Rs. 100/- for a three-seater plane ; waiting charges ; Rs. 10/- per hour.

ACCOM. There is no good hotel. Foreign visitors may stay at the comfortable Circuit House close to the railway station (to the south) with the permission of the Executive Engineer, P.W.D. Bhubaneswar Division. There is another small P.W.D. Dak Bungalow in the old city near the Kedar-Gauri Kund where visitors can stay with permission from the same authority. There is a Dist. Board Dak Bungalow to the south of the Lingaraj temple (permission : Chairman, Dist. Board, Puri). Grand Hotel and Bhubaneswar Sanatorium are cheap middle class hotels. There are several good Dharamasalas in front of the Great temple., and on the shore of the sacred Lake.

# PURI

A popular sea-resort on the eastern sea board of India and a great place of pilgrimage, especially sacred to the Vaishnavites, Puri draws every day quite a stream of visitors from Calcutta and the adjoining States.

But Puri's title to fame rests more on the famous temple of Jagannath or the Lord of the Universe, 192 ft.

high which stands at the centre of the town dominating the entire scene. The presiding deities are Jagannath (Lord Krishna), his brother Balaram and his sister Subhadra. Incongruous as it may seem, there is no caste barrier in the temple—a unique feature unknown anywhere else in India. This is perhaps due to the great act of Sri Sri Chaitanya Mahaprabhu, the fourteenth century *avatar* (god-incarnate) who, while praying in the temple ordained it open to all irrespective of caste and occupation. The great tradition remains. And today whoever enters this great temple and asks for *prasad* receives it, and the 'untouchable' and the Brahmin can eat off the same plate without scruple.

There are four gates to the shrine. The Lion Door on the east is richly decorated with sculptures symbolical of Hindu forms of worship and has a pyramidical roof. In front of the gate stands the famous black marble pillar, the Arun Stampha, brought from the Black Pagoda of Konarak, which is one of the most beautifully carved things in all India. The Sri temple (temple of Jagannath), a combination of four temples adjoining one other, was first built by Yayati Kesari in the 12th century A. D. and is now maintained by a vast endowment provided by the Rajas of Orissa. Maharaja Ranjit of the Punjab bequeathed the Koh-i-Noor to Jagannath, but his successors failed to carry out the bequest. 1484 priests in various capacities daily serve the Lord and altogether 20,000 persons earn their livelihood in the service of Jagannath. There is an endless chain of festivals at the temple; for there is always something on at Puri to proclaim Lord Jagannath's supremacy over the Universe.

But the Rath Jatra (Car Festival) in June-July, every year, is a great occasion when a mammoth congregation drawn from all parts of India assemble to watch the holy festival. Reposing on a huge chariot, 45 ft. high and supported on sixteen wheels the Lord moves on to his garden house, Gundich Bari, one mile away amidst wild rejoicings of a seething, almost hysterical, mass of humanity. In olden times devotees were known to have thrown themselves beneath the wheels, for it was considered a high virtue to die at the feet of Jagannath, but in recent times such practices have not been allowed.

**Sakshigopal :** Ten miles from Puri, is the celebrated Krishna temple at Satyabadi, near Sakshigopal, reached by bus or train. The temple is almost hidden by avenues of palms ; and the tank alongside which the temple is built adds much to the serenity of the spot.

Other places of interest in Puri are : Radhakanta Math ($\frac{1}{2}$ m. to the south of the Great Temple) where Sri Sri Chaitanya spent 18 years of his life in meditation. His slippers, water vase and blanket are preserved there : Sargadwar Gate (1 m. south of the temple) on the sea beach, where there are a number of *ashrams* : and the sea beach between Sargadwar Ghat and the Eastern Rly. Hotel.

\*　　　\*　　　\*　　　\*　　　\*

COMM. 310 m. from Calcutta and 38 m. from Bhubaneswar Puri is reached by train from Calcutta by a comfortable overnight jaurney, via Kburda Road. Local trains and buses are available for Puri from Cuttack and Bhubaneswar.

ACCOM. E. Rly. Hotel on the beach caters in European style, Middle class Indian hotels are Puri Hotel, Victoria Club. Sea View Hotel, Barons Hotel and Grand Hotel, all on the beach near Sargadwar and Bay View Hotel, on the Chakratirtha Road.

CONVEYANCE. Taxis are available, but cycle rickshaws and horse carriages are popular transport. There is a regular bus service to Bhubaneswar via Sakhigopal. Bus for Konarak is available only during summer (March-May).

# KONARAK

Twenty miles to the north-east of Puri along the sea coast, and 54 miles by motorable road via Pipli lie the stupendous remains of the wonderful temple of Konarak dominating the lonely grandeur of a fine sandy stretch on the Bay of Bengal. Built by Narasingha Deva 1, the Ruler of Orissa, in the 13th century in honour of the Sun God, the temple has no parallel in India for its profusion of sculptural wealth. It powerfully conveys the idea of the Sun-god speeding through the heavens in a chariot drawn by horses driven by Arjuna.

Though the elements have been merciless and man vandalic, yet sufficient remains to show that the Hindu builders possessed not only the poetic fancy to conceive great artistic creations, but also the technical skill to reproduce their dreams in stone on a gigantic, and yet highly imaginative, scale. Scrolls, images, animal figures, elephants, domestic scenes, scenes of battle and the chase, all are carved with amazing skill and with an extraordinary inspiration.

"Almost every inch of the outside surface is covered with carvings, portraying with a daring fidelity the vast panorama of life. All the variety of human experience, from its lowest to its highest expression is here depicted with a liveliness and exuberance of vitality which takes one's breath away. It is as though the master artist who designed this temple of the Sun had realised that since the Sun warms all life, every form and expression of it is sacred, from the most carnal to the most refined". Sir John Marshall says : "There is no monument of Hinduism, I think, that is at once so stupendous and so perfectly proportioned".

From the ruins that now remains, the sculptural splendour of the original temple can only be imagined; for the main shrine collapsed many years ago. All that now remains of the main temple is its adjunct, the audience hall which too had to be closed from all sides and filled up with rubble and sand to prevent collapse. But what still remains is breath-taking.

"Konarak is a living testimony to the speculative daring and artistic sensibility of an ancient people who

125

knew how to live, love, worship and create in heroic proportions".

A trip to Konarak is a veritable pilgrimage to India's glorious past. Visitors to Puri must not miss it whatever the inconvenience.

\* \* \*

COMM. Konarak is reached by bullock cart from Puri by an overnight journey along the sea coast (20 m). Two persons can travel in a cart; and the charge varies from Rs. 14/- to 16/- for a cart. There are bus services from Bhubaneswar and Puri (38 m. & 54 m. respectively) but the buses operate only for three months during summer, that is, from March to May. The 28-mile road from Pipli is muddy which makes the journey difficult. At Nimapara, midway between Pipli and Konarak, sweets, fruits and tea are available. There is also a cheap hotel at Nimapara. Bus fare from Puri : Rs. 5/- ; and Rs. 4/8/- from Bhubaneswar including return. Small planes are available from the Orissa Flying Club, Bhubaneswar for trip to Konarak (Details of charges are mentioned under Bhubaneswar).

ACCOM. There is a P. W. D. Inspection Bungalow at Konarak with a khansama. Tinned provision and stores should be taken ; for the Khansama may not be able to secure anything more than rice and vegetables. For longer stay in the Inspection Bungalow permission should be taken from the Executive Engineer, P. W. D. Puri. The sea-beach, before the temple is very wide; and the sea is two miles from the temple.

# GOPALPUR-ON-SEA

If you wish to take a quiet holiday in romantic surroundings, the ideal place is Gopalpur-on-Sea, an entrancing seaside town in Orissa, where there is a combination of all the best features of a seaside and a health resort packed into one. Here you will enjoy the towering cliffs. You can look up at them from the sandy beach or down from them on to a wonderful view across the watery waste to the dim blue line where earth and sky meet and mingle. You will enjoy immensely a few day's visit strolling around and taking it easy, the fascinating picture of a quaint Indian village with simple aboriginals, old temples, and woods wonderfully rich in flowers and bird life. In fact this tiny charming seaside resort affords a variety of scenic beauty which offers every distraction that the holiday maker could wish to find. Popular season is March-June, when the climate is mild and sea-bathing most refreshing. There are plenty of gay entertainments—golf, fishing and dove-shooting in back-waters. Surf-riding and yachting in the sea are most thrilling.

*     *     *

COMM. Gopalpur is 385 miles by rail from Howrah. 375 miles from Calcutta is Berhampur (Ganjam) the nearest rail-head whence Gopalpur is only 10 miles away reached by car or bus. There is a regular bus service from Behrampur.

ACCOM. The Palm Beach, an Oberoi hotel (Rs. 20/-), splendidly situated on the beach provides excellent accommodation and cuisine in European style. For middle class visitors accommodation is a problem. There are, of course, a number of middle class hotels run by Anglo-Indians, but they cannot be recommended for a variety of reasons. It will be better for them to stay at the Dak Bungalow. Family suites are available during the season at moderate rents.

## JAMSHEDPUR

156 miles west of Calcutta and close to Bihar's rich iron and coal fields, lies the mighty industrial town of Jamshedpur which bears the name of its founder. Set up in 1908 by Jamshedji Nauservanji Tata with the technical assistance of an American Engineer, Charles Page Perin, Jamshedpur today occupies a prominent place on the industrial map of the world, for its iron and steel factory is the biggest single steel manufacturing plant in all Asia. The five blast furnaces can produce 11 lac tons of pig iron per year, while the Duplex plant can turn out 3000 tons of steel a day. The industry employs over 10,000 persons. The story of how the obscure jungle village of Sakchi has developed into the India's picturesque "Steel Town", extending over an area of 25 sq. miles with a cosmopolitan population of about 2 lakhs is a stirring saga of human endeavour and perseverance that will inspire posterity for generations to come.

Sprawling between the Suvarnarekha and the Kharakai, Jamshedpur has its share of natural beauty that seems to lend charm to the matter-of-fact look of her vast blast furnace and sky-piercing chimneys.

\* \* \*

ACCOM. Jamshedpur lies on the Howrah-Bombay main line of the S.-Eastern Railway. Tata Guest House (Euro. style), Sakchi Dak Bungalow and Railway Retiring Rooms provide excellent accommodation for visitors. Guzrat Boarding & Lodging, Tisco Hotel and Jamshedpur Boarding House are good middle class hotels.

# CHAPTER II

# NORTHERN INDIA

*From the gleaming ramparts of the untrodden Himalayas spreads a vast sweep of land which, beyond Delhi, lies between the Jumna and the Ganges to form a most fertile stretch of land which takes a proud name of its own —the Doab or the Indo-Gangetic plain. On the banks of the two sacred streams flowing across this enormous expanse stand the holy cities of Hardwar, Brindaban, Allahabad and Banaras which draw millions of pilgrims from distant lands. As the original seat of the Indo-Aryans, Northern India has a rich heritage of historical associations of the old ages. In later times, here flourished the Grand Moghuls whose patronge gave a new impetus to the growth of literature, fine arts, architecture and crafts. And the monuments they erected were proportionate to their heroic deeds—the wonderful Taj Mahal, and the forts of Delhi, Agra and Fatehpur Sikri still stand over this land in deathless glory.*

## CHUNAR

Chunar, 20 miles north of Moghulserai, is a small, picturesque town, hedged between the river Ganga and the rocky spurs of the Vindhya Hills, and is well known for its historic associations. Besides, Chunar is famous from time immemorial for its stone quarries which supplied red and buff sandstones to the Indian kings beginning from Asoka to the late Moghul emperors, for their important sculptural and architectural constructions.

Of considerable historical interest is the old fortress which rises abruptly from the plain 400 feet high and commands a beautiful view of the Ganga. Its principal defence consists of a single stone parapet with watch towers built along the margin of the precipitous ridge. The fort played an important part in the stormy days of mediaeval India. In 1530, Chunar was the residence of Sher Shah who obtained it by marriage with the daughter of a local chief ; in 1537, Humayun captured it, but Sher Shah dislodged him soon after, and in the subsequent struggle between the Pathans and the Moghuls, Chunar formed the key to Bihar and Bengal. Since its conquest by Akbar in 1575 it remained with the Moghuls till 1750, when it fell to the Nawabs of Oudh. After his surprise defeat at the hands of Raja Chait Singh of Banaras, in 1781, Warren Hastings hurried to it for shelter and the house in which he lived still stands. The fort is about 2 miles from the station, and at present accommodates Government social service institutions.

Chunar has a good climate and a picturesque setting. There is a charming view of the Vindhya range which forms its western background. It has the virtues of a sanatorium for which it is resorted to by visitors who wish to have a quiet change.

*     *     *

COMM. 431 miles from Calcutta and 20 miles north of Moghulserai, Chunar is on the Howrah-Delhi main line. It is about 28 miles from Banaras via Moghulserai.

ACCOM. An Inspection Bungalow in the Fort, cheap eating houses in the town, and a Refreshment and Waiting Room at the station accommodate visitors. There is no good hotel. Transport consists of rickshaws and tongas. Taxis are not available.

## MIRZAPUR

From Chunar it is only half an hour's journey to Mirzapur, an ancient centre of brass and carpet industry and a great mart for cotton and grains, situated on the right bank of the Ganga.

There is a beautiful river-front studded with ghats and temples some of which contain good carvings. Six miles from the town, near the deserted cantonment town of Tara, there is a fine water-fall caused by the descent of a stream from the plateau of a Vindhya range. To the north-west of the town is the Civil Station wherein are situated the District Board and P.W.D. Dak Bungalows. Mirzapur enjoys a healthy climate and its water is exceptionally digestive and health-giving. So there is invariably a rush for water as the mail train s halt at the Mirzapur station.

*     *     *

COMM. Mirzapur lies on the Howrah-Delhi main li ne, 40 miles north of Moghulserai and 54 miles south of Allahabad. It can also be reached from Banaras by the Banaras-Allahabad meter gauge line changing at Madhosingh whence a short track leads to Chila passing through Mirzapur Ghat. From Chila there are ferries for Mirzapur and Vindhyachal. Roadways buses ply between Mirzapur Ghat and Allahabad and Banaras along the Grand Trunk Road.

ACCOM. Besides the Dak Bungalows in the Civil Lines there are cheap hotels in the town, near the station. All conventional conveyances including buses are available. There are lst. and 2nd. class Waiting Rooms and well-appointed Refreshment Rooms at the station.

## VINDHYACHAL

Vindhyachal, a notable pilgrim-place and a sanatorium, is really a continuation of Mirzapur, being only 4 miles to the north-west. The town is situated on a detached hill overlooking the Ganga which flows a mile below it.

Great sanctity is attached to the temple of Bindubasini, on the Ganga, who is worshipped with the greatest reverence. The Vindhya ranges start from here and on the top of the mountain, to the west of the railway line, are two other places of worship—the temple

131

of Astabhuja and Kali-khon—each a mile and a half from the station. The Kali temple, it is said, was once the rendezvous of the *Thugs*. Other places of interest on the hill-top includes the temple of Sri Krishna, Ma Anandamayee Ashram, Sita Kund and Bhairab Kund, all facing the Ganga.

Vindhachal owes its popularity to its fine climate and picturesque surroundings for which it is resorted to by visitors from all parts of India. From the top of the Vindhya ranges there is a charming view of the Ganga flowing at a little distance. One can have a beautiful view of the town from the passing train. It is an ideal place for those who want a quiet holiday in charming surroundings. The best season is November-March.

\*          \*          \*

ACCOM. There are no hotels, but there is a Dak Bungalow on the top of the hill. Beside, there are Dharamsalas and temple rest-rooms. Bungalows are available for hire at monthly rates. Ekkas and cycle rickshaws provide transport. There are Dak Bungalows, middle class hotels and Rly. Refreshment Rooms at Mirzapur which should be the best base for visit for the flying visitor

# BANARAS

422 miles from Calcutta, 950 miles from Bombay and 1330 miles from Madras is Banaras, the holiest of the holy spots of the Hindus and the centre and crown of Hindu India.

Timeless and pre-historic, Banaras has been the capital of Hinduism from the dawn of Indian life ; it is one of the oldest cities in the world. Here is a congregation of 1500 temples headed by the famous temple of Vishwanatha which magically sways the hearts of countless millions of this sub-continent. The holy city is the epitome of all that is best in Hindu religion and philosophy. Its rare sanctity, thousands of hallowed memories of saints and seers and great deeds of preachers

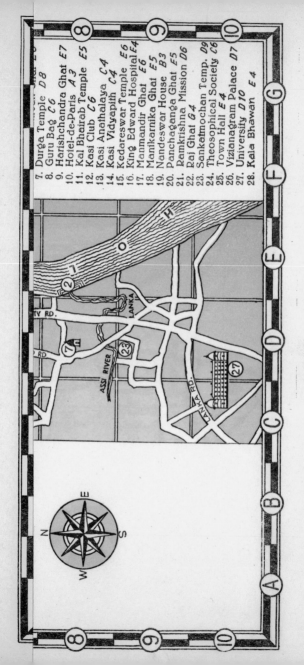

7. Durga Temple *D 8*
8. Guru Bag *C 6*
9. Harishchandra Ghat *E 7*
10. Hotel-de-Paris *A 3*
11. Kal Bhairab Temple *E 5*
12. Kasi Club *C 6*
13. Kasi Anathalaya *C 4*
14. Kasi Vidyapith *C 4*
15. Kedareswar Temple *E 6*
16. King Edward Hospital *F 4*
17. Manmandir Ghat *E 6*
18. Manikarnika Ghat *E 5*
19. Nandeswar House *B 3*
20. Panchaganga Ghat *E 5*
21. Ramkrishna Mission *D 6*
22. Raj Ghat *G 4*
23. Sanketmochan Temp. *D 9*
24. Theosophical Society *C 6*
25. Town Hall *E 4*
26. Vizianagram Palace *D 7*
27. University *D 10*
28. Kala Bhawan *E 4*

and reformers, its sacred temples and bathing ghats on the river—all make it the holiest and the most beloved city of the Hindus. Throughout the ages, men and women from all parts of India have yearned to visit Banaras to wash away their sins and to die at the feet of Siva which means salvation and eternal bliss.

With its array of temples, palaces, minarets and crowded ghats rising tier over tier above the water, Banaras is also the most colourful and picturesque of all the cities of India. It is a wonderful sight to see the vast crowd of worshippers, who throng the stone stairs as they stream up and down the river, to make their ablutions and repeat their prayers. As the visitor floats down the river in a boat he sees the most picturesque religious pageantry that the East can show, and imagination recalls through the dim vistas of time the endless procession of devout people wending their way down the narrow lanes to the temple with garlands to adorn their gods or to wreathe in devotion the emblem of Siva's divinity.

For miles this wonderful scene of devotion and colour stretches along the river-side as the devotees bathe in the Ganga and offer their prayers in the temple. Then they depart for their distant homes, satisfied that they have set their eyes on the most sacred places of their faith, and in sweep fresh thousands to take the place of each returning band.

## Places of Interest

The chief holy spots in the city are the temple of Vishwanatha or Golden Temple crowned by a dome covered with thin plates of gold; the temple of Annapurna embellished with delicately tinted sculptures; the Panchaganga Ghat; and Manikarnika, the sacred burning ghat. Other notable sights are: Dasaswamedh Ghat, the popular bathing ghat and the show-place of the city; Raja Jai Singh's Observatory, near Dasasawamadh Ghat; the Bharat Mata Temple which contains a gigantic relief map of India carved on white marble; the Durga Temple with its graceful architecture; Mausoleum of Vaskarananda; and, of course, the Hindu University which keeps alive the city's age-old tradition as a great centre of culture.

\* \* \*

ACCOM. The two western style hotels are: Clark's Hotel and Hotel-de-Paris (Rs. 20/- daily), both in the Cantonment. Good Indian hotels are: Central Hotel and Banaras Lodge at Dasaswamedh Ghat Rd., Grand Hotel at Nichi Bagh and Empress Hotel on Vidyapith Rd. There are 20 Dharmsalas in the city of which the most popular ones are situated at Godhulia. Strangers should ask the rickshaw puller to take them to Pare Dharamsala or Harasundari Dharamsala at Godhulia or to one of the hotels at the Dasaswamedh Ghat Road (as. -/8/- for the full rickshaw).

CONVEYANCE. Taxis, buses, cycle rikshaws and tongas. There is a city bus service which operates from Godhulia. Cantonment and Kasi Rly. stations are about 2 m. from Godhulia corner which is close to the temple and ghats, and where are situated the popular Dharamsalas and hotels.

SHOPPING. Banaras is world-famous for its exquisite silks, brocades and sarees. Enamelled brassware and lacquerad toys are also famous.

## SARNATH

About 5 miles north-east of Banaras lies the ancient relics of Sarnath, or holy Isipatana, where Lord Buddha delivered his first sermon 2,500 years ago and set into motion the Wheel of Law. Here was first revealed the cause of earthly suffering and the means to extinct suffering to the five disciples—Kondayana, Vishpa, Bhadrika, Mahanam, and Ashvajit—who had earlier deserted the Master at Uruvela. At the end of the sermon Kondayana came near the Buddha and said: "Lord, let us receive ordination from the Blessed one". And the Buddha said: "Come, O bhikkhus! Well taught is the doctrine. Lead a holy life for the extinction of suffering". At that moment there were only six holy persons in the world—the Lord himself and his five disciples.

The place soon became the principal centre of Buddhist learning from where the teachings of Lord Buddha spread throughout the length and breadth of the country. Here was built the first thatched hut (Mulagandha Kuti) to shelter the Master from monsoon. The illustrious monarch Asoka later added a new interest to the place by building a stupa (Dharmarajika) and a pillar in honour of his Master. Gradually, Sarnath became so important that in the Gupta era it surpassed Mathura as a great centre of image-making. In the 12th century, a queen of King Govindachandra of Kanauj invested it with new shrines and monasteries and the glories of Sarnath continued undiminished till it was destroyed by the Muslims.

After the terrible devastation of Sarnath by Kutbuddin in 1195, the place lay buried under ruins and jungle for nearly eight hundred years, lost from the view of the world. It was by a chance that the place was rediscovered at the beginning of the 19th century. In 1794, Jagat Singh, Dewan of Raja Chait Singh of Banaras, unknowingly pulled down a stupa in search for quarry, and that was no other than the Dharmarajika Stupa of Asoka. In the course of dismantling the Stupa, two marble vessels were found, one containing some human bones, and the other pearls and gold leaves. These bones, believed to have been the earthly remains of the Blessed One, were cast into the Ganga to the accompaniment of great ceremonies. An account of this was published by Mr. Jonathan Duncan, the British Resident of Banaras, and this attracted the attention of a distinguished line of scholars and archaeologists. To Sir John Marshall, however, goes the honour of rediscovering Sarnath for what it is today. This was successfully followed up by Anagarika Dharmapala of Ceylon and his successor, the Mahabodhi Society which by its constant effort has succeeded in re-establishing Sarnath to somewhat its former glory. The Mulagandhakukti Vihara completed by the Society in 1931 and which bears on its walls magnificent frescoes done by a Japanese artist, is a place steeped in peculiarly profound spiritual calm.

## Objects of Interest

**Chowkhandi** : At the approach to Sarnath, about half a mile below the main site, is a dilapidated stupa surmounted by a modern brick tower. This is probably the spot where the five disciples first met the Buddha before the sermon was preached to them. In later times, Emperor Akbar (1956-1605) raised a brick tower over it to commemorate his father's (Humayun) visit to Sarnath.

**Museum** : This preserves an enormous quantity of priceless relics and a large number of Buddha and Bodhisattva images, mostly of the Gupta era, dug out of Sarnath including the famous Lion-Capital which forms the emblem of the Government of India. In fact, the superb Buddha and Boddisattva images of Sarnath have earned for Gupta art the pride of place that it now occupies in the art-history of India.

**Dhamek Stupa** : At the centre of the main site and dominating the entire scene stands the Dhamek Stupa (143 ft. in height), the most remarkable monument extant at Sarnath. This is assigned to 500 A.D., for it bears intricate workmanship and floral decorations characteristic of the Gupta period. At the south-west of Dhamak is a Jain temple of modern date.

**Asoka Pillar** : At the north-west corner of the excavated area stands the broken stump of the Asoka Pillar which most probably marks the spot where the first sermon was delivered. Close to it is an enclosed area where once stood the Dharmarajika stupa of Asoka.

**Mulagandhakuti Vihara** : This is the modern temple built by the Mahabodhi Society in 1931 and the centre of present worship. It bears on its walls Ajanta-style frescoes painted by a Japanese artist depicting events from Lord Buddha's life. The Mahabodhi Library contains a rare collection of Buddhist literature. A little to the east is the Chinese Temple which contains a beautiful marble image of the Buddha.

\* \* \*

COMM.  Sarnath is connected by a fine metalled road with Banaras which is the base for pilgrimage to Sarnath.  Taxis and cycle rickshaws can be hired at Banaras for the trip.  Buses of the Uttar Pradesh Roadways operate on special occasions, such as the Anniversary of the Vihara in November and the Siva temple fair in August.  Sarnath is also connected by rail, but few people use the train due to inconvenient timings.

ACCOM.  There is a two-storied Dharamsala at Sarnath, a gift of the Birla family, where visitors can stay with permission from the Secretary, Mohabodhi Society.  There is no local bazar.

# AJODHYA

The ancient history of Ajodhya, the capital of Kosala on the Gogra river, 117 miles from Banaras on the Lucknow route, is lost in a myriad of legend and mythology.  The place is most beloved to the Hindus as the birth-place and the capital of Ram Chandra, the hero of Ramayana, and is held by the Puranas as one of the seven sacred places.  After the death of the last Solar king, Ajodhya which is said to have covered an area of 96 sq. miles, became a wilderness although it continued to be an important place throughout the centuries.  Lord Buddha travelled extensively in the kingdom and when Hiuen Tsang visited Ajodhya in the 7th century he found it a great place of worship.

King Vikramaditya succeeded in tracing the outlines of a considerable number of old buildings rendered sacred by association with the events in the life of Rama.  The most important of these are Ramkot, the birth-place of Sri Ram Chandra which is marked by a small temple adjacent to a mosque; Nageswarnath temple dedicated to Lord Shiva; Hanuman temple, the most imposing edifice of the town; Darshan Singh's temple; and the Maniparbat or the sacred mound.  Besides, there are many beautiful temples.  The temple dedicated to Sita Devi stands on the Sita Ghat.

COMM. Ajodhya lies on the Banaras-Lucknow main line of the N. Rly., and can be reached by through trains from all the cities of Northern India. Coming from Gorakhpur side, Ajodhya Ghat can be reached via Mankapur Junction. There is a regular motor launch ferry service between Ajodhya Ghat and Ajodhya.

ACCOM. There are Dharamsalas. But the best base for a visit to Ajodhya is Fyzabad, 4 miles away, where there are a number of middle-class hotels, a Circut House, Inspection Bungalow and a Dak Bungalow. Tongas and cycle rikshaws are are usual transport.

## FYZABAD

4 miles from Ajodhya is Fyzabad, the old capital of the Nawabs of Oudh which still contains many monuments and tombs of royal proportions. The capital w as transferred to Lucknow by Asaf-ud-daula in 1780 whence Fyzabad receded into unimportance and Lucknow sprang into prominence.

Of the monuments, the mausoleum of Babu Begam, the widow of Shuja-ud-daula, is the finest in Uttar Pradesh. Close by is the mausoleum of Shuja-ud-daula which is similar to that of the Begum.

There is a museum containing Jain antiquities and a library in the Guptar Park ("the Park of Disappearance"). Atone corner is a temple which is said to mark the spot whence Rama disappeared. Ajodhya is only 4 miles from the Cantonment approached by a fine road.

\*                    \*                    \*

ACCOM. There are a number of cheap, middle class hotels and Dharamsalas. The Dist. Board Dak Bungalow is near the Sadar Post Office. There is a Circuit House and an Inspection Bungalow is the Civil Lines. Cycle rickshaws and tongas are usual transport. There are bus services to the neighbouring towns.

## LUCKNOW

Lying on the bend of the river Gomati is Lucknow, the capital of Uttar Pradesh and one of the most beautiful cities of India. When it was the capital of the Kings of Oudh two centuries ago, Lucknow was virtually the "Paris of India", the centre of culture and gracious living. The city rose to a great height of prosperity in all India during the reign of Asaf-ud-Daula (1775-1779), when most of the outstanding buildings including the Great Imambara were built and when this city definitely replaced Delhi as the seat of Muslim culture and literature. Even today when much of its old splendour is lost, the city is a showplace. Seen from the Frazer bridge, the city appears one mass of beautiful buildings, crowned with domes of burnished gold while scores of minarets, palaces and tombs interspersed with rich foliage and fine parks lend to the scene that harmonious splendour reminiscent of old Oriental grandeur.

**History :** Legend connects the founding of the city with Lakshman, the brother of Rama, and the city was known as Lakshmanpur until the name was altered to Laknau during the reign of the Nawabs of Oudh.

The dynasty of Oudh was founded by a Persian named Saadat Khan who, for his signal service to the Emperor of Delhi, was rewarded with the Governorship of Oudh. He had his headquarters at Fyzabad. Saadat Khan made the most of his opportunity, consolidated his domain and amassed fabulous wealth. His successor, Sefdar Jang (1739-1753) was a favourite of Delhi and was promoted Vazir to the Emperor. He died at Fyzabad but his remains were transported to Delhi where they were interred in the beautiful mausoleum known as Safdar Jang.

The next Nawab Suja-ud-Daula (1753-1775) joined hands with the Moghul Emperor, Shah Alam, against the British but was defeated at the battle of Buxar. Though vanquished he was fortunate enough to retain his kingdom, but was forced by Lord Clive to pay a heavy war indemnity sufficient to cover the cost of the campaign. He resided at Fyzabad where he died.

Lucknow rose to the greatest height of prosperity it has ever known under Asaf-ud-Daula (1775-1797), a passionate builder and a patron of art and culture. He transferred his capital to Lucknow from Fyzabad. His court was famed throughout Hindustan for its lavish splendour. He built the Daulat Khana, the Great Imambara and its mosque, the Rumi Darwaza, Khurshid Manzil, the Banqueting Hall and the garden pavilions at Charbagh and Aishbagh. He was greatly loved by his subjects and is mentioned with affection and honour even to this day.

The next ruler was Saadat Ali Khan (1798-1814) who was installed by Sir John Shore after the deposition of a usurper. He, too, was a builder and spent large sums for developing Lucknow. Thanks to his efforts the city grew to very nearly its present size. He built the Moti Mohal, Dilkhusa gardens, the Throne Room (Lal Baradari) and the King's Stables.

Saadat Ali Khan was followed by his son, Ghazi-ud-Din Haidar (1814-1827), remarkable for his agreeable and polished etiquette and for the dignity of his court where art and literature received the most liberal patronage. He was made the first king of Oudh by the British. He built the Residency, the Kaizarbagh tombs, the tomb at Shah Najaf, the Kadam Rasul and the Wilaiyat Bagh. He also constructed the canal on the south side of the city. He lies buried at Shah Najaf, the white-domed mausoleum on the bank of the Gomati.

The next ruler Nasir-ud-din-Haider (1827-1837), a debased sovereign, built the Chhatter Manzil and the Tarawalt Kothi.

Muhammad Ali Shah (1837-1842), an able ruler, added to the beauties of his capital by building the Husainabad Imambara where he is buried, the Jama Masjid, the Tank and the adjacent structures.

The reign of the next king, Amjad Ali Shah (1842-

1847) was marked by increasing signs of disorder and decadence. He, too, was something of a builder. He built the Hazratganj Imambara in which he is buried, the Iron Brigade and the metalled road to Kanpur.

The fifth and the last King of Oudh, Wajid Ali Shah, ascended an already tottering throne. Pleasure-loving and indolent, Wajid Ali was not the man to save the situation. Under him matters moved from bad to worse. The state was plunged heavily into debt. His interest was centered in the harem whose three hundred and seventy members each enjoyed a separate suite of apartments. He was deposed in February 1856 and removed to Calcutta where he died in 1887. He built the Kaizarbagh palaces, only a fraction of which now survives, at a cost of eighty lakhs.

**Places of Interest** : For the purpose of sight-seeing the city may be divided into four parts :

(1) The old city called Chauk around which flourishes the bazars where are to be seen the art and crafts for which Lucknow is famous—sarees of various designs and hues, gold and silver brocades, silverware, clay figurines, pottery and a hundred other odd curios. (ii) The Royal Quarters, or Kaizarbagh, consisting of the Rumi Darwaza, the Great Imambara, Machhi Bhawan, the isolated palaces of Hosainabad, Chattar Manzil and Moti Mahal which together present a most spectacular panorama of architectural work and costly splendour. (iii) The Civil Lines between Moti Mahal and the Canal consisting of the Council House, Secretariat and Hazratganj with its fashionable shops, avenues and parks. (iv) The Cantonment area with the beautiful Dilkhusa gardens and open spaces.

**Great Imambara** : The Rumi Darwaza, and the Great Imambara together with the buildings of Hosinabad form an architectural groups which in point of size and splendour has been pronounced as one of the most imposing in India. The Great Imambara is Asaf-

141

ud-daula's glory and the pride of Lucknow. The Nawab is said to have spent millions on it. The central hall, measuring 162 ft. in length and 53 ft. in breadth, is the largest vaulted apartment in the world. The internal splendour of the Great Imambara, once fairy-like, has greatly diminished. A steep flight of seemingly endless steps through dark, tortuous corridors—almost a Chinese puzzle—leads upward to the sunlit flat, roof which affords a wondrous view of the surrounding panorama. Aurangzeb's mosque on the crest of Lakshman Tila towers in front, and the Husainabad Imambara, a poor imitation of the Great Imambara, lies to the west. At the west flank of the Imambara are the dilapidated buildings of the Machhi Bhawan (fishing palace) and beyond it are the buildings of the Lucknow Medical College.

**The Residency or Belle Garad :** To men and women of the British Isles, however, Lucknow is a place hallowed by memories, at once pathetic and heroic, of the Mutiny of 1857. As a memento of that stern struggle, the Residency has been preserved to this day as it stood at the end of that terrible six months. The walls still bear the marks of shot and shell ; the shattered gates show where assault after assault was delivered on the British garrison. The picture gallery in the central hall is interesting for the old paintings illustrative of the grim battle.

Other places of interest are : Hussainabad Imambara ("the palace of lights") ; the Old Clock Tower and gardens ; the Jama Masjid ; the Victoria Gardens, near Kaisarbagh ; Lal Baradari, now the State Museum ; Shah Najaf and Sikandra Bagh (now Government Horticultural Gardens) on the river ; and the Grand Chatter Manzil, once the residence of the royal ladies and now headquarters of the Central Drug Laboratory. In the Baradari, close to the Old Clock Tower gardens, are to be seen the life-size portraits of the Nawabs of Oudh. The Banarasi Garden attached to the Zoo, a little to the east of the Council Chamber, is Lucknow's pre-eminent beauty spot.

**Hints for Sight-seeing :** At least two days should be given to sight-seeing in Lucknow. In the first outing, visitor should proceed in a cycle-rickshaw from Aminabad Park (centre of the city) to the Great Imambara seeing Hazratganj, Kaisar Bagh, Lal Baradari (Museum) and the Residency on the way. Leaving the Great Imambara, the Clock Tower and Husainabad Imambara should be visited. On the return journey Jama Masjid and the Chowk may be seen. In the evening Shah Najaf and Sikandra Bagh (on the Gomati) can be visited. At nightfall it is pleasant to saunter at the fashionable shopping centre at Hazratganj. The Council Chamber, Government House, Banarasi Garden and Zoo (all close to one another) can be seen in another outing. Buses go to almost all the places from Charbagh station.

*      *      *

COMM. Lucknow is an important railway centre served by four broad gauge and two meter gauge lines. The Central Railway connects it from Bombay via Kanpur where, it meets the Northern Railway. It is reached by through trains from Delhi, Calcutta and other principal cities. Lucknow is also served by air. IAC booking office is at the Carlton Hotel.

ACCOM. Carlton Hotel at Shahanajaf Road is the leading European style hotel. Good Indian style hotels are : Kapoor's Hotel, Hazratganj ; Imperial Hotel and Majestic Hotel, Lal Bagh ; Central Hotel, Aminabad ; Bengal Hotel and Hotel Hindustan, both at Charbagh. Railway Retiring Room (N. E. Rly.) at the station (Rs. 4/8/- daily) is a fine place to stay.

CONVEYANCE : Rickshaws and tongas are popular transport. Uttar Pradesh Railways provide excellent transport in the city and beyond it to the neighbouring towns and places of tourist interest. Taxis are available.

SHOPPING : Gold and Silver embriodery, Chikan kurtas, table covers, silverware, clay figurines and potteries are famous. U.P. Govt. Emporium at Hazratganj deals in all the varieties.

143

# NAIMISHARANYA

Naimisharanya! the very name conjures up to memory a great vista of ancient India, when in the depths of the forests the Aryan Rishis meditated on the mysteries of the Universe and life and produced a philosophy which is the proudest of all our heritage. This ancient intellectual centre of imperishable renown is today marked by a small station on the Balamau-Sitapur section of the Northern Rly., about 45 miles north of Lucknow. Even today the place maintains much of its ancient calm which provided the forest ascetics the seclusion for their high metaphysical speculations. The river Gomati flows nearby. According to literary evidence here was evolved the metaphysics of the Aranayakas (forest portion of the Upanishads) and the later Upanishads.

The monthly Amavasya fair attracts large crowds. There are two Dharamsalas at Naimisharanya.

# BAREILLY

Bareilly (pop. 208,083), the largest city of Rohil-khand, is a busy trade centre, and is well known for the production of rosin, bobbin, catechu, matches and furnitures. A considerable volume of merchandise moves to the northern Himalayan region from this place. Besides, Bareilly is an important educational centre which contains a number of educational institutions and technical institutes. Historically, this was the headquarters of the Rohillas, a plundering Afghan tribe, who ransacked and conquered wide territories from Almora to Etawah and later provoked the Mahrattas to plunder their territory. Hafiz Rahamat Khan, the Rohilla ruler, was, however, a mild and popular prince and the British, at first, had no quarrel with him. But Nawab Sujauddaulah of Oudh coveted his territory, and Warren Hastings, in his insatiable greed for money, lent him a British brigade in an unholy alliance which came in for much criticism at the time. The Rohilla War (1773-74) that ensued involved much unnecessary violence, oppression, inhumanity and cruelty ; the British troops behaved barbarously and Hafiz Rahamat Khan was killed in battle. Faiz Ullah, a Rohilla scion, was later recognised by Nawab Asafuddaulah as the Rohilla chief from whom is descended the present Nawab of Rampur.

Bareilly contains a number of fine mosques of which the mosque of Shaikh Ahmad Khandan bears a Persian inscription of Balban (1284 A. D.).

**Ahhichatra :** About 20 miles west of Bareilly, in the village of Ramnagar, lies the excavated ruins of the ancient fortress-city of Ahhichatra which is mentioned in the Mahabharata as the capital of North Panchalas who helped the Pandavas in the battle of Kurukshetra. Excavations have unearthed a brick fortification with a perimeter of $3\frac{1}{2}$ miles, domestic buildings, temples, stupas, fine pottery, coins and terra-cotta images of Brahmanical deities ranging in date from the third century B. C. to the end of the tenth century A. D. The Panchala land was a great centre of Vedic culture. About 2 miles west of the fortified area are the ruins of some stupas, one of which is supposed to have been built by Asoka. Hiuen Tsang saw here ten Buddhist monasteries and nine Brahmanical temples in the 7th century A. D.

\*   \*   \*

COMM. 146 miles from Lucknow and 157 miles from Delhi, Bareilly is an important Rly. junction on the Moghulserai Saharanpur main line of the Northern Rly. A meter gauge line of N. E. Rly. runs from Agra Fort via Kasganj and Bareilly to Kathgodam (for Nainital). By road Bareilly is 63 miles from Kathgodam ; there is a regular bus service between Bareilly and Nainital through Haldwani and Kathgodam.

ACCOM. Of the hotels, Civil & Military Hotel and Royal Hotel in the Cantonment are preferred. There is a Dak Bungalow in the Cantonment and cheap middle class hotels in the town. But it is more convenient to stay at the Railway Retiring Room at the station (2 rooms with two beds each : charge Rs 5/- per room for 24 hours).

CONVEYANCE. All types of conveyances are available. U. P. Roadways buses go to many places including Shajahanpur, Sitapur, Rampur, Moradabad, Badaun, Haldwani and Nainital.

# RAMPUR

Rampur (pop. 134,277), 39 miles north of Bareilly, on the main line to Delhi and Saharanpur, is a classic town, rich with gardens and parks, monuments and temples, libraries and art galleries. This was the capital of the Rohilla State of Rampur now merged with Uttar Pradesh. It has a number of factories.

In the Fort is the famous library which contains a rich collection of Oriental manuscripts including a number of precious Moghul paintings. Of great interest is the little volume of Turki verse autographed by Babar and Shah Jahan. Other objects of interest include the Museum, the Juma Masjid, Khasabagh palace, Sahabad Castle and the temples.

\*       \*       \*

ACCOM. Rampur State Hotel is close to the station. There are a number of middle class hotels and Dharamsalas. Conveyance includes tongas, cycle rickshaws and taxis.

# MORADABAD

Moradabad (pop. 161,854), 17 miles from Rampur and 100 miles from Delhi, is an important railway centre and a large city in Rohilkhand noted for its ornamented and plated brasswares.

The city, named after Murad, son of Shah Jahan, lies on the Ramganga river ; to the north-west is the Civil Station and to the west is the Juma Masjid, a handsome building erected in 1631, on the bank of the river. To the north of the town are the ruins of the fort built by the Rohilla chief, Rustom Khan.

At Sambal, 22 miles south of the town, there is a mosque with an inscription which states that it was built by Babar. But this is doubtful. The Hindus claim it to be a shrine of Vishnu.

*  *  *

COMM. Lying on the Moghalserai-Saharanpur main line of the Northern Rly., Moradabad is an important railway junction: a line runs (100 miles) to Delhi via Hapur (change for Meerut) crossing the Ganga at Garhmukteswar ; and another to Aligarh (89 miles) via Chandausi. A metre gauge line runs to Kathgodam (for Nainital) via Kashipur and Lalkua. U. P. Roadways buses go to many places including Meerut, Chandausi, Haldwani and Nainital.

ACCOM. There is a Dak Bungalow (2 miles from station). Cheap hotels, Dharamsalas and Mussafirkhanas are there. All types of conveyances are available.

# NAINITAL

23 miles from Kathgodam, linked by a spectacular mountain road, and on the shore of a fairy-like lake, in a cup between pine-clad hills, is Nainital (6,500 ft.), a Himalayan hill station of great beauty.

Coming up from Kathgodam by car or motor bus the eye can hardly believe what it sees ; for, as the vehicle rises 6,500 feet, there lies this shining water, still and majestic, more than a mile long and surrounded by green slopes of idyllic beauty. A fine road (the Mall) passes along the eastern shore which is the show-place of the town, and on its side are situated most of the hotels, residences and shops. The lake lies north to south, and a horse-ride or walk from Talli Tal (southern end) to Malli Tal (Northern end) through the romantic setting of the eastern shore is the chief vocation of the visitors to Nainital. The highest peaks, Cheena, 8,568 ft. and Deapatta, 7,587 ft., are to the north and can be ascended to by the more hardy. A pretty ride on the west side of the Lake is a favourite pastime, the road ascending to a considerable height through wooded slopes. But the finest view is obtained from the east side, from Sher-ke-danda and its top Laria Kanta, whence the snowy ranges of Almora and Ranikhet may be seen.

There is seldom an hour of dullness at Nainital. Added to the invigorating climate there is a large choice of sports and mountaineering. Besides these, there is excellent yachting and boating on the lake and plenty of swimming and fishing in it.

## Excursions from Nainital

Nainital is the ideal base for excursions to the hill stations and the beauty spots of the Kumayun hills which, besides fishing, hiking and shooting, afford wonderful views of the snowy Himalayan peaks.

**Bhowali & Bhimtal :** 7 miles east of Nainital, through a romantic mountain road, is Bhowali, a quiet sanatorium hidden by tall trees and thickly wooded forests. Leaving Nainital, the bus to Bhimtal (14 miles by bus via Bhowali and 10 miles by pony by short-cut) halts for a few minutes at the Bhowali bazar and then proceeds another 7 miles south-east for Bhimtal which contains one of the largest lakes in the Kumayun hills. This triangular lake was once an ideal spot for mahaser fishing, but fishing is not allowed at present. A detached pavilion rising from the waters of the lake provides a charming picnic spot. At the south-east shore of the lake stands the palace of the Maharaja of Jind, who was a great connoisseur of dogs ; the south-west shore is fringed by picturesque wooded hills. From this point Kathgodam is only 7 miles by a bridle-path.

About two and half miles east of Bhimtal is **Naukuchia Tal,** the nine-cornered lake, reached by a newly-built, fine metalled road. The Tal, the largest in the Kumayun, is fenced by oak forests on three sides and is said to be 180 feet deep. There is a dreamy beauty about the spot which is also an ideal place for fishing. In the neighbouring village called Shilloh was born Pandit Gobinda Ballabh Pant. Nainital was also the haunting-ground of Jim Corbett, the famous author.

There is a spacious District Board Dak Bungalow at Bhimtal where one can stay for a few days while holidaying in Bhimtal, Naukauchia Tal and Sat Tal, another lovely spot on the way to Bhimtal. The Sat Tal group of lakes lie $1\frac{1}{2}$ m. south of the motor road, mid-way between Bhowali and Bhimtal.

**Ramgarh :** 8 miles from Bhowali and 15 miles from Nainital by bus is Ramgarh, one of the prettiest spots and the home of orchards. Beautifully set amidst luxuriant vegetation it has an excellent climate and presents a good view of the distant snow. The State Government has established a Fruit Preservation Factory at Ramgarh. There is a P.W.D. Dak Bungalow which can be occupied with permission from the Executive Engineer, Kumayun Prov. Divn., Nainital.

**Mukteswar :** About 30 miles from Nainital and 14 miles from Ramgarh is Mukteswar (7,500 ft.), a place of rare beauty, which abounds in fine walks and sights as delightful as any in Kashmir. This also is noted for its fruits and orchards; but by far the most fascinating is the lovely, dense verdure, ablaze with rhododendrons and an assortment of flowers, through which one gets a glorious view of the Himalayan snow early in summer and autumn. The place is well-known for the Veterinary Research Institute. There is a P.W.D. Dak Bunga-low. Cottages are available on monthly hire. There is a direct bus service from Kathgodam via Bhowali and Ramgarh.

*       *       *

COMM. Kathgodam is the railhead for Nainital, Ramgarh Mukteswar, Ranikhet, Almora and other tourist centres in the Kumayun region of the Northern Himalayas. Buses of U.P.

Govt. Roadways and Kumaon Motor Owners Ltd., run to all, these places and the transport is comfortable and cheap. There are many Dak Bungalows & Inspection houses lining the route. Permission for a long stay in these is given by the Executive Engineer, Kumayun Prov. Divisn. Nainital.

ACCOM. Western style hotels of Nainital are: Hotel Metropole, Swiss Hotel and Royal Hotel. Good Indian hotels are: Grand Hotel (Rs. 14/-) Waldort Astoria (Rs. 10/-), Elphinstone (Rs, 12/-) and Himalaya Hotel (Rs. 10/-). The Y. M. C. A. gives superb food and accommodation largely in European style for Rs. 7/8/- per day.

CONVEYANCE. Taxies, rickshaws and ponies.

# RANIKHET

"The finest place in the world", to quote Justice William O. Douglas of the United States Supreme Court, is Ranikhet, an important military hill station (6,000 ft.), 52 miles from Kathgodam and 37 miles from Nainital. The mountain-road to Ranikhet passes through enchanting sights. On the way is Garampani (half-way between Nainital and Ranikhet), where the way-side eating houses serve delicious refreshments.

Beautifully set on a narrow strip on the top of a thickly wooded hill, flaming with rhododendrons and a thousand species of flowers, Ranikhet is a glorious hill station surrounded by thick vegetation, forests of pine and oak, beautiful cedars and cypresses of indescribable beauty. In point of scenic grandeur it goes very near to Darjeeling. The views of snow-capped Himalayan range including the twin peaks of Nanda Devi from here are as near perfection as possible. The long snowline crowned by the Nanda Devi towers in front above the green hills. Best views can be had from the terrace of the Ranikhet Club, in the centre af the town, or from the observation platform in front of the Military Officers' Mess at Chaubatia, 6 miles to the south-east, reached by a fine motor road through the Government fruit gardens. The Nanda Devi (25,640) rises directly in front, while the Trisul (23,360 ft.) and Kamet (25,450) lie at the north-west. Ranikhet is also the base of one of the pilgrim routes to Kedarnath, Badrinath, Manas Sarobar and the Pindari Glacier. Ranikhet is extremely cold—minimum temperature being 26 degrees in winter. Visitors must take heavy warm clothing.

There are many pleasant walks and picnic spots in the nearby hills and dales with ample facilities for riding, shooting and fishing. Kosi and Ramganga rivers are ideal for fishing. Ranikhet Club provides billiards, table tennis, badminton etc. It has a library and a bar. There are a number of excursion spots in the vicinity with Dak Bungalows. No permission is necessary to occupy them. The Nanda Devi fair, held every year in August-September, provides colourful dancing and singing.

\*     \*     \*

COMM. Ranikhet is reached from Kathgodam via Bhowali by U. P. Roadways buses in 4½ hours. Bus fare : Rs. 4/8/-. It is also reached by bus from Nainital in 3 hours.

ACCOM. There are good hotels and bungalows at different heights. West View Hotel (Rs. 13/- daily), Norton's Hotel (Rs. 11/- daily) and Hotel Rosemount are attractive. There are cheap hotels near the bus-stand but they are not recommended. There are three Dak Bungalows : (1) Forest Rest House (permission from Sub-divisional Forest Officer, West Divn. Almora), (2) M. E. S. Inspection Bungalow (permission from Sub-Divisional Officer, M. E. S., Ranikhet), (3) P. W. D. Inspection Bungalow (permission from Secy, Dist. Board, Almora).

## ALMORA

Almora (5,400 ft.), 82 miles from Kathgodam and 32 miles from Ranikhet by bus, is an ancient hill station. It was the capital of the Chand Rajas in the 16th. century. The town is situated on a bare ridge from which an exceedingly fine view of the snowy peaks can be obtained. There are many religious ashrams and educational institutions in the town while in the neighbourbood are the famous Binsar and Jalna fruit orchards. Mahatma Gandhi had spent three weeks in Almora and was so impressed by the climate and scenic beauty of the Kumayun hills that he was "more than amazed why our people need go to Europe in search of health." The Ramkrishna Mission is situated at the West End, beneath the 'Brighton Corner', while the Ashram of Ma Anandmayee is at Patel Devi close to the Culture Centre of the celebrated oriental dancer, Sri Uday Shankar.

For sheer natural beauty some of the spots in and around Almora have few parallels. About four miles east of the town is the picturesque Kalimat ridge (6414 ft.) which provides an interesting peep into Nepal, 13 miles to the north and reached by a bridle-path through magnificent jungle scenery is the Binsar hill, covered with dense alpine forests which provides ample shooting. From its top, locally known as Jhandi Dhar (Flagstaff), there is a magnificent view of the surrounding panorama. In olden days this was the favourite summer resort of the Chand rulers of Kumayun.

Besides mountaineering, a huge lot of fishing and shooting is available in the lakes and forests of the Kumayun hills. The angler will find a paradise among the many *tals* and lakes in which excellent trout fishing is to be had. The main attraction for hikers is the Pindari Glacier reached by several marches. Many Dak Bungalows line the route, but visitors have to make their own arrangements for food. The best time for a trip is May or early October. The Deputy Commissioner, Almora, helps in securing conveyance and carriers. He also supplies printed literature on equipment and facilities available. Intending visitors should secure a copy of 'Pindari Glacier Notes' by Captain Mackintyre (Rs. 2/-) from the District Board, Almora, who also supply information about equipments, routes, transport and accommodation.

\*       \*       \*

ACCOM. Good hotels are Deodar Hotel (Rs. 13/-) Himalaya Hotel, Royal Hotel and Capital Hotel. Besides there is a

152

comfortable Circuit House and a Sessions House where visitors can stay with permission from the Dy. Commissioner In-charge, Kumaun Division, Nainital.

CONVEYANCE.   Cars, ponies and dandies.

# ALLAHABAD

Situated on the confluence of the Ganga and the Jumuna (505 m. from Calcutta and 844 m. from Bombay) Allahabad, or ancient Prayag, is an important place of Hindu pilgrimage and a principal city of Uttar Pradesh. Described as Tirthraj (king of the places of pilgrimage) it is still the scene of great devotion and piety. King Harshavardhana performed great sacrifices here every five years. On those occasions the Emperor used to give away in charity all the accumulated wealth of his empire to Brahmins and religious mendicants. The Kumbha Mela held every twelfth year draws mammoth gatherings from all parts of India.

**Fort :** During the Moghul rule, Allahabad was a place of royal residence. Overlooking the Sangam stands the great fort of Akbar (built in 1575 A.D.) in which Jahangir lived for sometime. The gateway to the fort is Grecian, and in front of the inner gateway is an Asokan pillar, 35 ft. high, with an edict of Asoka inscribed on it (242 B.C.). It contains a later inscription by Samudra Gupta recording his victories and another by Jahangir commemorating his accession to the throne. The pillar was brought from Kosambi. In a wide vault underneath the fort are many stone images of Hindu pantheon. The original Akshya Bat is somewhere near the place, yet unaccessible to worshippers. On the extensive plain just below the fort gathers a vast concourse of pilgrims for the Magh Mela bathing every winter.

**Akshya Bat :** The *Akshya Bat* as is shown today in the Patalpuri temple at the corner of the fort is a fake tree ; the real tree lies within the fort. The tree was seen by Hiuen Tsang who visited Prayag along with

Harshavardhana in 540 A.D. The Chinese pilgrim gives a graphic account of the holy tree and the great merit one could acquire by making sacrifices under it. After the construction of the fort, access to the holy tree was discontinued and worship was diverted to this branch of the sacred tree, which practice was kept alive by the British for security reasons. Only recently the original Akshya Bat has been located in the fort although the worship of the fake tree still continues.

**Kkasru Bagh :** Near the railway station is a small Moghul garden, the Khasru Bagh, which contains the mausoleum of Prince Khasru who rebelled against his father Jahangir. Other notable buildings are : the Government House, the University, the High Court, and the Allahabad Municipal Museum which contains interesting relics excavated from Kosambi and Bihta.

**Kosambi :** 34 miles from Allahabad, up the river Jumna, lies the ruins of the prehistoric city of Kosambi, where the Vatsa King Udayana, a contemporary of Gautama Budha, ruled in the sixth century B.C. and where the Lord himself stayed from time to time at the Ghositarama monastery. According to tradition, the city was founded by a descendant of the Pandavas of Hastinapur and it continued to be a leading political centre in North India till the beginning of the Christian era. Hiuen Tsang in the 7th century saw the ruins of the great Ghositarama monastery which contained to be occupied by Buddhist monks till the century before him.

Kosambi to-day is an archaelogist's paradise. "No site in India is richer in surface-finds than Kosambi. Enormous quantity of coins, beads and terracotta figurines have been collected from the surface and have found their way to the museums of India and abroad" (Archaelogy of India). The other find is a shrine which contains two fine tarracotta images belonging to the pre-Maurya period. Two miles west of Kosambi is the Pabhosa Rock which bears important inscriptions.

To-day it is a place of pilgrimage of the Jains.

There are two road routes to Kosambi. The shorter (unsafe in rainy season) leads from Allahabad to Sarai Akil (22 miles by bus) and thence 12 m. by tonga along a kachha road. The other route (65 m.), motorable throughout the year, is the G.T. Road and then along the Jumna canal road. Irrigation authorities issue permits to drive along the canal bank.

**Bihta** : 11 miles south-west of Allahabad, on the other side of the Jumuna, is Bihta, where excavations have unearthed the remains of a well-planned settlement which flourished from the pre-Maurya period down to the Gupta period. Among the antiquities found are terracotta figurines, vessels and coins ranging in date from the 2nd, century B.C. to 2nd. century A.D. The seals of ivory, bronze and stone are interesting because they furnish the names and addresses of the householders and merchants and of the places and persons with whom they were in correspondence. The place must have been a centre of great commercial activity.

*     *     *

ACCOM. European style hotels of the city are : Barnett's Hotel at Canning Road and Royal Hotel at South Rd., both in Civil Lines (east of the railway station). Indian style hotels are: Sind-Bombay Hotel and New Tajmahal Hotel, Johnstonganj and Roorki Hotel, all in the city (West of the railway station). There are a number of hotels, eating houses and Dharamsalas on the Hewett Road and the nearby bazar. Bus stand is at the Zero Road, in the city. Cycle rickshaws are plentiful and exceedingly cheap. Taxis are available.

# KANPUR

One of the great industrial cities of India, Kanpur (pop. 705,383) is often described as "the Manchester of India". Kanpur is an entirely modern city, created by trade and enterprise. It has a number of busy mills which turn out immense quantities of woollens, cottons, brushes and leather goods.

Kanpur will always be remembered for the stirring events of the Mutiny of 1857. The heroic exploits of Tantia Topi and the equally gallent defence of Wheeler's Entrenchment and the tragic massacre of the helpless Englishmen at the Sati Chaura Ghat and in the Bibighar still recall a history which is at once thrilling and pathetic. The Memorial Well (recently obliterated) marks the spot where the bodies of British women and children, murdered in Bibighar were thrown into the well.

Most historic of all is the **Sati Chaura Ghat** ('Massacre Ghat' in the Cantonment), where about 500 English captives were butchered by the mutineers under Nana Sahib of Bithor, the adopted son of the exiled Peshwa, Bajirao II. An inscribed label "In memorium 27th, June, 1857" bears the sad remembrance of the grim tragedy. This is also the most popular bathing ghat of the city.

**Bithor** : 15 miles north of Kanpur is Bithor, where the Brahmavarta Ghat on the Ganga is held in high reverence by Hindus. Legend has it that the great god Brahma performed a sacrifice here on the creation of the Universe. On the steps of the ghat can be seen the footmark of Brahma which is the present object of worship. On an eminence, a mile to the south, is the Balmiki Ashram where the great sage sank himself in meditation and then compiled the original Ramayana. According to tradition, here Sita gave birth to Lava and Kusa while in exile. There is a beautiful view of the Ganga from the terrace of the Ashram. The tall temple on the other side of the river marks the village Parihar ('banishment') where Sita was at first left off in exile and from where the great sage Balmiki brought her to his *Tapoban* to gave her shelter. In modern times, Bithor shot into prominence when the last Peshwa, Bajirao II, after his defeat at the battle of Kirkee (1817) was kept in internment here by the British on a princely pension. There are the remains of many temples and palaces which the Peshwa Bajirao II and the Mahratha nobles built at Bithor, which was then a prosperous town with a population of 60,000 people. After its destruction in the battle of Bithor (1858) the place receded to the background and Kanpur came into prominence. There are eighteen ghats on the Ganga of which the Pathar Ghat is an architectural beauty. It was built by a Hindu minister of the Nawab of Oudh. Just on the main road can be seen the ruins of the palace in which Peshwa Bajirao II and later Nanarao Peshwa lived. It was totally destroyed by the British in the battle of Bithor which took place in the course of suppression of the Mutiny. The National Flag perpetually flies over the beloved spot where lived the last Peshwa who even in exile endeared himself to the people of Northern India by many deeds of piety. Bithor to-day is a small village charged with a spiritual calm. Its legendary association with Balmiki, Dhruva and Sita Devi makes it a fit place for meditation and piety. There are in the village a number of Maharashtrian Brahmins, successors to those who settled here with Peshwa Bajirao II.

A branch line of the N. E. Rly. (meter gauge) from Kanpur terminates at the Brahmavarta Ghat (18 miles), but it is more convenient to reach the place by road (bus service ; 15 miles), taking the Nanarao Peshwa Rd. which branches off from the G. T. Road at Kalyanpur. There is a P. W. D. Dak Bungalow at Bithor.

\* \* \*

GETTING ABOUT : Kanpur lies at the north-west side of the station. The junction of the Mall and the Birhana Road is the chief commercial centre (1 mile from station, reached by bus or cycle rickshaw). There are situated the G. P. O., the principal banks and the hotels. Around it lies the market place of the city and the offices. Strangers should do well to get into some hotel at the Rail Bazar (at the back of the station) or at the Mall-Birhana Road junction.

ACCOM. Barkely House, Civil Lines, (1 m. from station) caters in European style. Indian style hotels are : Station View Hotel, opposite Rly. Station ; Kanpur Hotel, Birhana Road ;

157

Orient Hotel, the Mall ; Kashmir Hotel near G. P. O. ; Central Hotel, Rail Bazar ; and New Calcutta Hotel, Birhana Rd. Charges vary from Rs. 5/- to Rs. 8/- per head per day. There is a commodious Dharamsala adjacent to the station platform.

CONVEYANCE. Cycle rickshaws go anywhere and are exceedingly cheap. There is a city bus service. Taxis are available. Buses of the Uttar Pradesh Roadways link almost all the neighbouring towns and places of historic interest. Buses go to Bithor (16 miles) and Kanauj (52 miles) at frequent intervals.

# KANAUJ

Today a small town on the Ganga, 52 miles north of Kanpur, Kanauj (ancient Kanyakubja) was for many centuries the imperial capital of Northern India and a great centre of Indian culture. In its palmy days—from early seventh century to the end of the twelvth century A.D.—it was a city of incredible wealth and beauty, of shining palaces, temples and parks, and was inhabited by a prosperous people who loved learning and the arts. As the proud capital of Harshavardhan, the greatest Indian Emperor after Asoka, it became the premier city in all India to whom the entire Eastern world turned in homage. For six centuries since then Kanauj, like Delhi of later times, remained the symbol of imperial power—a glorious trophy which went as the crowning prize to the ambitious potentate who proved himself the bravest in battle.

**History** : After the fall of the Imperial Guptas, three states rose into power in Northern India—the Maukharis of Kanauj, the Guptas of Malwa and the Vardhans of Thaneswar. Of these the House of Kanyakubja became the leading power in Northern India under Isanavarman (554 A. D.), who, in the hope of restoring the fallen fabric of imperial unity of Northern India, waged and won many battles against the kings of Andhra, Bengal and the Hun invaders, and for the first time assumed the imperial title of *Maharajadhiraja*. His successor Grahavarman Maukhari married Rajyasri, the daughter of King Pravakaravardhan of Thaneswar and sister of the still more celebrated Harshavardhan. But the alliance of the two most powerful royal houses of Northern India did not deter the king of Malwa, a descendant of the Later Guptas, to lead a campaign against the Maukharis of Kanauj in which Grahavarman was killed and his queen Rajyasri made a prisoner. Rajavardhan, the new king of Thaneswar, who hurried to the support of his brother-in-law, also fell to Sasanka, the king of Bengal and an ally of the Guptas. When, shortly afterwards, Harshavardhan ascended the throne of Thaneswar his immediate task was to avenge the death of his brother-in-law and to rescue his sister Rajyasri. Waging an incessant warfare against the 'Five Indies' Harsha completely defeated the Guptas and their allies, rescued Rajyasri and became the undisputed master of Northern India, his empire extending from Kathiawar in the west, to Bengal in the east and the Vindhyas in the south. His two formidable opponents were Sasanka of Bengal and Chalukya Pulakesin II of Vatapi. Grahavarman left no heir and so at the request of his sister and the nobles of Kanyakubja, Harsha ascended the vacant throne of Kanyakubja. The two kingdoms were united and Kanauj became the capital of the greatest empire that came into being after the Mauryas. Bana, the celebrated author of 'Harshacarita' and 'Kamdambari', who enjoyed Harsha's patronage, has left an account of the great deeds of his master. Hiuen Tsang, the great Chinese pilgrim, who arrived at the court of Harsha at Kanauj in 630 A. D., has left a glowing account of the splendour of the imperial city of Kanauj and the great power that its Emperor exercised over the faudatory kings.

Even after the death of Harsha in 647 A.D., the imperial aura of Kanauj continued undimmed through the succeeding centuries ; and ambitious rulers of the farthest parts of India considered it the greatest achievement to have "captured Mahodaya Sri", that is, Kanauj, the proud seat of Harsha and the symbol of imperial power. "What Babylon was to the martial races of West-

159

ern Asia, what Rome was to the Teutonic barbarians and Byzantine to the mediaeval world of Eastern and Southern Europe, that was Mahodaya Sri (Kanauj) to the upspringing dynasties of the eighth and the ninth centuries A.D."

A century after Harsha's death, a prince of the name of Yasovarman largely revived the imperial tradition of Kanauj by feats of arms recalling those of Harsha, but hardly had he consolidated his powers when he fell to Lalitaditya, the ambitious king of Kashmir. The great poet Bhababhuti flourished in Yasovarman's court.

In the ninth and the tenth centuries, Kanyakubja was ruled by the Gurjara-Pratiharas who became the greatest power in Northern India. The two most remarkable Pratihara kings were Mihira Bhoja (840-885) and Mahendrapala I (885-910) who followed Harsha and Yasovarmana in encouraging art and letters. Poet Rajasekhara adorned the latter's court. But at length the power of Gurjara-Pratihara was weakened by the repeated attacks of the Rastrakutas of the Deccan till the king of Kanauj became a figurehead and the feaudatory chiefs like the Chandellas of Bundelkhand became all powerful. In 1018, when Rajyapala was the king of Kanauj, Mahmud of Ghazni sacked the city and with this the Gurjara-Pratihara rule in Kanauj virtually ended. More terrible things were to happen in the North-Western frontier : Mahammad Ghori, following the example of Mahmud of Ghazni, was making a supreme bid for the crown of Hindusthan. In Kanauj the Pratihara rule was now replaced by that of the Gahadavala of which the greatest ruler Gobindachandra, a great patron of Buddhism, ruled for about half a century (1104-1154) over an extensive kingdom. His grandson, king Jaychand of Kanauj, frittered away his energy and resources in petty jealousies with Prithvi Raj, the king of Ajmer, even when Mahammad Ghori was devastating the plains of the Punjab and threatening the doom of Hindu rule in Northern India. Prithvi Raj Chauhan was finally defeated in the battle of Tarain in 1192. The Muslims took Delhi and Ajmer. It was now the turn of Kanauj, the symbol of Hindu power. "The power of the Gahadavalas was shattered on the plains of Chandwar in 1193 and the agony of Imperial Kanauj was soon hushed in the stillness of death."

## Places of Interest

**The Old Fort :** Kanauj today is a small sub-Divisional town noted for the manufacture of fine perfumes. Nothing now remains of its ancient glories, of the "city of ten thousand temples" to which Hiuen Tsang paid eloquent tribute, except some ruined temples and ruined ramparts of the old Fort. At the back of the town, to the east, are a series of high mounds, about a mile long, which mark the ruins of the fortress-palace of the ancient Hindu kings. At places, the broken outer walls of the fort are clearly visible from a distance. Archaeological excavations, now in progress, confirm that the site contained old Hindu palaces of successive ages and the latest one, that of Jaychand, has been definitely identified. Further excavations are expected to reveal palaces and temples belonging to the reign of Harshavardhan. On an eminence, on the flank of the mound, there is a pair of temples known as Balapith (Baleswarnath Siva) which has been in Muslim hands since the conquest of Kanauj by the Muslims. The Muslim claim them to be tombs ; but the architecture is definitely Hindu. At this point the ramparts of the ancient Hindu fort are boldly visible. There are still many old temples, some half-broken, despite repeated Muslim vandalism.

**Makdum Jania :** To the south of the main road to the town (mid-way between the station and the town), are the ruins of ancient Hindu temples superimposed by a later mosque. This spot is believed to have been the sacrificial altar of King Harshavardhan, but it is now called Makdum Jania. This, too, is in Muslim hands. The ruins of the platforms for sacrificial offerings are clearly visible.

COMM. From Kanpur, the Grand Trunk Road passes through Kanauj to Delhi. There is a regular bus service between Kanpur and Kanauj (51 miles : fare Rs. 2/4/-) besides the metre gauge line of the N E. Rly. which runs parallel to the Grand Trunk Road. Buses stop just behind the Kanauj Rly. station, on the Grand Trunk Road, whence the town is about 3 miles by tonga.

ACCOM. There is a District Board Dak Bungalow near the station-cum-bus stand. Here are a number of clean eating houses run by Kanauj Brahmins. The Kunj Beharilal Dharamsala is in the town. One can reach Kanauj by the morning bus and return to Kanpur by night after a day's sight-seeing.

*  *  *  *

# KUSINARA

Thirty-two miles east of Gorakhpur is holy Kusinara, which the Buddha chose for his entry into *Mahaparinirvana*. After forty-five years of strenuous wanderings for the salvation of men, here the Lord arrived on his 'last pilgrimage' and died in the arms of his faithful attendant Ananda, under the cool shade of the twin *sala* trees in the grove of the Mallas.

Time has stood still over this lonely spot, and a tone of brooding melancholy still seems to fill the air. It is as though the earth and the spirit, the shrubs and the ancient trees, all are united in mourning for the departed Lord, the Light of the World. The story of his death has been told with moving pathos in the Mahaparinirvana Sutta (the 'Great Decease') of the Digha Nikaya. Today, even after the lapse of many centuries, the sight of the reclining statue of the dying Lord moves even the casual visitor to tears.

At the time of the Buddha, the Mallas constituted a republican state as tributary to the king of Magadha ; they were noted for their reverence for the Buddha. Kusinara shot into unprecedented limelight and glory when the ageing Lord, three months before his actual death, chose the place for his *Mahaparinirvana* to the exclusion of the other great cities of India. Soon after the death of the Buddha, the place became a great centre of worship, and many *chaityas* and *viharas* were built

162

around the great stupa in which the Malla princes had enshrined the relics of the Buddha. About three centuries after, the Emperor Asoka added a new interest to the place by raising a temple, a stupa and a pillar just on the spot where the Tathagata passed away into *Mahaparinirvana*. Hiuen Tsang, who visited Kusinara in the 7th century, saw the Asokan buildings in a ruined state, including the pillar, which is now missing. The pillar probably lies somewhere around, awaiting the excavator's shovel. The place continued to be a chief centre of Buddhist worship till the beginning of the 13th. century, when it, like Sarnath and other holy places, suffered terrible destruction at the hands of Muslim invaders. After this Kusinara ceased to be a place of worship, so that after a time its very identity was forgotten. Gradually, thick jungles grew over the sacred *sala* grove, and for five centuries it lay as an unknown waste in the midst of rice-fields. Fortunately, the village was still known by its ancient name—Kusinara or Kusinagar—by which it has been mentioned in the Pali texts. Following this clue, General Cunningham, the celebrated antiquarian, came to Kusinara in 1861 and declared the neglected, brick-strewn wood as the spot of the *Mahaparinirvana* of the Buddha. Subsequently, Mr. Carleyle of the Archaeological Department of the Government of India explored the site in 1876, when the *Mahaparinirvana* stupa and the famous 20-feet stone statue of the dying Buddha were uncovered. Excavation work was resumed at the beginning of the present century under the supervision of Dr. Vogel and Pandit Haranand Shastri, and to them goes the credit for re-establishing Kusinara to what it is today.

Chief among the objects of interest is the **Mahaparinirvana Shrine**, an unimpressive, flat-roofed temple, which has a surprise even for the most knowledgeable visitor ; for it contains the magnificent 20-feet recumbent image of the Buddha in the 'lion posture', his head to the north, exactly corresponding to the description of the Buddha's last sleep as given in the

Mahaparinirvana Sutta. The great image is the present object of worship. At the base of the flower-adorned image is a Sanskrit inscription which clearly indicates the identity of the donor of the statue and its maker. The inscription runs : "This is the token of the supreme offering (mahadan) of Swami Haribal to the *Mahavihara*. The image has been made by Dina of Mathura". Although no date is given, from the character of its language and workmanship it appears to be a work of the Gupta period (500 A.D.).

The adjoining **Mahaparinirvana Stupa**, as it was found in the excavation of 1876, was probably a renovation by the same Haribal over the earlier Asokan stupa. But it had been repaired again and again down the centuries by wealthy devotees, so that today it is in a perfect state of preservation. The stupa, as it stands today, is 75 feet high and has a gold varnished dome which, mingling with the bright rays of the rising sun, produces an entrancing spectacle.

About 400 yards west of the stupa, on the road to Ramabhar, is a small temple which contains a large image of the Dhyani Buddha of the Mahayana pantheon. The temple is locally known as Matha Baba Murti Mandir.

A mile south of the Mahaparinirvana Stupa is the **Cremation Stupa**, locally known as Ramabhar, which has been recently renovated. This is said to be the spot where the Tathagata was cremated. A large banian tree covers its entire top and flanks, its trunk turned into a tiny hermitage by a Chinese monk who lives a life of great piety and simplicity. To the east of the stupa flows a branch of the river Hiranyavati, and to its south is the village Anuradhapur which marks the site of the ancient Malla capital.

Kusinara owes much of its present revival to the noble efforts of the Venerable U. Chandramani Maha Thera, an Arakanese Buddhist and close associate of the late Ven. Dharmapala. Among the modern buildings he caused to be built are a Buddhist Dharamsala, which contains a temple and a library of Buddhist sacred texts, and a school where the study of the Dhammapada is encouraged. Also notable is the Birla Dharamsala-cum-temple built by Seth Jugal Kishore Birla, who has aptly been called the "Anathapindika of modern times". There is also a small but fine Chinese temple which contains another beautiful image of the Buddha. Then there is a college. known as the Buddha College, and a Post Office at Kusinara. Yet Kusinara is a small, quiet village far removed from the modern amenities of life.

\* \* \* \*

COMM. Kusinara is 32 miles to the east of Gorakhpur town, reached by U.P. Government Roadways buses (2½ hours' journey). The bus goes to Kasia via the sacred site of Kusinara. Coming from Bihar or Banaras it can be approached from the Deoria Sadar railway station, on the Bhatni-Gorakhpur section of the N. E. Rly. There is a bus service between Deoria and Kusinara via Kasia. There is a P.W.D. Dak Bungalow at Kasia (1½ miles from Kusinara). But it is best to base oneself at Gorakhpur town where there are a number of hotels and Railway Retiring Rooms. Every two hours there is a bus for Kusinara.

ACCOMMODATION. The Birla Dharamsala and the Buddhist Dharamsala accommodate visitors. The Government has recently built a Rest House which offers all amenities. Casual visitors should carry lunch boxes from Gorakhpur and return by the evening bus after a rest in one of the rest houses.

# AGRA : THE ROYAL CITY

Agra, 122 miles from Delhi and 785 miles from Calcutta (via Tundla), is the most romantic of all the cities of Hindustan, for it contains not merely the imperial city of mighty forts, echoing courts and awe-inspiring gateways but that crowning glory in marble, the Taj Mahal, the masterpiece of Moghul architecture, exquisite beyond words.

**History :** The history of Agra begins with Sikindar Lodi, who made it his capital in 1500 A. D. Babar captured it in 1526 after his resounding victory at Panipat, and solemnly declared that his invasion of India was not merely a raid but a permanent conquest. The descendent of the terrible Timur thus assumed the title of Emperor of Hindustan, and ruled from Agra till his death in 1530. Babar was a nature-lover ; he laid out fruit and pleasure gardens, but very little remain today of his flower gardens and baths except Ram Bagh and Zohru Bagh. His son Humayun preferred Delhi, where he met his death by falling down the steps of the Old Fort. But Agra rose to prominence when Akbar, the greatest of the Moghuls, made it the seat of his power and proposed to make it a worthy capital commensurate with the glory of his far-flung empire. To this end be founded the modern city of Agra, opposite to the old city of Babar, on the right bank of the river, and built the Fort on the site of on old Pathan castle. The results of his efforts, supplemented by those of his successors, converted Agra into the most beautiful, wealthiest and most famous capital in all the world. Shah Jahan stayed at Agra from 1628 to 1637, when the Fort received many splendid additions and the work on the Taj started. Havell truly remarks that "It was one of the greatest epochs of Indian architecture". But from the hour of Shah Jahan's confinement in the Jasmine Tower, a prisoner in his splendid palace, Agra's greatness began to wane and it perished with Aurangzeb, who removed his capital permanently to Delhi, which henceforth became the capital of Hindustan and the headquarters of the successive shadow emperors. Agra would have dropped to the level of an ordinary provincial town but for its majestic monuments, which rank among the greatest achievements of Moghul architecture.

In 1761, Agra was captured by Suraj Mal of Bharatpur and his Jats, who caused much damage to the city and its monuments. Thenceforward it went as prize alternately to the Mahrattas and the Muslims, whoever proved the strongest ; the Mahrattas held it for quite a time till Lord Lake took it in 1803.

# The Fort

Overhanging the Jumna, in the shape of a crescent, stands the Fort of Agra (1565-73), 'one of the most outstanding structural achievements of Akbar, who displayed in it an originality and spontaneity of a new era of architecture'. Its battlements of red sandstone tower 70 feet from the ground, the wall runs a mile and a half in circuit, and the immense mass of masonry dwarfs the modern town. "Within the fort is a maze of palaces, halls of state, pavilions, corridors, balconies, kiosks, wrought in dazzling white marble and decorated with the most beautiful carving and exquisite tracery in stone, the cost of each of which would be a king's ransom".

The fort, as it stands today, represents the contributions of three Moghul emperors. Originally designed by Akbar to suit military needs, it was added to by Jahangir, while to that immortal builder, Shah Jahan, we owe the grand white marble edifices which by virtue of their rare beauty stand in happy contrast to the stern character of the older work.

Entering through the Amar Singh Gate (where passes are sold) one comes to the **Moti Masjid** (Pearl Mosque), built by Shah Jahan, of pure white marble and unequalled in India for its refinement and purity of its proportions and design. A boldly written Persian inscription records that the mosque was built by Shah Jahan and likens it to a precious pearl. Turning right, through the Mina Bazar, the road leads to the courtyard of the **Diwani-Am** (Hall of Private Audience), which was commenced by Shah Jahan and, by some accounts, was completed by Aurangzeb. The throne of the great Emperor was set in a raised alcove wondrously decorated with mosaic flowers, semi-precious stones and gilding. Here sat the Grand Moghul to give audience, to receive ambassadors and to administer justice. At the foot of the alcove is a marble platform on which stood the highest ministers to submit petitions to the Emperor and to receive his commands.

To the north of the **Diwani-Am** is the **Inner Mina Bazar**, where mèrchants sold costly jewellery, silks and brocades to the royal ladies. "Sometimes the Great Moghul and his court would amuse themselves by holding a mock fair in which the prettiest of the wives and daughters of nobles would act as traders, and the Emperor would haggle for the value of an anna, and the ladies would feign indignation, scold his Majesty roundly and tell him to go where he could suit himself better". (Havell)

"But when at length", says Bernier, ' the bargains are struck, the Begums as well as the Emperor pay liberally for their purchases, and often, as if by accident, let slip out of their hands a few gold instead of silver *roupies*, as a compliment to the fair merchant and her pretty daughter. Thus the scene ends with merry jests and good humour".

At the back of the Diwani-Am is the **Macchi Bhawan,** which was once a fairy-like garden laid out in marble with golden fish tanks, flower beds and fountains. It was destroyed by the Jats and the beautiful objects were carried off to the palace of Suraj Mall at Dig. Close to it is the **Nagina Masjid**, a three-storeyed beautiful mosque built by Aurangzeb for the ladies of the Zenana.

Going east towards the river-side, the visitor will see the **Diwani-khas** and the **Mahalla-khas**, the pride of the Agra Fort, which, according to Havell, "rank with the Diwani-khas at Delhi as the most exquisite of Shah Jahan's buildings", barring of course the magnificent Taj Mahal, which stands by itself". The Diwani-khas (Hall of Private Audience) is a large, white marble pavilion of wondrous beauty which clearly shows the influence of Persian art and the Persian love of flowers, which almost amounted to flower worship. An inscription states that it was erected in 1637, the 11th year of Shah Jahan's reign. Architecturally, we notice here a great contrast between the styles of Akbar and Shah Jahan, the former being stern, red sandstone structure built with an eye to defence and the latter elegant and effeminate white marble edifices of mellow beauty where one could enjoy leisurely all the pleasures of life without bothering for security, which was now fully assured in a mighty and prosperous empire.

On a nearby terrace overlooking the river is a black throne with a white seat opposite it. The **Throne Terrace**, as it was called, was the favourite seat of Shah Jahan, where he amused himself by casting fishing lines in the tank below. Beneath the Throne Terrace is a wide enclosure where contests between elephants and tigers took place.

A doorway from the Diwani-khas leads to the **Saman Burj**, or Jasmine Palace, so called because of the flowers in delicate mosaic and brilliant gilding with which it is adorned. This was probably built by Jahangir. Later, Shah Jahan occupied the Jasmine Palace with Mumtaz Mahal, the lady of the Taj. Here, again, in full view of the Taj Mahal, Shah Jahan, the captive Emperor, breathed his last attended by his devoted daughter Jahanara, who shared his captivity for seven years. Adjacent to the Samman Burj are three white marble pavilions which form the famous **Khas Mahal** of Shah Jahan built in the typical elegant style of the period. Havell says, "There is an indescribable grace and charm about all this quarter of the palace, to which the beauty of material, the perfect taste of the ornament and elegance of the proportions, the delightful background of the landscape and historical associations contribute". The niches of the wall all contained portraits of the Moghul Emperors which, like so many other things, were looted by the Jats of Bharatpur. A number of similar paintings are preserved in the Calcutta Museum. Again, the little vaults in the walls have a pretty story told of them. "Occasionally, the Emperor would drop surreptitiously a jewel into one of the niches. The fortunate finder was thereby entitled to be his companion for the day". An inscription says that it was built in 1636.

The great quadrangle in front of the Khas Mahal is the **Anguri Bagh**, which was once a splendid Moghul garden with exquisite flower beds and fountains. To its west is the Mina Masjid, the smallest Moghul mosque ever built, and to the north is the **Sish Mahal** (Palace of Glass) the walls and ceilings of which were spangled with fragments of looking glass set into gorgeous gilt and coloured stucco. This was the bath of the royal ladies. The suite, with its fountains and artificial cascades, served as the dressing room to the harem. To the west of the Khas Mahal, on the entrance to the Jahangir Mahal, is a small apartment which contains the "Somnath" gates, captured from the tomb of Mahmud at Ghazni in the Afghan expedition of 1842 and brought to India at the request of Maharaja Ranjit Singh of the Punjab.

Next comes the **Jahangir Mahal,** a most remarkable building in which is noticed a fine admixture of Hindu and Muslim styles of architecture. Most probably it was the residence of Jahangir's Hindu mother, Mariam Zamani and his Hindu wife, Jodh Bai. Although it bears Jahangir's name it is beyond doubt that it was planned and constructed by Akbar with the same architects who built Fatehpur Sikri. "Nothing could be more striking", says Havell, "than the contrast between the extreme elegance, bordering on effeminacy, of the marble pavilions of Shah Jahan's palaces, and the robust, virile, yet highly imaginative architecture of this palace of Akbar". Nearby is a suite of small rooms known as **Akbar Mahal** which even in their dilapidated condition show a perfect adaption of stately solidity and commanding symmetry with admirable carvings in red sandstones inferior to nothing else in the whole of the Fort. From the outer courtyard there is a beautiful view of the winding Jammuna and the distant Taj charmingly silhouetted against the sky.

**Jumma Masjid :** Outside the fort and towering over the Agra Fort railway station stands the Jumma Masjid, erected in 1644 A. D. by Jahanara Begam, eldest daughter of Shah Jahan. It is built on the pattern of

Shah Jahan's splendid mosque at Delhi, but is far inferior in merit.

## Taj Mahal

Every visitor must pay homage to the Taj Mahal, the most glorious tomb that grief ever raised in memory of love, and one of the wonders of the world.

According to the *Badshahanama*, Arjumand Banu, better known by her titles Mumtaz Mahal, Exalted of the Palace, and Mumtaz-ul-Zamani, the Wonder of the Age, was married to the Emperor Shah Jahan in 1612 when she was twenty-one. Although his second wife, Mumtazi-Zamani enjoyed the undivided love of the Emperor. She bore him fourteen children and died in child-bed in a camp at Burhanpur during a campaign against Lodi Khan, in 1631. The bereavement, too great for the Emperor, turned his hair grey. The beloved body was temporarily buried at Burhanpur; six months later, a vast funeral cortege accompanied it to Agra, where it was laid in the garden of the Taj, which belonged to Raja Jai Singh at the time. The Taj was begun in 1631 and together with its appurtenances—a mosque on the west, a congregational hall (Jamat Khana) on the east and the main gateway on the south—was completed by 1653. In his determination to raise to her memory a monument which should keep her name immortal, the emperor employed 20,000 men daily upon it. The most famous artists and workmen of India were gathered to this task, which entailed an expenditure of 400 lakhs of rupees.

The Taj Mahal, the glory of Agra and the most beautiful building in the world, is set in a garden with a marble platform at the centre and is surrounded by dark cypress trees, green turf, flowers and fountains ; "the song of birds meets the ear, and the odour of roses and lemon flowers sweeten the air". Seen by day-light the perfection of its detail and its most wonderful beauty and magnificence delight the connoisseur, but seen by moonlight it is a radiant vision of beauty, and the charm of its lovely form is felt to the full. "The great domes seem to swim in the silver light, and the stately minarets shoot up towards the dark blue of the sky, and the scene is one of unearthly beauty" which no language can express. "The beauty of the Taj", says Havell, "as in all great art, lies in its simplicity. One wonders that so much beauty can come from so little effort. Yet nothing is wanting, nothing is in excess; one could not alter this and that and say that it is better".

"Glorious as is this mighty building in the mass, it is just as full of beauty when examined closely and in detail. Every part is covered with the most graceful and exquisite designs inlaid in marbles of different colours. Every wall, every arch, every portal, is ornamented and finished as if the craftsmen had been engaged upon a precious casket instead of a corner of an immense palace tomb". Around the arches run inlaid verses of the Koran beautifully shaped in black marble, and it is said the whole of the Koran is thus inlaid in the Taj.

The heart of the building is the central chamber where Shah Jahan and his wife sleep together, for he was laid beside her. The tombs are of the purest white marble, inlaid most beautifully with designs formed of agate, cornelian, lapis-lazuli, jasper, and other precious stones. The tombs are surrounded by a pierced marble screen which in itself is a master-piece. Fergusson says that no words can express the chastened beauty of the hall seen in the soft gloom of the subdued light coming from the distant and small openings. The cenatoph was originally enclosed by a screen of gold studded with gems. This was removed by Aurangzeb and replaced by the present exquisite screen of pierced marble.

The real graves, however, lie elsewhere—in a vault immediately under the central chamber. A steep passage leads down to the vault, where the bodies rest level with the surface of the ground, beneath plainer tombstones.

Although they are now plain to bareness, the encircling walls and ceilings were once covered with sheets of purest gold.

Dear as Mumtaz Mahal was to him, Shah Jahan never intended to lie beside her in the Taj. His idea was to construct a still more majestic mausoleum for himself on the opposite bank of the Jamuna and to connect the two by a white marble bridge. The project was interrupted shortly after the foundations were laid and was never completed. The idea did not appeal to Auranzgeb. That austere Muslim ultimately laid his father beside his mother in the Taj Mahal.

The two mosques on either side of the Taj greatly add to the beauty of the cemetery. The one on the west was used for prayers and the other on the east for congregational discourse. The Taj also possessed formerly two wonderful silver doors. These were looted and melted by the Jats in 1764.

**Tomb of Itmad-ud-daulah :** The tomb of Itmad-ud-daulah, another beautiful monument, is on the left bank of the Jamuna, about 3 miles north of the Taj and is reached by the bridge across the Jamuna. The mausoleum was built by the Empress Nur Jahan for her father, Itmad-ud-daulah, who was grandfather to the lady of the Taj. Mumtaz Mahal's parents also lie in one of the rooms of this monument. The mausoleum built of white marble, stands in the centre of a garden and is one of the finest examples in India of inlaid work in a style derived from Persian mosaics. The marble lattice work of the passage admitting light to the interior is extremely fine, and the rich paintings on the ceiling and walls and carvings on the archways have few parallels in India.

**Ram Bagh :** Half-a-mile north of Itmad-ud-Daulah is the Chini-ka-Rauza or the China tomb, said to be the burial place of Afzal Khan, a Persian poet, who was Prime Minister to Shah Jahan. Further north is the Ram Bagh, the first Moghul Garden in India, said to have been laid by Babar. On his death in 1530, the body of Babar lay for six months in Ram Bagh prior to its removal to Kabul for burial. In later times the Ram Bagh was a favourite resort of the Empress Nur Jahan. The two pavilions jutting out over the river possess a number of subterranean chambers. These have been modernized and are now let out to picnikers.

### Sikandra

At Sikandra, 6 m. from Agra, just on the Mathura Road, is the tomb of Akbar, as dignified and unusual as the great emperor who lies there. The village, however, derives its name from Sultan Sikandar Lodi, the first sovereign to make his capital at Agra.

The road from Agra passes by numerous crumbling tombs and palaces and remains of archaelogical interest which show that the area once contained many palaces and gardens of the prominent nobles of the Moghul court.

The mausoleum of Akbar stands in the midst of a vast garden covering an area of 123 acres and enclosed by four giant gateways. The one on the west bears an inscription in Persian which states that the mausoleum was completed by Jahangir in the seventh year of his reign, that is, in 1612 A.D. Originally designed and commenced by Akbar himself, the grand mausoleum, Havell observes, "is different in plan from any other Moghul monument, being distinctly Hindu in character and resembling the many-storied pavilions, used as assembly halls in Hindu and Buddhist monasteries, of which the Panch Mahal at Fatehpur Sikri is an example."

The building rises in terraces something in the form of a pyramid, the lower stories of red sandstone and the top storey of white marble. With its arabesque tracery, Hindu carving and Buddhist form, this curious and beautiful building bears witness to the composite faith of the Great Moghul who sleeps therein. An inclined passage beneath a lofty achway leads to the high vaulted chamber in the centre of the lowest storey, where a simple marble tombstone covers the earthly remains of the great Akbar. The vaulted ceiling was originally covered with marvellous frescoes in gold and blue, now obliterated by whitewash. In the chamber, besides the tomb, were placed such precious relics as the Emperor's armour, clothes and books, which in later times were looted by the Jats of Bharatpur—those soulless fanatics who caused much damage to the beautiful monuments of Agra. The top floor, which is open to the sky, is surrounded by beautiful white marble cloisters, the outer walls of which are filled with lattice-work wrought in the most beautiful patterns. In the centre stands the grandly simple tomb of the Emperor, engraved with the 99 glorious names of Allah, exactly over the place where his body rests in the vaulted chamber below.

The elaborately carved small, marble pillar by the side of the tomb served as a stand for burning incense.

**Baradari of Sikandar Lodi :** Half a mile west of the mausoleum of Akbar, in the compound of a Christian Mission, is a red sandstone building which is the only surviving structure of the capital of Sikandar Lodi. It is known as Baradari and dates from 1495. Jahangir converted the palace of the former Afghan monarch into a mausoleum of his mother, Mariam Zamani, the Rajput wife of Akbar. Her cenatoph stands in the central hall surrounded by fifty small apartments.

*　　　*　　　*　　　*

COMM. Geographically situated at the centre of India, Agra is reached by through mail trains from almost all the important towns of India. The city is served by the three principal rajlways—Central, Western and Northern Railways. There are three stations—Fort, City and Cantonment—which are equidistant from the city and the hotels.

ACCOM. Lawries Hotel on Mahatma Gandhi Road is the leading European style hotel in the city. Others are Imperial Hotel and Empress Hotel, on the same road. Agra Hotel (Rs. 11/- daily), at 165 Metcalf Road, is a reputed Indian style hotel which

also caters in European style. Calcutta Hotel in the bazar is a
cheap Bengali style hotel. For parties of motorists, the Circuit
House (Euro. style) on the Taj Road, near the Taj, is ideal. The
khansama prepares food and charges fixed rates. Daily rent for
occupation is Rs. 2/8-. Advance reservation should be made with
the Dist. Engineer, P. W. D. Agra. There is also the P.W.D.
Dak Bungalow on Mahatma Gandhi Road.

CONVEYANCE. Taxis and station wagons are available
at moderate rates. These may be hired for the trip to Sikandra
and Fatehpur Sikri. Besides, there are Govt. bus services to these
places. The bus-stand is near the Fort Rly. station. Tongas and
cycle rickshaws are available in plenty.

SHOPPING. The stone-craft of Agra is famous. Stone-made
articles both useful and decorative make excellent souvenirs.

# FATEHPUR SIKRI

At Fatehpur Sikri, 26m. south-west of Agra, just on
the spot where Saint Salim Chisti had foretold a son,
Akbar built a marvellous city where every building
is a palace and every palace a dream carved in red sandstone.

Akbar suffered bereavement of his twin children. He
was childless. "Stories of the miraculous powers of the
Divine Salim Chisti of Fatehpur Sikri reached his ears.
When men of science failed him, he turned to the man of
God. His prayer was granted. The babe was given the
name of the saint. This son Salim, born at Fatehpur
Sikri, succeeded Akbar as Jahangir". In gratitude for the
divine favour Akbar erected this beautiful city and transferred his capital to the place which for half a century
witnessed the most benevolent rule of the mightiest of
the Moghul emperors. It was the proud witness of
many noble thoughts and deeds, and even after its
desertion long ago, it stands today as an authentic witness
to Akbar's splendid efforts to achieve a synthesis of the
Hindu and Muslim cultures.

The capital was about 7 miles in circumference, surrounded on three sides by high battlemented walls
pierced by nine massive gateways and open on the north-
west side, where it relied for protection upon a large

176

artificial lake which measured some 20 miles around the banks. Akbar held court at Fatehpur Sikri for 13 years—from 1574 to 1586 A.D.—and then transferred it to Agra so that the saint in whose honour Fatehpur Sikri was founded might have the peace and solitude he sought.

In 1583 Queen Elizabeth of England addressed a friendly letter to "the most invincible and the most mightiest prince, Lord Zelabdin Echebar" requesting trading facilities which ultimately brought into being the East India Company. The small band of Englishmen who brought the letter to the Emperor Akbar at Fatehpur Sikri found it 'much greater than London and very populous'. The surprised Englishmen saw there 'many fine carts' and 'much merchandise of silk and cloth and of precious stones, both rubies, diamonds and pearls'.

The road from Agra climbs the ridge past the Nahabat Khana, a triumphal gateway where musicians played during state functions. Further up lies a ruined block of stables traditionally known as the **Mint**, and opposite it are the remains of the **Treasury**. The road next leads to the courtyard of the **Dewani-Am**, where from the elevated Judgment Seat the king looked upon the petitioners in the court below. Behind this, to the west, is a large paved courtyard laid out in black and white squares known as the **Pachchist** court, where the emperor played chess, using slave girls as living pieces from square to square.

To the south of the Pachchist Court, is the **Turkish Sultana's House**, a small chamber encircled by a verandah, which is considered the most beautiful building in Fatehpur Sikri. Every inch of both the exterior and interior is exquisitely carved, the facades being unrivalled in India for elaboration of detail. The roof is carved in imitation of old Italian tiling, while a remarkable series of naturalistic panels adorn the interior walls. Southward again is **Khwabgah**, "House of Dreams", reputed to be Akbar's sleeping chamber and containing fine mural paintings and inscriptions.

To the north of the Pachchist Court rises the most astonishing building of Fatehpur Sikri, the **Dewani-Khas**, from the central chamber of which rises a huge column of red sandstone with a spreading capital surrounded by a balustrade. The Emperor's seat was placed on the top of this mighty pillar, and from it ran four bridges to the galleries surrounded by walls. Here, "Akbar sat centrally enthroned high above the ground with his counsellors on four sides yet rendered separate and remote by the intervening open spaces."

The history of this unique building is still shrouded in obscurity. It is said that in 1575 Akbar completed a building at Fatehpur Sikri known as the Ibadat Khana, the Hall of Worship, where men of learning assembled on Friday nights for religious debates. Since the Dewani-Khas answers much of its description, some have identified it with the Ibadat Khana. But the supposition is highly improbable, for it is known that the Ibadat Khana was pulled down by Akbar himself after his new faith, Din Illahi, failed to attract adherents. It stood by the apartment of Abul Fazal and Faizi, near the great mosque.

Near at hand is the **Ankh Michauli**, where the Emperor is said to have played hide-and-seek with the ladies of the harem. At the southern corner of this is a small square platform which is remarkable for the elaborate struts that support the flat roof. The style resembles Jain architecture of the eleventh century. Known as the **Astrologer's Seat**, it was the abode of a Hindu Yogi. Abul Fazal tells us how greatly Akbar favoured this class of Hindu saints. In his desire to penetrate into the hidden mysteries of life and the Universe, the Emperor spent many hours in the dark, in secret discourse with Brahmins on the Astrologer's Seat.

To the west is **Panch Mahal**, an extraordinary five-storied building as its name implies. It was probably erected for the ladies of the harem as a pleasure resort. Planned on the lines of a Buddhist *vihara*,

178

each successive storey contracts until the fifth floor is merely a dome supported by four sculptured columns.

Standing immediately south of the Panch Mahal is the house of Mariam-ul-Zamani, originally called the "Golden House" on account of the profuse gilding on the walls. Daughter of Raja Bahar Mal of Jaipur, Mariam was the mother of Prince Salim, afterwards the Emperor Jahangir. At the south-west of Mariam's palace is the so-called **Jodh Bai's Palace**, the biggest apartment in the palace. The building is self-contained and displays carvings of a pronounced Hindu style. This was probably the principal harem. A wing runs north to form the Wind Palace, which was a favourite resort in warm weather. Opposite this is the Zenana garden, which stretches down to the Hiran Minar, an odd tower at the edge of the dry lake, studded with false elephants' tusks in stones.

At the west stands the two-storied **Bir Bal's Palace**, rivalling that of the Turkish Sultana in beauty and elaboration of its exterior and interior carvings. It commands a fine view of Hathi Pool (Elephant Quarter). Hiran Minar (Deer Minaret) and Karvansarai are to its north, while on the west it overlooks the lake, once gay with the flotilla of imperial barges. South of Birbal's house are the stables for horses and camels, which are still in tact.

At the south-west corner of the fortress-palace is the Jumma Masjid, the largest and grandest building in Fatehpur Sikri. It is celebrated throughout the country as a place of worship because of its close proximity to the tomb of Salim Chisti.

At the centre of the courtyard of the mosque is the tomb of the Saint, a magnificent building of the finest white marble, enclosed with exquisite pierced walls. This is one of the sacred places of pilgrimage in the country. The cenotaph occupies the centre of the marble floor beneath a beautiful canopy of *sheisham* wood beautifully inland with mother-of-pearl. The shrine is visited by thousands every year. Childless women, both Hindu and

Muslim, resort to the tomb and pray for the saint's favour. Close to the north wall of the great mosque are the houses of Abdul Fazal and Faizi, which are of no merit. Commanding the south wall of the palace is the Buland Darwaza, or Gate of Victory, described by Fergusson as the "noblest portal in India, perhaps in the whole world". 176 ft. high and the finest example of Moghul gateways, the Buland Darwaza was erected by Akbar in commemoration of his conquest of Khandesh in 1576. The Buland Darwaza like most other buildings of Fatehpur Sikri were so solidly constructed and so well preserved that many of them to-day are as good as they were when first built.

Of Fatehpur Sikri the celebrated British archaeologist Stuart Piggott says : "There can be few places where the visitor so surely finds himself confronting across the centuries an outstanding personality every aspect of whose subtle and dominating character has been impressed on the buildings he caused to be built".

*     *     *     *

COMM. A good metalled road connects Agra with Fatehpur Sikri (26 miles). Quaint milestones, some 20 ft. high, are encountered at intervals. These date from the days of Babar and are known as 'kosminars' (a kos equalling about 2 miles). There is a regular bus service. Taxis and station waggons can be hired at Agra for the trip. The Agra-Byana line of the Western Rly. passes through Fatehpur Sikri : there are convenient trains.

ACCOM. There is a palatial Archaeological Dak Bungalow at Fatehpur Sikri at the entrance to the palace. There are Khansamas, and meals are charged according to fixed schedule. Visitors from Agra can arrange for lunch and tea by previous intimation to the care-taker or to the Superintendent of Archaeology, Agra Division, 20 Mall Road. Agra. There are cheap restaurants in the nearby bazar.

# MATHURA

Mathura, situated on the west bank of the Jumuna, in the centre of the holy land of Vrajamandal, between

Delhi and Agra, is one of the oldest and most sacred cities of India, being the celebrated birth-place of Lord Krishna. It is the greatest centre for the worship of Vishnu, as Banaras is for that of Siva. Mathura has been the centre of Bhagbata religion from the beginning of Indian life, much before the birth of Jainism and Buddhism. As the centre and nucleus of the devotional movements centering round the name cf Krishna this holy land has reigned supreme in the mind of the people throughout the ages. Ancient visitors to India were invariably attracted by its antiquity and unique sanctity which made it a great centre of pilgrimage for Hindus, Buddhists and Jains alike.

Historically, the city dates from the pre-Mauryan times. Successive waves of foreign invasions passed through it ; and the cultures of the Greeks, the Parthians and the Saka-Kushans enriched the life and culture of this cosmopolitan city. In the first and second centuries A. D., during the memorable reign of the Kushan kings, Kadphises II and Kanishka, Mathura was a seat of royalty and it was then that it saw the beginning of a period of intense art activity which is rightly called the "Golden Period" of the Mathura School of sculpture. Mathura then became the richest emporium of Buddha images in India and these found their way to Sanchi, Sarnath, Sravasti and Kusinagar, and, outside India, to China and Japan. Inspired by the great art traditions of Bharhut and Sanchi, the Mathura school, for the first time, evolved image-making, set forth the rudiments of iconography and thus greatly influenced and shaped Classical Indian art which found culmination in the Age of the Guptas. The Mathura school was thus the prelude to the glorious epoch of artistry that emerged under the Imperial Guptas.

"Kanishka's capital was established at Peshawar, but that Mathura must have played an important part in the government of the Kushans is shown by its selection as the site for a royal gallery of sculpture representing the members of the royal family". But the outstanding statue, worth a visit to Mathura for itself alone, is that of the great Kanishka, a unique life-size statue which shows the king's costumes and weapons with a life-like expression. "If ever a man's soul was portrayed even in his boots, it is in this astonishing statue". Apart from archaic art, statues of kings, Buddha and Bodhisattas, there is in the Curzon Museum a great mass of remarkable figure-sculpture belonging to the first two centuries, which form what is usually referred to as the "Mathura School of Art". In addition, it contains a rich crop of figure-sculpture of the contemporary school of Gandhara which flourished in the North-West Frontier and Afghanistan under the patronage of the Scythian kings and which shows, though externally, new forms of Western influence on Indian art ; for, it has been rightly said that the Gandhara artist had the hand of a Greek but the mind of an Indian.

After the Kushans, Mathura came under the rule of the Guptas. The glory of Mathura as a centre of art was still in the ascendant and some of the finest images of the Mathura school belong to the Gupta Age. The best among them is the standing image of the Buddha dedicated by monk Yasadatta.

The creative genius of the Mathura sculptors was on the decline when we come to the early medieval period (600 to 900 A. D.). Art had lost its creative fervour and profane subjects largely appeared in the field which Cunningham delightfully called "the smirk-ing of unabashed nudities" of voluptuous girls ; and by the time we reach the medieval period (900 to 1200 A. D.), the art history had well nigh run its course.

During the middle ages, Mathura continued in its prosperity and fame, but its great fame was also the cause of its great misfortune. Mahmud of Ghazni pillaged and burnt the city in 1017 A. D. and carried off fabulous wealth. The city was again pillaged by

Sikandar Lodi in 1500 when the temples and shrines suffered irreparable damage. Mathura flourished again under Akbar's liberal patronage and a number of great temples were built, and Mathura and Brindaban became great centres of religion and culture. But the peace of Vrajamandal was short-lived ; Aurangzeb's iconoclastic fury fell upon the holy city and almost all the temples were destroyed including the great temple of Kesava Deo at Mathura and Gobindji at Brindaban. Lying on the high road between Delhi and Agra, Mathura was far from peaceful during the anarchy following the break-up of the Moghul empire. Again it suffered a terrible ravage at the hands of Ahmed Shah Abdali; and it was only with the British occupation of the city in 1803 that the place began to recover from the terrible shocks of the past and reestablish herself once again as a great centre of religion and pilgrimage.

### Places of Interest in and around Mathura

**Katra :** Of the chief and oldest shrine of the city, the Brahmanical temple of Kesava Deo, in the Katra area, only the basement now remains. It occupies the site where once stood the celebrated Buddhist monastery called Yasa Vihara. The great temple of Kesava Deo was finally destroyed by Aurangzeb who built a mosque over it (which still stands over its ruined basement) and renamed the city Islamabad. This is the exact spot where Krishna was born in Kamsa's prison and is regarded with great reverence by Hindus. A stone sign-board with the inscription "Birth-place of Krishna" has been raised to mark the holy spot and a committee has been formed to restore the temple of Kesava Deo which for centuries occupied the sacred site. At the south of the ruins of the Kesava Deo temple (now marked by Aurangzeb's mosque) is Potara Kund, a paved, ancient tank in which Krishna's baby linen was washed.

**Vishram Ghat :** A fine view of the holy city with

its pavilions and galleried ghats descending to the rippling waters of the Jamuna can be obtained from a boat. Occupying a central position is the Vishram Ghat which everyday draws a large stream of pilgrims. According to tradition, this is the spot where Lord Krishna rested after killing the tyrant Kamsa. The Jamuna *arati* (worship of the Jamuna) which takes place daily at dusk is a solemn ceremony in which thousands of oil lamps are floated on the river and cows and turtles are fed to the accompaniment of an enchanting melody of temple bells and devotional hymns. Nearby is the Sati Burj, a red sandstone medieval tower (1574 A. D.) which commemorates the *sati* sacrifice of a wife of Raja Bahar Mal of Ambar.

About a mile to the west of Vishram Ghat, in a congested area, is the temple of Dwarakadhish, a modern structure, which is the present centre of worship. Nearby is the Jumma Masjid, a fine edifice adorned with four minarets each 132 ft. high. The mosque was built in 1660 A.D. Mathura is a city of festivals— Janmastami and Holi are great occasions when the temples are decorated, conches blown and hymns sung in glory of Krishna. Vana-Vihara festival falls on the Vaisakhi Purnima day, while the Pancha Tirtha Mela begins in July-August.

**Mahaban** : 7 miles south-east of Mathura, on the east bank of the Jamuna and reached by road across the railway bridge, is Mahaban, the sacred spot associated with the infancy of Lord Krishna; and a mile off is Gakool, the celebrated spot where the Lord spent his sportive boyhood days in company with the herd-boys and herd-girls and performed many miracles. These places, unusually sacred, are visited by thousands of pilgrims, particularly during the birth-anniversary of the Lord in July-August. Overhanging the Jamuna at Mahaban is an old building which is identified with the palace of Nanda. 5 miles from Mahaban, on the same route, is Baldeo which is another place of pilgrimage. These places can be reached by tonga from Mathura. There is a bus service to Baldeo.

**Gobardhan & Radha Kund :** 16 miles west of Mathura, across a low range hills, lies Gobardhan, a picturesque spot and a great centre of pilgrimage. Gobardhan is reached by the Dig Road, by car or bus. There is a regular bus service. It is said that Krishna lifted up the hill itself and held it aloft on a single finger for seven days and seven nights to shield his worshippers from the floods poured down upon them by Indra. Close to the Manasi Ganga, a large masonry tank of Divine creation, stands the beautiful temple of Harideva erected by Raja Bhagawan Das of Ambar during the reign of Akbar.

Three miles to the north of Gobardhan is Radha Kund, a village clustering round two small lakes, and it is said Lord Krishna himself bathed here in self-purification. On the road to Radha Kund are seen the tombs of Suraj Mall of Bharatpur and his two queens in picturesque surroundings. In front of the cenotaph is an artificial lake and behind an extensive garden.

**Barsana :** 15 miles to the north of Gobardhan and 10 miles south of Kosi (on the Delhi-Agra main road) is Barsana, the birth-place of Sri Radha, the principal devotee of Lord Krishna and therefore a great place of pilgrimage. There is a regular bus service from Mathura to Barsana via Kosi.

**Dig :** 8 miles to the west of Gobardhan and 40 m. from Mathura is Dig which contains the splendid palace of the great Jat ruler, Suraj Mall. Commenced about A. D. 1725, it is the finest and the most original of the Indian palaces of the period which, Fergusson tells us "for extent of shadow and richness of detail surpasses any similar ornaments in India either in ancient or modern buildings". The Jat chief carried to it a great deal of loot from the Fort at Agra. There are a number of highly decorated marble pavilions in the palace ground interspersed with charming gardens. At a short distance is the Rup Sagar Lake where rises the historic fort which was the scene of fierce battles during the British occupation of Northern India. There is a bus service from Mathura to Dig.

\*             \*             \*             \*

COMM. 90 miles from Delhi, 771 miles from Bombay and 825 miles from Calcutta, Mathura lies on Delhi-Bombay main line of the Central Rly. The Delhi-Bombay high road passes through Mathura and beyond it through Agra and Gwalior. U.P. Roadways buses ply between Delhi and Agra through Mathura.

ACCOM. European Travellers can stay in the M. E. S. Dak Bungalow in the Cantonment. It has a Khansama and food is charged at fixed rates (Break-fast : Rs. 1/5/-; Lunch or Dinner : Rs. 3/-). Advance reservation should be made with the Supdt., M. E. S., Mathura. The Railway Retiring Room at the main station (Central Rly.) however provides excellent accommodation and should be occupied, if available, without looking around for other accommodation. There is a P.W.D. Dak Bungalow (no Khansama) near the Court (2 m. from station) in charge of the Dist. Engineer, P. W. D. Mathura. Agra Hotel at Bengali ghat and Modern Hotel near the bus-stand cater for middle class Indians. There are numerous Dharamsalas on the river-front.

On the main road between Mathura and Brindababan is Gita Mandir, a magnificent modern temple-cum-dharamsala built by that devout soul, Raja Birla.

CONVEYANCE. Ekkas and rikshaws are cheap and plentiful. Taxis, if available, are expensive. U.P. Roadways transport buses run regular service between Mathura and Brindaban, 6 miles away. Tongas can be hired for the trip to Mahaban and Gakool ; buses go to Gobardhan, Radhakund and Dig.

# BRINDABAN

Six miles north of Mathura is Brindaban, a name which conjures up the futility of mundane affairs. It is the land of faith where almost every house is a temple and every temple a solemn centre of devotional songs and worship in honour of the Lord. Here in Nikunja Ban (now a thickly wooded garden enclosed by a high wall) the Lord appeared and danced and sang with the devotees for their satisfaction and deliverance. With the deepest reverence and throbbing heart the devotee approaches the spot today and here he sits  and weeps in solitude for the divine favour.

## The Temples

At the entrance to the town, on the left, is seen the lower half of the splendid temple of Gobind Deo which, even in its broken state, is a gem of architecture and the artistic glory of Brindaban.  The temple was built by the two principal disciples of Sri Chaitanya—Rupa and Sanatan—in 1593 under the partronage of Akbar, with red sandstone supplied by the Maharaja Man Singh of Ambar.  Aurangzeb demolished the three upper stories of this great temple so that the blaze of its huge oil lamp at the top might not torment his eyes and distress his soul.  Fergusson describes it as "the most interesting and elegant edifice that Hindu India has ever produced at least in Upper India and the only one perhaps from which an European architect might borrow a few hints".  But Growse (in his *Mathura : A District Memoir*) goes further and amends Fergusson saying :  "I should myself have thought that 'solemn' or 'imposing' was a more appropriate term than 'elegant' for so massive a building and that the suggestions that might be derived from its study were many rather than few".

Opposite the half-demolished temple of Gobind Deo, stands the modern temple of Ranganath built in Dravindian style by Seth Radha Krishna and Seth Govind Das of Madras. This huge temple, almost entirely of white marble with an abandon of gold, stands in a vast enclosure with three *gopurams*. Close to it rises the temple of Lala Babu, a Bengali devotee, who gave away the whole of his fabulous wealth in religious endowments and himself turned a sanyasin.

Brindaban is sacred beyond measure, every nook and corner being associated with some events in the life of Krishna. There are the Kunja Gali, the Mana Gali and Dhana Gali, where the Lord is said to have revealed the meaning of His Being in what is commonly known as the *Ras Lila*. Nearby, on the Jamuna, is the Chira-harana Ghat, where the Lord is said to have stolen the clothes of his devotees.

The other great old temples of Brindaban are : Gopinath, Madan Mohan, Balaram, Jugal Kishore and Radha Ballabh, all built by the Bengali Vashnavites with materials and funds given by Maharaja Mansingh of Jaipur during the reign of Akbar. Brindaban is studded with groves where the devotees sing the great glories of God at all hours of day and night and where religion is the only pursuit known on earth.

\*        \*        \*        \*

ACCOM   There are a number of Dharmasalas.  The Hotel Hindusthan at Gopinath Bazar (Rs. 6/- daily) caters for middle class Indians.  Accommodation is available at the Municipal Dak Bungalow and Bharat Sevasram Sangha.  It is convenient to visit the place from Mathura by taxi or cycle-rickshaw or ekka.  There is a metre-guage rail connection from Mathura. Buses of U.P. Roadway leave Mathura every hour for Brindaban.

# JHANSI

Jhansi (pop. 127,156), seven hours by express train from Kanpur, is an important trade centre which derives an added importance from the military and railway establishments. For the masses of India the very sound of the name lets loose a flood of dreams connected with the heroic exploits of the Rani of Jhansi, who in a blinding flash of courage, unparalleled in the whole history of heroism, made herself and her city immortal in the annals of India.

The walled city is dominated by a medieval fort built by Bir Sing Deo of Orcha (1605-27). At the break-up of the Moghul empire, the Mahrattas over-ran and annexed the Orcha State, which then receded to un-importance, and founded the city of Jhansi. Successive Mahratta chiefs ruled the State under the East India Company till 1853, when, on the death of Gangadhar

Rao, the dynasty ended, and the territory lapsed to the British Government. The young Rani of Jhansi, the widow of Gangadhar, was given a pension, but was not allowed to adopt a heir. Smarting under disappointment, the Rani soon found a chance to avenge her wrong : she/plunged headlong into the Mutiny and became its foremost leader and a formidable enemy of the British. The high-light of the Fort, which is otherwise of no interest, is a platform on the western rampart from which the Rani dashed off to Kalpi, when Sir Huge had secured its submission on April 4, 1858. She then seized Gwalior and scared away Scindia who was an ally of the British, but eventually died fighting in a heroic battle at the head of her faithful troops. Her principal lieutenant, Tatya Topi, a general of uncommon military ability, whose mighty deeds stir up the blood of Indians even today, was at last captured and hanged. The residential palace of the Rani in the heart of the city was long ago converted into the Kotwali by the British, but the room in which the Rani lived has been preserved, and has since become a veritable shrine of pilgrimage, resplendent with a deathless glory.

**Orcha** : 7 miles south of Jhansi and 3 miles south of the Orcha Rly. station, amidst a beautiful landscape on the Betwa, is Orcha which contains the magnificent fortress-palace of Bir Singh Deo. At the height of its glory, Orcha with its magnificent palaces and temples covered a much more extensive area, and was the premier State in Bundelkhand, but to-day it is only a village. Its great ruler, Bir Singh Deo, was a notable figure of the 17th century and an intimate associate of Prince Salim, afterwards the Emperor Jehangir. He killed Abul Fazal, Akbar's favourite historian and Minister, at the instigation of Prince Salim wherefore Akbar sent a force to chastise him, but on the accession of Jehangir to the throne he recovered his former power and enjoyed great influence at his court.

Rising above a wooded island in the Betwa, spanned by a many-arched stone bridge, is the palace in which

Bir Singh Deo held his court. Dense, green forests skirt the rivulet which flows on with a silvery music. Although much of its old grandeur is gone no great imagination is required to realize how grand it must have been in its palmy days. There is also the apartment built for Emperor Jehangir but never used. Resembling a French chateau of the 18th century the palace of Orcha is most impressive even in its present condition. The palace apart, Orcha still retains many marks of its past greatness : scattered around the palace there are many stately buildings, pleasure pavilions and awe-inspiring temples which still attract worshippers to their mighty portals.

**Datia :** 16 miles north of Jhansi, on the main line to Delhi, is the former princely State of Datia noted for its great medieval palace, also built by Bir Singh Deo. Occupying an eminence on a ridge to the west of the town rises the Gobinda Palace with its beautifully sculptured windows, balconies and copulas which according to Fergusson is "perhaps the best example of Rajput architecture of the 17th century." The wide view from the balcony at the rear far into the distant land across a lake is exceedingly panoramic.

*      *      *      *

COMM. Jhansi lies on the Delhi-Bombay main line of the Central Rly., 225 miles from Delhi and 133 miles from Agra, via Gwalior. A branch line from Jhansi runs to Allahabad via Orcha, Harpalpur (for Khajuraho) and Banda (for Kanpur) while another runs straight to Kanpur (137 miles) via Kalpi, an ancient town of considerable historical interest. This was the birth-place of Raja Birbal, a most famous minister of Akbar, and the scene of grim battles during the Mutiny of 1857-8.

ACCOM. There are a number of middle class hotels at Sipri Bazar, at the back of the station, of which Central Hotel and Sipri Hotel are popular. The other good hotel is the Jhansi Hotel at Sadar Bazar (3 miles from station). The Circuit House and the P.W.D. Insp. Bangalow are both to the east of station.

CONVEYANCE. Tongas and cycle rickshaws are transport, Taxis are scarce. Buses go to Datia, Lalitpur and Shivapuri.

# DEOGARH

66 miles south of Jhansi, on the Delhi-Bombay main line of the Central Railway is Jakhlaun station, whence the classic Gupta temple of Deogarh (c 500 A. D.), which is of supreme importance to archaeologists, is 8 miles to the west.

On the crest of a thickly wooded hill overlooking the Betwa river is the famous Dasavatara temple, which contains some of the finest sculptures and in which "the early Gupta style had reached its culmination". The conical tower or *sikhara* which became the most characteristic feature of North Indian temples first came into fashion in this temple as in another at Bithargoan (in Kanpur District). But at this stage it was ponderous and heavy and had not yet developed that graceful, tall, curvilinear spire which was perfected in the temples of Bhubaneswar in the early medieval period. The most striking feature of the Dasavatara temple at Deogarh are its porticos which are four in number projecting from each side of the central structure and reached by a flight of steps. The plain walls on the three sides of the sanctum are relieved with recessed panels or false windows each carved with a superb figure composition within a framework of graceful pilasters and architraves. The images of Siva, Vishnu and other Brahmanical gods are superbly sculptured, lending to them a majestic serenity that is enchanting. "When complete", says Percy Brown, "this building was unquestionably one of rare merit in the correct ordering of its panels, all alike serving the purpose of practical utility, yet imbued with supreme artistic feeling. Few monuments can show such a high level of workmanship, combined with a ripeness and refinement in its sculptural effect as the Gupta temple at Deogarh".

\*　　　\*　　　\*　　　\*

COMM. Jakhlaun station is reached in three hours from Jhansi and one hour from Bina. Express trains do not stop at

191

Jakhlaun. Tongas and bullock carts can be hired at Jakhlaun for the 8 miles trip to Deogarh along a kaccha road which is not negotiable in rainy season. The best base for visit is Lalitpur, a small town, 10 m. above Jakhlaun, where all facilities are available.

ACCOM. There is a Forest Dept. Dak Bungalow at Deogarh to occupy which permission should be taken from the Divisional Forest Officer, Bundelkhand Region, Jhansi. There is a Jain Dharamsala below the temple. Secretary, Jain Prabandhak Committee, Deogarh, P.O. Lalitpur, arranges for all facilities on previous intimation.

# ALIGARH

Aligarh, which boasts of the great Muslim University, does not begin and end with that University alone. It has a long and chequered history, boasts of historic sites and monuments, ancient and great, and has much to offer to the sightseer and the student of history alike.

Koil, the ancient name of Aligarh, has left its mark on the history of India. It is mentioned in the Puranas as the capital of the dreaded demon-king called Coel or Koil, and the ruins of the prehistoric fortress of Koil, which are to be seen on an eminence to the west of the railway station, are supposed to be the remains of the legendary citadel of the said demon chief. Buddhist remains excavated from the site tend to prove that the place is of great antiquity and a custodian of remote history. For centuries, during the historic period, Koil was the stronghold of the powerful Dor Rajputs who eventually lost their independence to the all-conquering Kutbuddin in 1194. From the middle ages through the period of turmoil following the disintegration of the Moghul power to the begining of the nineteenth century Aligarh was a storm centre. Its strategic situation coupled with its prosperity attracted the scourge of Timur, the Terrible, who swooped upon the city with fire and sword and massacred the inhabitants without mercy. Early in the 18th. century, Sabit Khan, a general of Emperor

Muhammad Shah, renamed the city Sabitgarh after his own name and built the great mosque which is the chief architectural glory of present-day Aligarh. In the middle of the eighteenth century, Aligarh became the bone of contention between the various claimants for power in India—the Afghans, Jats, Mahrattas and the Rohillas. In 1757, the Jat ruler, Suraj Mall of Bharatpur, occupied the city and renamed it Jatgarh. Shortly afterwards the Jats were dislodged from power by the raid of Ahmad Shah Durrani (1759), and in the confusion that followed Najaf Khan finally drove out the Jats, occupied the city and changed its name to Aligarh. But the Afghan victory was far from decisive; it only plunged Aligarh into a ceaseless, bloody strife between the Afghans and Jats in which both parties completely exhausted themselves. Seizing this opportunity, Mahadhaji Scindhia, captured the city by a lightening dash (1784 A.D.) and made it the headquarters of his northern army. During the twenty years of Mahratta occupation Aligarh shot into the political map of India as the invincible stronghold of Mahadhaji, who even after the other great powers had come to terms with the British, aspired to the hegemony of India. In this period was built the great fort of Aligarh where the Mahratta troops were drilled by the French generals De Boigne and Jean Perron in advanced European methods. It was here, again that in 1802 Scindhia and the Raja of Nagpur entered into an alliance against the combined powers of the British, Nizam and the Peshwa. At length all political speculations were set at rest when, in the Second Mahratta War, Wellesley defeated Scindhia and the Raja of Nagpur and Lord Lake repulsed the forces of Perron and captured Aligarh and Agra (1803).

To the east of the railway station is the Civil Station which contains all that modern Aligarh has to show, that is, the University, the Judge Courts, District office and the Government of India Form Press. Aligarh is justly proud of the Gandhi Eye Hospital.

Notable among the objects of interest is the Muslim Anglo-Oriental College founded by Sir Saiyad Ahmad Khan in 1875. This formed the nucleus around which the great Muslim University of Aligarh was built.

The University consists of a number of institutions of which the buildings are built on the pattern of Oxford and Cambridge Universities. The University draws students from all parts of India, Pakistan, Turkey, Egypt, South Africa, and where there are Muhammadans.

About 4 miles west of the town is the great fort of Scindhia with which were associated the French generals De Boigne and Jean Perron and which played a great role in the period of confusion and turmoil prior to the British conquest of Northern India.

In the old city of Koil, on the G. T. Road, lies the historic Achal Tank around which are small Hindu temples nestling amicably on tall, ancient trees. Not far from it is the Bala Kila, the ancient fortress of Koil, which is surmounted by the great mosque built by Sabit Khan in 1728 A. D. With its tall minarets and ponderous craftsmanship the imposing edifice dominates the whole scene and can be seen from the passing train. Aligarh is usually associated with butter and lock industries which provide livelihood to a great section of the populace. Every year in February a cattle fair and industrial exhibition is held in the city.

\* \* \* \*

COMM. 79 miles from Delhi, 81 miles from Meerut and 816 miles from Calcutta, Aligarh occupies the central position among the historic towns of Uttar Pradesh. It lies on the Delhi-Moghulserai main line of the Northern Railway. The Grand Trunk Road passes through the city. U.P. Roadways buses go to many places such as Bulandshahar, Meerut, Agra.

ACCOM. There is a Dak Bungalow on the Samad Road, between the city and Civil Station. Imperial Hotel, near the station, Green Hotel, in the city, and Shamshad Hotel, near University, are popular. Tongas and cycle rickshaws are transport.

# MEERUT

Meerut (pop. 233,183), the headquarters of the Meerut Division and a chief city of Uttar Pradesh, is centrally situated in the Doab, between the Ganga and the Jumuna 40 miles north-east of Delhi. It is a great mart for agricultural produce, a notable centre of education and has a very large military establishment— the headquarters of the Eastern Command of the Defence Department.

Meerut, together with Delhi, was the earliest cradle of Muslim power in India. Its immense wealth attracted the notice of Timur who, after the terrible sack of Delhi, sent a strong force in 1399 to plunder the city, but the strong walls of the city defied even his picked generals. The ruthless conqueror then appeared before the city walls with the swiftness of a tornado, devastated the city and put every soul to the sword. The carnage of Delhi and Aligarh was repeated in Meerut.

But Meerut has left a deep mark on history as the birth-place of the Mutiny. After a few warnings in Bengal, the Sepoys of the 3rd. Bengal Cavalry and the 11th. and 20th. Bengal Infantry mutinied at Meerut, on Sunday, May 10, 1857. A small well, in front of the temple of Aghornath (Siva) at Kali Paltan ground, on the west of the cantonment town, became the scene of ghastly murder. The insurgents broke open the gaol, released their comrades who had been put into prison for their refusal to accept greased cartridges, murdered every European they came across and then marched off to Delhi. The Europeans in Delhi were butchered, and the dethroned Emperor Bahadur Shah was proclaimed the Padshah of Hindustan, on May 11, 1857. The Mutiny spread like wildfire, and the whole country from Meerut to Kanpur was on fire ; nearly the whole of Rohilkhand and Oudh slipped from British hands.

The city is divided into two parts : the old walled

city, distinguished by the Clock Tower (Kambo Gate) and containing congested bazars and metal workshops for which Meerut is famous, is at the south ; while the Cantonment town called Sadar (also thickly populated lies a mile to the north. Modern shops, hotels, restaurants, military barracks, offices and colleges are situated in the Cantonment which is very extensive with fine roads, parks, gardens and clubs. St. Johns Chruch (1821), built in Italian style, was the first Chruch to be constructed in Upper India. At Suraj Kund, at the eastern suberb of the city, there are a number of small temples, *sati* stones and Dharamsalas. In the old city and its environs, there are a large number of mosques, tombs and imambaras some of which are very old. The Makbara of Salar Masa-ud Ghazi was probably built by Kutbuddin Ibak early in the thirteenth century ; the Jumma Masjid dates from an earlier date. The Darga of Shah Pir, a fine structure of red sandstone, was erected by Nur Jehan in honour of the pious fakir.

With its groups of buildings, hostels and playgrounds, the Meerut College presents a fine spectacle and is probably the largest in the State both in point of size and roll of students. East of the college, near Surajkund, is the Nauchandi grounds where a very large fair takes place every March. Traders and manufacturers from every part of India take stalls at the Nauchandi Fair which becomes a show-place for varied and beautiful merchandise and cultural performances.

\*       \*       \*       \*

COMM. 40 miles north-east of Delhi, on the Delhi-Saharanpur line of the Northern Rly., is Meerut reached by through trains from Delhi, Gaziabad or from Khurja via Hapur. It is convenient to detrain at the Meerut City station where there is plenty of conveyances both for City and Cantonment towns. U. P. Govt. Buses also ply every hour between Meerut and Delhi. Govt. buses to Dehra Dun and Hardwar pass through Meerut.

ACCOM. There are a few hotels in the old City near the Kambo Gate. But it is better to stay at the Cantonment town

(Sadar) which is central, cleaner and affords better hotel and transport facilities. Royal Hotel at the Mall Road (Rs. 10/- daily) is a good middle class hotel. Then there are the Meerut Hotel, Ranjan Hotel and a number of restaurants near Begam Bridge. Wheelers Club on the Mall Road offers excellent food and accommodation in European style. There is also the Circuit House.

CONVEYANCE consists of taxis, tongas and cycle-rickshaws. Service buses ply to the neighbouring towns including Hapur, Bulandshahar, Mujafarnagar, Mowana, Hastinapur and Garmukteshwar.

## HASTINAPUR

The ruins of Hastinapur, the epic city of the Mahabharata, where a court intrigue between the sons of the blind old King Dhritarastra and Pandu led to the sanguinary battle of Kurukshetra, lies 24 miles north-east of Meerut, in a alone region near the Ganga. On a high ground covered with woods and ancient bricks, there are still traces of ancient temples, wells and domestic buildings which the local guides assign to Dhritarastra, Draupadi or some Pandava hero. The pensive tranquility of the place where a few Sadhus meditate has not been disturbed by modern influence ; the Ganga flows a few miles away. Recent excavation of some mounds have yielded traces of settlement datable to a very early period.

In the open, at the west of the sacred pre-historic spot, there is a comparatively modern Jain temple with a Dharamsala. The temple authorities take care of the visitors. Hastinapur for long has been a petty out-of-way village, but in recent years it has attained development owing to refugee settlement and National Extension Scheme. Visitors should carry refreshments from Meerut or Mowana.

\*       \*       \*       \*

COMM. There is a bus service from Meerut to Mowana (16 miles) whence Hastinapur is eight miles to the east, across sandy tract. There is a bus service from Mowana to Hastinapur. Cycles can also be hired at Mowana for the trip.

# HARDWAR

Hardwar, a sacred city of great antiquity, lies at the foot of the Siwalik Hills through which the sacred Ganga bursts upon the plains of India. The holy city lies in the gorge beside the river. The city has one principal street running along the bank, studded with temples, dharamsalas and ghats. From the terrace of the Brahmakund ghat the wide view across the blue waters of the Ganga is exceedingly panoramic.

The Gangadwar temple on the Hari-ki pairi (foot-print of Hari) is the centre of pilgrimage. It stands just above the sacred bathing pool known as Brahma Kund. It is so holy that on auspicious days like the Kumbha sometimes a million pilgrims attempt to throw themselves simultaneously into the water. Hardwar has earned immortality as the chief venue of the Kumbha Mela which takes place every twelve years. Here, due to its close proximity to the Himalayas, is seen the largest concourse of Sadhus.

'Kapilsthan' is the ancient name of the sacred city; for here the great sage, Kapil passed many years in austere meditation. General Cunningham has identified the actual spot with Mayapur, a little down the river.

2½ miles below is Kankhal which has a congregation of temples headed by that of Dakheswar (Siva). The place is picturesque and is favourite with the Sadhus.

**Hrishikesh**, situated on the thickly wooded slopes of the Siwalik hills on the Ganga, is 14 miles to the north reached by rail or road.

Hrisikesh is a small town from where the people of the neigbouring hill districts get their supplies.

Three miles from the bazar bus-stand is the Lachmanjhula ghat reached by foot or tonga. Here the river can be crossed by ferry or by the hanging bridge for a visit to Swargashram of Kali Kamliwala and the

Gita Bhaban both of which are on the other side of the river. There are other ashrams in beautiful settings.

\*         \*         \*         \*

COMM. 915 m. from Calcutta (via Lucknow), 163 m. from Delhi (via Saharanpur) and 45 m. from Dehra Dun, Hardwar is situated on the Laksar-Dehra Dun section of the Northern Railway. Calcutta-Dehra Dun Express passes through Hardwar. It can be easily reached from Delhi by U. P. Roadways buses (4 hours). The bus service is frequent and comfortable.

ACCOM. Railway Retiring Rooms at the station are comfortable (Rs. 3/- per bed). Food can be procured from the Refreshment Room or from outside. There are many comfortable Dharamsalas on the riverside, a few cheap hotles and a Dak Bungalow near the station. Taxis and Tongas are available.

# DEHRA DUN

211 miles from Delhi by rail and 157 miles by express tourist buses from New Delhi, Dehra Dun is a beautiful valley set in picturesque surroundings between the Himalayas and the Siwalik hills. Its bracing climate throughout the year and its lovely natural beauty have made it a favourite residential city and an important educational centre in Northern India. Many delightful excursions can be made from the city : its environs abound whith big and small game and plentiful fishing. On its suberbs is the famous Rajaji Sanctuary. The Dehra Dun- Hardwar forest road affords a wonderful drive through superb forest scenery and natural animal life. At Kalsi, 32 miles from Dehra Dun on the Chakrata road, is an Asokan rock edict on the Jumna.

Dehra Dun is well known for the Military Academy and the Forest Research Institute which are situated at a beautiful spot about 3 miles south-west of the city.

Dehra Dun is the rail head for Mussorie which is reached by taxies or U. P. Roadways buses. Another bus service runs to Chakrata, a hill station, 66 miles away.

**COMM.** Dehra Dun is directly connected with Calcutta Bombay, Delhi and other chief cities of India by express trains. It can be reached easily from Delhi by express tourist buses (5½ hrs.) which pass through Meerut and Roorki.

**ACCOM.** The Western style hotel of the city is Hotel White House. Indian style hotels are ; Gresham Hotel, Royal Hotel, & Snow View Hotel. Transport consists of taxis, buses, and tongas. Taxis, station wagons and 32-seater buses may be hired for sight-seeing from the U.P. Roadways Service which has a central office at Dehra Dun.

## CHAKRATA

66 miles from Dehra Dun to the north is Chakrata, a celebrated hill station on the foothills of the Himalayas, about 7000 ft. above sea level. Chakrata is primarily a military hill station : it also does a good trade in potatoes. Half way to it is Khalsi where the Jumna first flows into the plains with a mighty roar and where fishing is plentiful. Here, on the roadside, stands a famous edict of Asoka which is still in tact. Chakrata is connected with Saharanpur by bus and with Mussorie and Simla by bridle paths.

\*　　　　\*　　　　\*　　　　\*

**ACCOM.** There is no good hotel. Visitors can stay in the Rest House or the District Board Dak Bungalow. Transport consists of buses, taxis and mules.

## MUSSORIE

From Dehra Dun a short drive of only 22 miles brings the visitor to Mussorie (6580 ft.), one of the most popular hill stations of Northern India famous for its gay social life and entertainments. Its excellent summer climate coupled with its close proximity to Delhi makes its a popular refuge from the heat of the capital.

Life here goes in a swing. "Every night there is something to do : new films, dancing with cabaret and good orchestras, may be a dramatic show too, for this is Mussorie's Festival time. There will be exhibitions,

horse-racing, theatrical shows, concerts, illuminations, sporting events, competitions and many other amusements".

The whole of Mussorie is made for visitors. The Mall is always thronged with holidays crowds. Mussorie is also the most level of all hill stations with beautiful walks. There are no stiff climbs, and yet the more adventurous can make thrilling excursions into the hills or the spectacular Jumna Bridge where the river Jumna flows out of its tortuous mountain valley into the plains below.

\*　　　\*　　　\*　　　\*

ACCOM. The western style hotels are: Charlevile, Hackmans's and Savoy—all charging Rs. 14/-daily. Good middle class hotels are: Silverton Hotel, Hotel Kashmir, Doon View Hotel. Libarary Club Hotel and the Y. M. C. A., all charging between Rs. 7/8/- and Rs. 10/- daily.

COMM. 1055 m. from Bombay, 957 m. from Calcutta, 233 m. from Delhi and 22 m. from Dehra Dun, Mussorie is reached by bus or car from Dehra Dun station. At Rajpur, 3 miles above Dehra Dun, at the root of the Mussorie hill, ponies can be hired for ride up the hills to Mussorie. Kingcrain is the bus head for Mussorie whence ½ mile's climb leads visitors to gay Mussorie.

Bis fare from Dehra Dun : Upper class — Rs. 2/- ; Lower class—Rs. 1/6. Toll Tax—Rs. 2/- per head. Rickshaws, Dandies and ponies are local transport.

# DELHI

The romance of Delhi with its crowded history— of great names and gallant deeds, of pomp and pageantry, of conquest and of being conquered, of quick rise and fall of empires — is as varied as it is thrilling. Lord Curzon described it "as the deserted cities of dreary and disconsolate tombs"; for in the course of 800 years, seven times on the plains of Delhi, great empires have risen and fallen, sometimes one upon another and sometimes one beside the other, their ruins alone now marking the spot where they once stood. Indeed history is writ large everywhere in

Delhi, on crumbling stones, decaying tombs and ruined ramparts littered across a hoary tract stretching on all sides. The seven old Delhi which rose phoenix-like from the ashes of the past, swayed for a time the length and breadth of Hindusthan and then crumbled into the dust were : Lal Kot, Siri, Tughlakabad, Jahanpannah, Firozabad, Purana Killa and Shahjahan-bad, each with a storied past and invested with an aura of romance.

**History** : According to legend, Delhi first became the capital of India in the days of Mahabharata and the fort of Indrapat, also called Purana Killa, is supposed to mark the site of that legendary capital. Firishta records a tradition that in the 8th century the city was named Dilli by king Dilu of Kanauj after his own name. Historically, however, Delhi dates from the middle of the eleventh century, when the princes of the Tomara clan had established their capital at Suraj Kund, near Delhi, and then transferred it to Mehralli, in the fort of Lal Kot built by Ananga Pal Tomar in 1050 A. D. The dynasty lasted just a century, until 1151, when it was supplanted by Visaldev, a Chauhan chief of Ajmere. His successor, Prithvi Raj or Rai Pithora, ruled both Delhi and Ajmer and built another fort around Lal Kot (the Qutub Minar area) which he named Rai Pithora. From Delhi, in 1191, Prithviraj led his formidable forces to defeat Mohammad of Ghor at Tarain, but in the following year he was himself defeated at that place. With his death the history of Hindu Delhi ends and that of Mohammadan Delhi begins. These two forts, the two Asoka pillars, the Iron Pillar at the Kutub and the tank of Surajkund are the only remains of the Hindu period now left in Delhi.

The earliest Muslim capital was established at Killa Rai Pithora, the seat of Prithviraj, conquered and fortified by Kutubuddin-Ibak in 1193. A century later, Siri, built by Alauddin Khilji about 1303, became the capital of the Sultans of Delhi. Tughlakabad was built by Tughlak Shah in 1321, and Jahanpannah by the next Tughlak sovereign, Mohammed Shah in 1327. Firozabad (sometimes called Firozshah Kotla) was built by Firoz Shah about 1354 A. D. At the end of the fifteenth century, the Lodis removed their capital to Agra. Purana Killa, otherwise known as Indrapat, was started by Humayun and completed by Sher Shah ; the latter, however, retained his capital at Agra. Akbar and Jahangir lived mainly at Agra, Lahore or Ajmer, because they did not like Delhi. For this reason, Delhi has very little or nothing to show of the great architectural achievements of Akbar the Great, which are mainly confined to Agra, Fatehpur Sikri and Allahabad. The last great Muslim Delhi that we inherit to some extent its former shape is Shajahanabad with its majestic marble palaces and famous mosques, built by Shah Jahan, the most magnificent of the royal builders of India. He also built the Jumma Masjid and opened the Western Jumuna Canal. From this time Delhi remained the capital of the Moghul emperors. Aurangzeb, a stern and fanatical puritan, did not bother himself with the art of building and with him began the decadence of Moghul architecture which reached the zenith of glory in the time of his father. With the death of Aurangzeb in 1707, set in the disintegration of the great Moghul empire. In 1737, during the reign of Muhammad Shah, Peshwa Baji Rao challanged the authority of the Moghuls and appeared before the gates of Delhi. During the nominal rule of the later Moghuls, Delhi was raided twice by foreign invaders ; first in 1739 by Nadir Shah, the Persian, who ordered a general massacre of the inhabitants and carried off the Peacock Throne, and then by Ahmed Shah Durrani, the Afghan, in 1756.

During the titular rule of Shah Alam, Delhi became the bone of contention between the Afghans and the Mahrattas. Madho Rao Scindia captured the city in 1771 and restored the emperor to the city of his ancestors. From 1788 a Mahratta garrison permanently occupied the palace, and Shah Alam remained a prisoner in the hands of Scindia until Lord Lake conquered the city in 1803 and took the emperor under British protection. Again, in 1804, Delhi was besieged by the Mahratta chief, Jaswant Rao Holkar, but was successfully defended by Col. William Burn. From that time till the Mutiny of 1857 Delhi remained under British protection although the shadow emperors were allowed a show of royalty. The last king Bahadur Shah was taken prisoner in the course of suppressing the Mutiny and with his death in Rangoon, in 1862, the Moghul dynasty disappeared from the pages of history. Delhi was formally annexed to the British crown by the Declaration of 1858. The city however rose to its present position of importance when the capital of British India was transferred there from Calcutta in 1911.

## Red Fort

The most outstanding land mark of Delhi today is the Red Fort around which lies the 'seventh Delhi', the Delhi of Shah Jahan. As the train approaching the Delhi Central Station slows down over the Jumna Bridge, the fortress-palace of Shah Jahan suddenly looms large and the visitor is at once overwhelmed by its bewildering dimensions and architectural splendour characteristic of great Moghul edifices. The fortress-palace of the Moghul emperors who followed Shah Jahan, the Red Fort is surrounded by a towering wall built of gigantic slabs of red sandstone and contains within it palaces, courts and pavilions which for their magnificence and costly splendour "became the envy of the art galleries of the world".

Entrance to the Fort is gained through the Lahore Gate whence a vaulted hall, 375 feet long, praised by Fergusson as "the noblest entrance to any existing palace', leads to the inner gateway called the Naubhat Khana. From this multi-storied Music Chamber royal bands played at frequent intervals. The French traveller Bernier, who at first was defeaned by the loud music of imperial drum and orchestra eventually discovered grandeur, solemnity and even melody in it'. On the second floor of the Naubhat Khana is now housed the War Memorial Museum.

*Diwani-am* : The first wonder inside the imperial enclosure is the Diwani-am, the Hall of Public Audience, a splendid building which still vividly recalls the pomp and pageantry of the imperial Moghuls. Bernier, who had the privilege of attending the Durbar, was awe-struck by its magnificence and grandeur. In a recess of the centre of the back wall is the imperial chamber splendidly panelled with marble and inlaid with precious stones. Most of the jewelled panels were looted by British troops after the Mutiny of 1857. Nearly fifty years later, Lord Curzon discovered some of them in London and had them replaced to their original position. Below the imperial seat is a marble dias used by the Prime Minister when presenting petitions and receiving orders from the emperor seated under the golden canopy above. The floor space was reserved for the "whole body of great nobles, the Rajas and the ambassadors all standing, their eyes bent downwards, and their hands crossed", while "high up in the recess, like a picture in the wall, glittered the dazzling figure of the grand Moghul, a figure to strike terror, for a frown meant death".

*Mamtaz Mahal* (now the Museum) : Behind the Diwani-am, overlooking the Jumna, is a court containing the imperial seraglio, where the Moghul emperors dreamed and dallied amidst the most fantastic splendour that the East has ever seen. One would do well to start with southernmost building, the Mumtaz Mahal which once formed part of the harem. In later Moghul days, it served as a military prison and till recently as a Seargent Mess. Here, as elsewhere in the Fort, time and men have wrought havoc and its original splendour is completely lost. It is now a bare building, a skeleton of its glorious past. It now accommodates the Museum of Archaeology. Here are to be seen some of the specimens of Moghul costume, pictures and calligraphy.

The adjoining building to the north is the Rang Mahal (Palace of Colour) which was the largest and the most beautiful of all the apartments of the royal seraglio. In the great days of Shah Jahan it was the palace of the Padshah Begum and was studded with paints and gilts and jewels of unearthly beauty. The Court Chronicler flew into ecstasy in describing that 'in excellence and glory it surpassed the eight-sided throne of heaven, and in lustre and colour it is far superior to the palaces in the promised paradise'. In a shallow chanal through its marble floors flowed the celebrated *Nahari Bhisti* or the Stream of Paradise 'like a quick fall of stars' creating a fantasy which no language can adequately describe. Falling in a rippling cascade down the Shah Burj at the extreme north and feeding the flowers and foliage of the famous Hayat Khan Garden it flowed silently through the chain of imperial salons—Hamman, Diwani-Khas, Khwabagh or Imperial Bedchamber—culminating in the stately Rangmahal, the favourite resort of the Emperor. "It is easy to imagine the Emperor, wearied by the ministration of justice or bored by an audience of foreign embassies seeking relief in the cool of the Rangmahal, resplendent with colour and marble, and musical with the subdued murmur of falling waters and the voices of his chosen ladies". But now all is gone and one can only imagine what it must have been in its palmy days.

*Khas Mahal* : From the Rangmahal one walks to the private apartments of the Emperor which bears the famous Scales of Justice, inlaid with gold. This was the Khas Mahal or Khwabagh where the Emperor rested or entertained his intimate friends. This suite of three rooms was most fantastically decorated with floral design in gold and gilt and various colours. Count Von Orlich, who visited the palace in the twilight of Moghul glory in 1843, was impressed by the Scales of Justice and the grandeur of the imperial bedroom, where he saw a rhapsodish engaged in lulling the Emperor to sleep with sweet tales reminiscent of the fashion of the Thousand and One Arabian Night Tales.

Adjoining the eastern wall of the Khwabagh, and overlooking a vast space on the shallow bed of the Jamuna, is the famous domed balcony called the Mussamman Burj. This was the scene of 'Darshan' or 'Showing' ceremony. Here the Emperor came every morning to salute the rising sun and to receive the salutations of his subjects. In recent past that colourful ceremony was once revived by the British who foolishly fancied themselves to be the successors of the Grand Moghuls. So, after the Delhi Durbar of 1911, the King George V and Queen Marry were led to this Golden Tower to receive obescience from the people in imitation of the Moghul emperors.

*Diwani-Khas* : Next comes the Diwani-Khas, or the Hall of Private Audience, a magnificient pavilion which baffles description. "The whole is of white marble, asseen in the sun ; but that is the least part of the wonder. Walls and ceilings, pillars and many-pointed arches, are all inlaid with the richest, yet most delicate colours. What it must have been like, you ask yourself, when the Peacock Throne blazed with emerald and sapphire, diamond and ruby, from the now empty pedestal, and the plates of burnished silver reflected its glory from the roof." And it is no wonder that Shah Jahan had chosen to inscribe on its exquisite walls a couplet in gold : "If there is paradise on earth, it is this, it is this."

In this court the nobels of the highest rank were wont to wait upon the Emperor. Here, on the marble dias dazzled in myriad colours the Peacock Throne of Shah Jahan worth above 10 million rupees. In giving a vivid account of the splendour of the Court Sir Thomas Roe says in awe-struck words : "High in a gallery, with a canopy over him and a carpet before him, sat in great and barbarious state the great Moghul". An eminent historian tells us that poet Milton must have had this dazzling scene in mind when he wrote in Paradise Lost.

"High on a throne of royal state, which far

Outshone the wealth of Ormuz and of Ind,
Or where the gorgeous East, with richest hand,
Showers on her kings barbaric pearl and gold,
Satan exalted sat".

Once the symbol and epitome of Moghul glory
this building was again dragged down by destiny to
witness the stupendous drama of the fall of the House
of Timur with the utmost refinement of humiliation and
cruelty. Here, Nadir Shah received the submission of
the Moghul Emperor, Mohammad Shah, in 1739, and
deprived him of the most valuable treasure of his ancestors—the Peacock Throne. The Mahrattas, the Jats
and the Rohillas, who became the nightmare of the
shadow emperors, despoiled it of its remaining treasures ; while in this building, it is said, the aged helpless
Emperor Shah Alam (1759-1806) was blinded by the
brigand Ghulam Quadi. When at the frantic invitation
of that Emperor, Lord Lake entered the palace in 1803
to afford him British protection against the predatory
raids of the Mahrattas, he found the Emperor sitting
under a tattered canopy 'almost alone'. It was here
again that in May 1857 the mutineers proclaimed Bahadur Shah once more emperor of Hindusthan, all un-
witting that seven months later he was to be tried in the
same hall for his life.

The muse of history had thus chosen this building
to be the scene of sunset of Moghul glory and the sun-
rise of another. But even in its departed glory the
Diwani-Am is a feast for the eyes ; the ceilings still
bear exquisite floral designs in gold and gilts the price of
which alone, according to the Court Historian, was no
less than 9 lakhs of rupees.

*Hammam* : To the north of the Diwani-Khas are
the Royal Baths (Hammam) consisting of three large
rooms connected by a shallow water channel. They
were lighted by windows of coloured glasses in the
roof and in the centre of each room is a fountain
of white marble. The baths were a favourite resort

of the Moghul emperors and within their cool marble walls important affairs of State were often transacted. Sir Thomas Roe was interviewed by Jahangir in the Hammam of the Agra palace.

*Moti Masjid*, close to the Hammam, was built by Aurangzeb in 1659. The austere puritan is said to have spent no less than 160,000 rupees on this private royal chapel. Much of its interior decorations, jewelled lamps and many other glories have long since disappeared, and yet the 'Pearl Mosque' stands like a 'beautiful case robbed of its gems'.

*The Gardens* : Proceeding north one enters the palace gardens which were laid out in flowered parterres and were watered by marble channels and fountains. The chief among them was the Hayat Baksh Garden which is bounded on the north and south by two pavilions named after the two monsoon months—Sawan and Bhadon. On the west of this, now occupied by military barracks, was Mahtab Garden or the Garden of Moonlight. Time and men have caused havoc to the Gardens and palaces of the Fort. In the small days of the Moghuls, waves of adventurers and raiders laid their hands on the fittings with which the royal palaces and the gardens were adorned. "After their cupidity was satiated, came others who removed the marble baths and sundry objects of art across the sea". Simultaneously with this barbarous loot modern utilitarian buildings raised their ugly heads at random to spoil what remained of the grand poem that Shah Jahan wrought in stone.

*Chandni Chowk* : From the Red Fort, Chandni Chowk is within a stone's throw to the west. The historic avenue runs from the Lahore Gate of the Fort to the Fatehpuri Masjid, and in its great days the avenue was skirted by the famous *nahar* (water-course) of Ali Merdan Khan. Once renowned as the richest market in the world, Chandni Chowk even today is a busy market-place and the centre for jewellers, ivory workers and brocade weavers who boast that they can spin

209

silver and gold as fine as any mill in Lancashire can spin cotton.

*Jumma Masjid* : A little to the south of Chandni Chowk, opposite the Red Fort, is the far-famed Jumma Masjid, standing out boldly from high ground. Built by Shah Jahan about 1658 A.D., it is a vast, splendid mosque and the largest of its kind in India. Its front courtyard, 450 feet square, is approached from three sides by a magnificent flight of steps so long, so majestically wide that they form what might be called a stone mountain. The mosque itself, a splendid structure, is crowned with three domes of white marble which command a view of the whole city. Inside the mosque are preserved some precious relics—a slipper of Mohammad, a hair of the Prophet, his footprints in stone and a piece of green canopy that once covered his tomb.

*Mosques of Shajahanabad* : Half a mile south of the great mosque is the Kalan Masjid, embedded in a poor locality near the Turkman Gate. This was built by Firoz Shah's Prime Minister, Khan Jahan, in 1386 in the pattern of a typical Arabian mosque. Khan Jahan, a converted Hindu, also built the Khirki Masjid, close to the walls of Jahanpannah near the Kutub.

Another notable mosque is the Fatehpuri Mosque at the western end of Chandni Chowk. This was built by Fatehpuri Begam, a wife of Shah Jahan, in 1650 A.D. Though architecturally far inferior to the great mosque this has been a centre of worship ever since the reign of Shah Jahan. The fine mosque at the back of Daryaganj called the Zinat-ul-Masjid was built by Zinat-un-Nissa, one of Aurangzeb's daughters. Of great historic interest is the Sonheri Masjid, opposite the Fountain on Chandni Chowk. It was from its roof that Nadir Shah watched the massacre of Delhi citizens on the 22nd March, 1739. He stopped the horrible bloodshed only on the piteous entreaties of Emperor Mahammad Shah saying : "The Emperor of Hindusthan must not beg in vain". Another mosque of great beauty is the Fakhr-ul

210

Masjid at the western side of Kashmiri Gate. This was built in 1728 by Fakhr-un-Nissa, wife of one of Aurangzeb's nobles.

*Raj Ghat* : At the back of Daryaganj, about a mile south of the Red Fort, is a hallowed spot, the Raj Ghat. Here, Mahatma Gandhi was cremated after his martyrdom on January 30. 1948. Surrounded by exquisite flower-beds, green, velvety turf and shrubs it is indeed a beauty-spot steeped in a profound spiritual calm. Every day streams of people—townsmen and simple village folks—visit this shrine of pilgrimage to lay flowers on the tomb of the greatest man of modern India, the Father of the Nation.

## NEW DELHI

**Connaught Place** : Between Chandni Chowk, the heart of old Delhi, and the Secretariat, that of the new, the distance is four miles. For the approaching visitor the first glimpse of New Delhi is Connaught Place, a symmetrical series of buildings, circular in design, which accommodate countless fashionable shops, hotels, restaurants, commercial houses and newspaper offices. From Connaught Place a number of wide tree-shaded avenues radiate in all directions—Parliament Street leading to the House of Parliament, the Secretariat and Rastrapati Bhawan, which all lie at a distance of about a mile and a half south of Connaught Place.

A neatly planned city with a vista of tree-lined avenues, green lawns and fountains, New Delhi is the creation of the British wherein European architecture, mingled with Indian, finds the noblest expression. It was designed by the famous architects, Sir Edwin Lutyens and Sir Herbert Baker and completed in 1931.

**Jantar Mantar** : Proceeding along Parliament Street one comes across the Old Observatory—Jantar Mantar—built by Maharaja Jai Singh about 1725 A. D. This is one of the five observatories that the astronomer king built at Banaras, Jaipur, Mathura, Ujjain and Delhi.

**Parliament House :** At the southern end of Parliament Street rises the imposing Parliament House. The building is circular, as fitting its size, an equilateral triangle. There are three sections built at equal angles round a central dome, 90 ft. in diameter. It is a novel edifice of modern architecture and certainly a thing of beauty. Permits to go inside the building are available only when Parliament is not in session.

**Rastrapati Bhawan :** Close to the Parliament Building are the two imposing Secretariat Buildings which stand at the approach to the crowning glory—Rastrapati Bhawan, one of the finest buildings in the world. The Processional Way leads through a high railing, between fountains and trees to the majestic building where lives the President of the Indian Republic. Thirty-two broad steps lead to the domed State Room which is the venue of colourful state functions. Beyond its surrounding marble-lined corridors are grouped the principal reception rooms. At the back of the building, lies the private garden of the President, Moghul and intricate, with innumerable flower beds and water channels like the pleasure dome of Kubla Khan.

North of Rastrapati Bhawan is the historic Talkatora garden, the exact spot where the Mahrattas first defeated the Moghuls in 1733 and overran Delhi.

**Rajpath and Maidan :** The great steps and the columned portico of Rastrapati Bhawan face and command a panoramic view eastward between the domes of the Secretariat down to the far avenues of Rajpath and the water channels of the Maidan. At its eastern end stands the India Gate which, along with its beautiful environs, is the show-place of the capital.

On both sides of the Great Place can be seen the palaces of the former princes of India. On the left, on the Janpath, is the National Archives of India, while on the left stands the National Museum. Nearby, on King

Edward Road, is the imposing Vigyan Bhawan, which is the venue of all important conferences.

**Birla House:** At 21 Albuquerque Road, recently renamed "Tees January Marg", is a private house which has come to be vested with infinite sanctity having been the scene of Mahatma Gandhi's martyrdom. Here, on the southern lawn of the Birla House, on the afternoon of January 30, 1948, Mohandas Karamchand Gandhi fell to his assassin's bullet. The sacred spot where the Father of the Nation shed martyr's blood has been marked by a small tablet and has since become a shrine of pilgrimage.

**Lakshminarayan Temple:** About a mile to the west of Connaught Place and a few minutes walk from Gol Market lies the beautiful Birla Mandir which, with its spacious lawns, fountains and pavilions, provides a most lovely setting for a restful and inspiring relaxation. Built by Raja Baldeo Das Birla in 1938 at a cost of millions of rupees, the temple is dedicated to all the religions of India.

## Monuments of the Old Delhis

Scattered over a tract of country of some seventy square miles on the right bank of the Jumuna there is an endless array of ruins of what are referred to as the 'Seven cities of Delhi': a mound that was once a gateway, a broken wall that was once the corner of a fort, a tumbling tower, and ruined dome. As you drive along the Mathura Road past Kotla Firozshah and Purana Qila, to Humayun's Tomb, and thence to Tughlakabad by the Badarpur Road and then return to Delhi via the Kutb along the Mehrauli Road, completing the circle, you pass through many ruined capitals covered with shattered palaces and tombs of dead and forgotten kings before the Delhi of today came into being. To wander without any fixed itinerary may be a most enjoyable way of seeing the sites, but for those who wish to see as much as possible within a limited time it is better to follow a set plan.

**Asoka Pillars :** Half a mile south of the Delhi Gate in Dariyaganj, on the left side of the Mathura Road, is Kotla Firoz Shah, the ruined capital of Firoz Shah (1331-1388), which contains a highly polished Asoka Pillar. The pillar was brought by Firoz Shah from Ambala. Around it lie the scattered ruins of the palaces and mosques of Firozabad, the 'fifth' city. The other Asoka pillar is on the Ridge near the Hindu Rao Hospital. This pillar can be reached by the Hindu Rao Road, which branches off from the Rajpur Road in the Civil Lines.

**Indraprastha or Purana Killa :** Two miles south of the Kotla on the Muthura Road and two miles due east of the Rastrapati Bhawan is the Fort of Indrapat, also known as Purana Killa (Old Fort). Nothing now remains of pre-historic Indraparasta, the legendary capital of the Pandavas. The present fort was begun by Humayun and completed by Sher Shah, who ousted Humayun and ruled in Delhi for five years (1540-45).

It is worth while to go up the massive gateway of Purana Killa, for the whole site is charged with a spirit of solitude and massive grandeur. At the north-east corner of the vast enclosure, now occupied by a refugee settlement, is Sher Shah's mosque, one of the most beautiful in Delhi. Opposite this, to the south, is a octagonal building known as Sher Mandal. From the stair-case of this building Humayun slipped while descending to offer evening prayer and died of his injuries three days later (January 1556).

**Humayun's Tomb :** A mile and a half further down the Delhi-Muthura Road is seen the tomb of Humayun, one of the really outstanding buildings in Delhi. It was built after the Emperor's death by his widow in 1565 A. D. This noble building of red sandstone, artistically picked out in relief with white marble and surmounted by a white marble dome, was built by a Persian architect who first introduced to India the idea of surrounding royal tombs with lovely formal gardens The actual tomb of Humayun, of polished white marble, occupies the place of honour in the large central chamber, surrounded by a large number of vaulted apartments. Each of these rooms contains graves of members of the Moghul family and there are so many of them that the tomb of Humayun is sometimes called the 'Dormitory of the House of Timur'. One contains the tomb of Dara Shikoh, the favourite son and heir-apparent to Shah Jahan, who was brutally murdered by his brother Aurangzeb after his victory in the battle of succession. There are more pathetic tales about the tomb of the Emperor, whose own career was wrapped in deep melancholy. It was in one of these dimly-lighted rooms that the last Moghul Emperor, Bahadur Shah, surrendered unconditionally to the British and finally died an ignoble death in exile in Burma.

Outside the southern wall of the garden tomb, close to the main gate, is another beautiful tomb with a mosque around it. This is the tomb of Isa Khan, a friend of Sher Shah. It was built by Islam Shah, son of Sher Shah, in 1547 A.D.

**Shrine of Nizamuddin :** Opposite Humayun's tomb, on the west side of the Mathura Road, is the sacred tomb of Nizamuddin, the great Muslim saint who possessed wonderful spiritual powers, and many tales are still told of cures wrought by a visit to the shrine, prayers miraculously answered and boons conferred. Around the courtyard of the shrine are innumerable tombs of kings, members of the royal family and famous poets and historians of Delhi. The most conspicuous among them are the marble cenotaphs of Jahanara Begam which is open to the sky (at her desire) and covered by green grass and the splendid white marble tomb of Emperor Mohammad Shah, who suffered humiliation at the hands of Nadir Shah.

**Safdar Jang :** A road from the Minto Bridge runs south directly through Connaught Place and two miles south of the Secretariat, on the Mehrauli Road, is the tomb of Safdar Jang (1753), which indicates the decadent phase of Moghul architecture and wherein lies the second Nawab of Oudh, who was for several years the favourite Wazir of Emperor Ahmad Shah II. A little to the east of Safdar Jang is Lodi Park, containing the tombs of the last Pathan Kings of Delhi (1450-1526). These tombs form an architectural style of their own, distinguishable from Moghul buildings by their octagonal shape surmounted by low domes. The tomb of Sikandar Lodi stands inside a large walled enclosure, indicating a transition from the Pathan style and a step toward the great garden enclosures of the Moghuls.

**Hauz Khas :** Proceeding further along the Mehrauli Road and past the Vinaynagar Road is seen a road that branches off to the west, to Hauz Khas. Here, Allauddin Khilji built a magnificent tank for his private use over an area of 70 acres. Lining its bank in the shape of a horse-shoe are a number of pleasure pavilions and buildings from which the wide view across the lake far into the distant land is exceedingly panoramic. Later, Firoz Shah repaired the tank, its bathing enclosures and pavilions and built a *madarasa* on its bank. The place was so beautiful that Firoz Shah built his own tomb in one corner of the tank, which is even to-day in a good state of preservation. Timur (1398) rested himself by the cool grandeur of Hauz Khas after his resounding victory over the forces of Mohammad Tughlak. Despite the ravages of time Hauz Khas is today one of the show-places of Delhi and is resorted to by picnic parties in winter.

**Siri :** Returning to the Mehrauli Road, one can see on the left-hand side, between the rows of newly-built houses, the ruins of Siri. Here, Allauddin Khilji built a new capital for himself. Nothing much now remains of that splendid capital, the 'second' Delhi, from which Allauddin carried his arms to all parts of India. "Allauddin's palace of a thousand pillars, which witnessed so many triumphs and tragedies, has completely gone to ruins." What still remained of the palaces, mosques and monuments of the once famous Khilji-Delhi has now been cleared to make room for the expanding capital city.

**Jahanpannah** : Nearby to the North, can be seen the scanty remains of the Jahanpannah, the invincible capital city built by Mohammad Tughlak after he had abandoned Adilabad. That unbridled tyrant, the Nero of the East, forcibly removed the entire population of Delhi to his new capital Daulatabad near Aurangabad in the Deccan. Nearby is Vijay Mandal which shows the remains of Mohammad Tughlak's palace.

**Rai Pithora** : Further down the Mehrauli Road, past the signpost Vijaymandal and bordering on the Kutub enclosure are the remains of Rai Pithora where Prithviraj Chauhan, the last Hindu King of Delhi, built his capital. In the citadel of Lal Kot can still be seen the remains of the Tomar dynasty which ruled Delhi in the eleventh century. First inside the fort of Lal Kot and then beyond the same at Siri, Kutbuddin and his successsors built the first Muslim Delhi. The Kutb enclosure begins at the east side of Lal Kot fort.

**Kutb Minar** : About 11 miles due south of Delhi is the far-famed Kutb Minar. This great tower was commenced by Kutubuddin in 1206 and completed by Altamash. A tower of sand-stone (circumference 47 ft. 3 inches at the bottom and 9 ft. at the top : height 280 ft.) the minar is regarded as the most beautiful example of a perfect tower known anywhere in the world. Legend goes that this tower of victory was first erected by Prithviraj and later reconstructed by the Muslim rulers. It is possible to ascend the lofty tower by a flight of 379 steps. A magnificent view of the historical buildings of the Delhi region lying dead flat on an infinite chess-board of green and brown country can be had from the top of the tower.

At the foot of the Kutb is the *Quwwatul-Islam* mosque (1196 A. D.), the first mosque in India. This was built on the plinth of a destroyed Hindu temple. Although an architectural failure it is an example of the liberal fusion of Islamic and Hindu sculptural modes. The finest among the later additions to the mosque is the so-called Alai Darwaza, the south gateway to the mosque enclosure built by Allauddin. That monarch was a megalomanic, "but in the so-called Alai Darwaza he has left us a very charming and delicate little building which may be considered to mark the culmination of early Indo-Muslim art".

**Iron Pillar :** In the courtyard of Quwwatul-Islam mosque stands the Iron Pillar, one of the most wonderful antiquities of ancient India (c.375 A.D). Neither time nor the elements seem to be able to rust or tarnish this perfect example of India's ancient metallurgical skill. In a few lines of Sanskrit poetry the Iron Pillar records the glory of a king Chandra who is held by Dr. Vincent Smith to be Chandravarman, King of Pushkarama (near Udaipur) and a contemporary of Samudragupta. The monument was probably brought from Mathura by Kutbuddin.

**Alai Minar :** A hundred yards to the west of the Kutb stands the Alai Minar (87 ft. high), the unfinished tower of Allauddin which was intended to be more than double the height of the lofty Kutb Minar. Allauddin was a dreamer and his vast project was abandoned immediately after his death.

**Fort of Tughlakabad & Adilabad :** About 5 miles to the west of the Kutb, on the Badarpur Road, are to be seen the colossal walls of the ruined fortress of Tughlakabad, built by Tughlak Shah in 1327 A.D. In front of the fort is seen the tomb of Tughlak Shah rising high above the dry plain on the right of the Badarpur Road. The tomb is outside the walls of Tughlakabad and stands in the midst of an artificial lake. On a high ground to the west of the tomb can be viewed the ruined ramparts of the fort of Adilabad.

**Tank of Surajkund** : By the side of Tughlak Shah's tomb a *kuccha* road leads south across a rocky tract to Surajkund, about 2 miles away. The road is very near from the Tughlakabad railway station. The famous tank of Surajkund is set amidst the bareness of rocky, open country. A huge masonry tank in the form of a semi-circle with steps all around it, Surajkund is one of the interesting monuments in Delhi. The tank marks the site of the 'first' Hindu Delhi founded by Ananga Pal Tomar about 1050 A.D. The capital was subsequently removed to Lal Kot in the Kutb area. The remains of the 'first' city—walls, pillars and ruins of temples—are clearly discernable. And on the rocks above the bund is a pavilion where Ananga Pal used to sit in warm weather. A visit to the tank is highly recommended, but the trip should not be made in summer as it is a somewhat difficult excursion and involves two miles walking from the Badarpur bazaar.

\*　　　\*　　　\*　　　\*

COMM. Delhi is almost equidistant from Calcutta and Bombay. It is the junction of many railways. Fast mail and express trains directly connect Delhi with Calcutta, Bombay, Madras, Amritsar, Pathankot, Jaipur, Ajmere, Lucknow, Banaras etc., while a network of air-lines brings the capital within easy reach of almost all the cities and towns of the vast sub-continent.

ACCOM. There is a large number of hotels in Delhi and New Delhi of various standards to suit all pockets. A list of them appears in the General Information Section. Of the Western style hotels, Asoka Hotel is the best. The next best is Janpath Hotel, centrally situated on Janpath. There is a well furnished P. W. D. Dak Bungalow at the Kutb Minar garden.

CONVEYANCE. Transport is plentiful but comparatively costlier than Calcutta and Bombay. A large fleet of Government buses ply through Delhi and New Delhi. Private bus services (starting from Delhi Central station) connect the city with Chandigarh, Patiala and other towns in the Punjab. U.P. Roadways buses leave for Muthura, Agra, Hardwar, Mussourie etc. from Ajmere Gate (midway between Delhi & New Delhi). Taxis are plentiful and cheap. Motor-rickshaws (2 seater) are still cheaper. Motor coaches are available on hire from the Delhi Transport Authority, Scindia House, New Delhi, for sight-seeing parties. They also supply elaborate guide maps of Delhi.

# DELHI : GENERAL INFORMATION

## HOTELS

Asoka Hotel,
  Diplomatic Enclave.
Ambassador,
  Sujan Singh Park, N. Delhi.
Hotel Janpath,
  Near Western Court.
Cecil,
  2 Underhill Road, Delhi,
Oberoi Imperial,
  Janpath, N. Delhi,
Maidens,
  Alipore Road, Delhi.
Swiss,
  Alipore Road, Delhi.
Y. M. C. A. Hostel,
  Jai Singh Road, N. Delhi.

### Indian Style

Agra Hotel,
  16, Daryaganj, Delhi.
Broadway Hotel,
  Asaf Ali Rd., N. Delhi.
Central Court Hotel.
  Connaught Cir., N. Delhi.
Grand Hotel,
  Underhill Rd., Delhi.
Hotel Royal,
  Queens Road, Delhi.
Maharaja Hotel,
  Queens Road, Delhi.

## NEWSPAPERS

Hindusthan Times
Statesman
Times of India

## INFORMATION

The Regional Tourist Officer, Janpath, (Phone 2742) supplies guides, information de-luxe tourist coaches for sight-seeing. He also arranges for permits for visiting Parliament House and Rastrapati Bhawan.

## TRAVEL AGENTS

American Express Co. Inc.
  Conn. Place, New Delhi.
Iyer & Sons,
  United India Building.
Orient Express Co.,
  70 Janpath, N. Delhi.
Mercury Travel,
  Hotel Imperial N. Delhi.
Trade-Wings,
  60 Janpath, N. Delhi.

## BOOK SELLERS

Bhawnani & Son.,
  Connaught Place, N. Delhi.
E. D. Galgotia & Co.
  Connaught Cir., N. Delhi.
English Book Depot.,
  Connaught Cir., N. Delhi,
Oxford Book & Statv. Co.,
  Scindia House N. Delhi.

## ART DEALERS

Shanti Vijay & Co.
  52 Janpath, N. Delhi.
Ivory Palace,
  Chandni Chowk, Delhi.
Girdharilal,
  Connaught Pl., N. Delhi,
Kheratilal & Sons,
  Janpath, N. Delhi.

## RESTAURANTS

Embassy,
  Connaught Pl., N. Delhi.
Gaylord,
  Connaught Cir., N. Delhi.
Moti Mahal,
  Darayaganj, Delhi.
York
  Connaught Cir., N. Delhi.
Volga,
  Connaught Pl., N. Delhi.
Wenger's,
  Connaught Pl., N. Delhi.

# CHANDIGARH

Chandigarh, 151 miles north-east of Delhi, is the capital of the Punjab. Situated in the shadow of the Himalayas, Chandigarh is entirely a new city designed by the well-known French architect, Le Corbusier, on the latest ideas of town planning. Like New York the city of Chandigarh is laid out as a square ; a grill of neat roads running at right angles divides the city into several sectors, each sector containing beautiful houses, lanes for slow-moving trafic, tracks for cyclists and paths for pedestrians. The architectural style of Chandigarh, though somewhat monotonous, is based on the utilitarian needs of the people. Here a new architectural feature, the sun-breaker, has been used on a mass scale. To the north of the city is the Capital comprising the Government House, the High Court and the nine-storied Secretariat. To the west are the educational buildings of which the engineering college is the most beautiful. In Sector No. II, are situated the residences of ministers and high officials. This also contains the Assembly Hall and the Mount View Hotel. The heart of the city however is Sector No. 22 which contains the shopping centre and cinemas.

**Pinjore** : 12 miles from Chandigarh, on the main road to Kalka, lies what is perhaps the loveliest and oldest Moghul garden in Northern India—the garden of Pinjore. This beautiful garden, a replica of the famous Salimar Gardens of Srinagar, was laid out by Fidai Khan, a foster brother of Aurangzeb. With the lower range of the Himalayas in the background and crystal spring water running through its rare plants and flowers the garden has a beauty which is almost romantic.

\*     \*     \*     \*

COMM. Chandigarh, on the main line to Kalka, is reached by through trains or buses from Delhi via Ambala. From the railway station the town is 5 miles.

ACCOM. Hotel Mount View (Rs. 22/- daily) is a fine Western style hotel. Hotel Aroma (daily charge Rs. 11/-) is in Sector No. 22. There are two rest houses in the same Sector. Cycle rickshaws are the main transport. There are a few taxis.

# SIMLA

Simla ! The name conjures up a picture of a delightful spot on the Himalyan slopes where the privileged ones can retire from the sweltering heat of the plains and spend their time in a whirl of gaiety and enjoyment. Simla is like a gay Swiss city isolated on a mountain top, with dark ilex forests around it, blue hills beyond, and the horizon ever whitened by snowy ranges.

"Leaving the thermometer with its mercury somewhere in three figures in the plains, you find Simla radiant and smiling in the delicious spring garments of a temperate climate. With the snow but a few weeks melted, the deodars and the hill pines welcome you with arms waving their new year's verdure. Wild flowers decorate the grassy slopes. Gorgeous crimson rhododendrons smile upon you from trees thirty and forty feet high".

A remarkably cosmopolitan crowd throngs the bazar and with it mingle the Aryan and Moghul peoples of Hindusthan, the Dravidians from the south, the primitive hill folks of the villages about Simla itself, the hill men of Kahsmir and adjoining Tibet. But gone are the days when competition amongst the Simla *memsahibs* to be voted the owner of the smartest rickshaw lent to the Mall a delightful panorama of colour and social life which was once her pride, for Simla is no longer the summer capital of India.

There are many beautiful walks and views around the hills. Visitors desirous of hikes and picnics may go to Jakko, Olen, Prospects Hill, Taradevi and Summer Hill, where the Rastrapati Bhawan is situated. There is good golf at Naldera, and racing, cricket and soccer at Annandale, a fair valley of 1200 ft. below the Ridge. There are splendid walks and scenery around the woods of Mashobra and Mahasu, 5 and 8 miles from Simla.

The more adventurous can take a wonderful holiday at Narkanda, 39 miles beyond, which offers splendid views of the snowy peaks east of Kulu. A regular bus service runs to Narkanda and Kotgarh (49 miles) and the holiday makers from Simla can come back from these places within the day.

Sport consists of lawn tennis, horse-racing, pheasant and partridge shooting snd open-air skating in the early and late days of summer. In the height of summer the rains interfere with outdoor amusements. A bright social life always fills the evenings.

From the begining of October to about the middle of December, Simla (7,200 ft.) enjoys the best climate in the world, but throughout the year it is equable.

\*　　　\*　　　\*　　　\*

COMM. 226 m. Delhi and 60 m. from Kalka, Simla is reached from Kalka, by a mountain railway meandering its way through 102 tunnels. For upper class and air-conditioned passengers, luxurious rail motors are run ; the scenery enroute is superb. At Kalka motor cars and buses are available for journey by road which is quicker (3½ hours). Simla can be reached from Delhi by car in half a day.

ACCOM. Western style hotels are : Cecil Hotel and Clark Hotel, on the Mall. Other good hotels are : Marina Hotel, Blessington Hotel, Royal Hotel, Hindu Hotel and Central Hotel. There are two P.W.D. Dak Bunglows and Railway Retiring Rooms at the station. There is a Y.M.C.A. hostel as well as a Y. W. C. A. hostel.

# AMRITSAR

320 miles north-west of Delhi and 18 miles short of the Indo-West Pakistan border is Amritsar, the religious capital of the Sikhs, famous for the Golden Temple. It is said that the surrounding tank, known as the "Pool of Immortality" was a favourite resort of Nanak. Ram Das, the fourth Guru, founded the city

in 1577, upon a site granted by Emperor Akbar and excavated the holy tank, which was eventually completed by Guru Arjun Singh who also erected the temple. Ahmed Shah Durrani destroyed the city in 1761, blew up the temple and defiled the shrines. Arjun Singh rebuilt it in 1764. Maharaja Ranjit Singh, the Sikh ruler, enriched the shrine and covered its dome with sheets of copper, overlaid with gold.

The sacred pool is surrounded by a pavement of white marble brought from Jaipur. In the centre of the pool, on an island, rises the Darbar Sahib (Golden Temple), the glory of Amritsar, with blinding radiance in the bright sunshine and mirrored in the placid water which laps the foot of its walls. The temple itself is reached by a white marble causeway, 204 ft. long, flanked on either side by nine gilded lamps. Three open doors of chased silver give access to the sanctuary itself. Here under a silken canopy lies the Granth Sahib, the sacred book of the Sikhs, read occasionally by the high-priest to sweet music. The devout crowd around all day long.

With the permission of the President, Darbar Sahib Committee, the visitor can gain admittance to the Temple Treasury over the portal of the causeway where are preserved 31 silver pillars, 9 ft. long, and 4 large ones. In a chest is kept a canopy of pure gold weighing 10 pounds, a magnificent array of jewellery, rubies, diamonds and other precious stones worth a king's ransom. All these are used when the Granth Sahib is taken in procession.

In the Temple Garden or Guruka-Bagh to the south is the Baba Atal Tower which is richly painted with frescoes depicting scenes from the life of Guru Nanak. Besides, there are numerous other places of interest such as the Akal Takhat temple which is the venue of the Supreme Religious Council, the Ram Bagh Gardens laid out by Maharaja Ranjit Singh and Jallianwalla Bagh, the scene of the ghastly tragedy of 1919.

**Tarn Taran :** 15 miles to the south of Amritsar is Tarn Taran, a place of pilgrimage for the Sikhs. Here, Ranjit Singh built a temple with beautiful frescoes and a tower by the side of a magnificent tank, which was the residence of Guru Arjun. There is a bus service.

\*   \*   \*   \*

ACCOM. Western style hotels are ; Amritsar Hotel, (Rs. 15/-) and Imperial Hotel (Rs. 15/-) on Queens Rd. the Volga Hotel caters for middle class visitors. There is a District Board Dak Bungalow. Taxis and tongas are the usual transport.

## ANANDPUR SAHIB

52 miles from Sirhind and 52 miles from Chandigarh, via the historic town of Rupar, is Anandpur Sahib, founded by Guru Tegh Bahadur, the ninth Guru who was put to death by Aurangzeb. It was here that the Sikh religion acquired its final militant shape. It is also one of the four religious thrones known as "Takhat Sahibs". The fortress-shaped temple, once the scene of fierce fighting, attracts thousands of pilgrims, especially on the occasion of the festival known as "Hola Mohalla" which takes place during February-March every year. There is a dak bungalow about a mile away from the station. Pilgrims are accommodated in the Gurdwara premises.

At Sirhind there is the famous Gurudwara of Fatehgarh, where the two sons of Guru Gobind Singh were bricked alive. This was avenged by Banda who razed the entire city to the ground.

## BHAKRA NANGAL

64 miles from Sirhind by rail and 60 miles from Chandigarh by bus is Nangal which is the centre of activity of one of the biggest multi-purpose projects undertaken in this country and offers immense potentialities in the irrigational and power development of the Punjab and the neighbouring States. Bhakra, nearly eight miles from Nangal, is the mouth of the great canal system that flows from the Sutlej.

225

Here, at the foot hills of the Himalayas, a 680-foot high dam is being built. At Nangal, 8 miles below, a 91-foot high diversion dam has been completed to regulate the supply of water from the Bhakra Dam.

This great project ranks with the other great multipurpose project of India—the Damodar Valley Project. The canal, the world's longest, was opened by the Prime Minister of India in July 1954. The two rest houses, one "first class" and the other Field Hostel (permission from Executive Engineer, Nangal Township) accommodate visitors.

## KASHMIR

When the Emperor Jahangir, the most pompous of the great Moghuls, was dying on the way to Kashmir, the generals and the great nobles of State pressed round his couch, begging for his last commands. Their Lord could think of only one thing : "Only Kashmir" —was the emperor's last wish.

Set within a girdle of snow-capped mountains of the most beautiful scenery imaginable, Kashmir, described by poets as 'a Paradise on Earth' is a land of rich forests and upland pastures, of slow flowing graceful rivers, of swift running glistening mountain torrents and placid lakes. If you imagine Venice set in the heart of Switzerland, that is Srinagar, the capital of Kashmir, the tourists' paradise which baffles all description.

**Srinagar :** Life is worth living as you glide in a houseboat when the lotus has blossomed and the banks of the Jhelum are a mass of beautiful tapestry of infinite colour with the snow-capped mountain peaks in the background. One of the most beautiful spots in the world is the Shalimar Garden on the Dal Lake just beyond the city. Srinagar itself is built along the banks of the Jhelum in the centre of the valley, and the two sections of the beautiful town are connected by nine wooden bridges which add considerably to the wonderful panorama. Srinagar, meaning the city of wealth and knowledge, was for centuries known as Pravarapura after king Pravarasena II who ruled in the 6th century. Rajatarangini, written by the great Kashmiri scholar, Kalhana, records the great position of honour that the city enjoyed as a centre of culture in the 12th century.

All worship this beautiful valley. Akbar first grasped its immortal beauty. The Moghuls left fair gardens and gave Kashmir the noblest tree in the world —the chenar. Jahangir loved Shalimar as a woman and, like a woman he adorned her. "All will-of-the-wisp, for the real giver of this revel are the sky, the snow, the rivers and the lakes. No such mountains—the Alps and the Rockies are mere foothills. And for rivers, the valley is old and clings to her ancient friends, the fabulous Hydaspes, in whose venerable progress the gallant Sind and the lovely Lidar join their cool streams. Lakes ! There is the largest in all India, the Wular (Ullola, "with high-going waves"), and the loveliest in all the world, the Dal". (Sir Walter Lawrence).

## Beauty Spots in and around Srinagar

Of the beauty spots the Dal Lake, on the suburbs of Srinagar, takes the pride of place. Vying with the Dal are the terraced Moghul gardens, the most beautiful gems that adorn the valley. Five miles from Srinagar is the Chashma Shahi (Royal Spring), the smallest of the Moghul gardens laid out by Shah Jahan, and two miles beyond it is the world-famed Nishat Bagh rising from the Dal in terraces of flower-beds and cascades, exquisite beyond words. Opposite this, overlooking the Dal, is the Naseem Bagh containing magnificent shady chenar trees. Two miles beyond Nishat is the queen of the Moghul gardens, the Shalimar, the inevitable goal of all. On the crest of a 1,000 ft. high hill, called Takht-i-Suleman, stands the Sankaracharya temple (6th century) commanding a splendid view of Srinagar.

For those who are sports-minded, Kashmir offers a variety of big and small games as well as fishing in its several trout waters. And for the lover of nature, there can be nothing more pleasant than a trek to the beautiful valley of Lolarb or the mountain meadow of Sonemarg.

**Gulmarg :** 29 miles west of Srinagar and 3,000 ft. higher is Gulmarg, a place of uncommon beauty which casts an irresistible spell in June. It is also a winter resort with facilities for ski-ing and skating. Its golf course is among the finest in the world. A four-mile climb from Gulmarg brings the visitor up to Khilinmarg (10,0000 ft.), a lovely spot carpeted by an abundance of plant life and colourful flowers. This is a 'Botanist's paradise'. Gulmarg is supplied with hotels.

**Wular Lake :** About 35 miles north of Srinagar is the world-famed Wular lake, a jade in colour, which is the largest in all India. It is full of fish, especially mahseer, and can be reached either by houseboat or bus.

**Pahalgam :** 60 miles east of Srinagar is Pahalgam, a place of wondrous natural beauty yet unspoilt by urbanity and sophistication so characteristic of Gulmarg. Pahalgam is the base for a trek to Amarnath, 29 miles away. Pahalgam is reached by bus from Srinagar. There are a number of hotels of all categories.

**Amarnath :** 29 miles from Pahalgam is the celebrated cave temple of Amarnath in the upper reaches of the Himalayas (12,762 ft.) reached in three days' trek from Pahalgam through wonderful lakes and mountain meadows, gay with flowers and ringed with the snow ranges. The presiding deity is the great god Shiva who manifests his great glory in the form of a **lingam** which naturally comes into being and waxes and wanes with the moon. The most auspicious day for worship is the night of the full moon in the month of Sravan (July-August) when pilgrims from all corners of India flock there to have a darshan of the mysterious, holy lingam.

**Season :** The season is from April to the middle of October. Autumn begins with September when the weather is most delightful. June-July is the most pleasant in Gulmarg. During the season temperature varies from 35° to 95° F. Light woollens with overcoat must be taken.

*  *  *  *

PERMITS. Indian visitors to Kashmir must possess permits issued by Distt. Magistrates. Foreign 'tourists' can have permits from the Regional Tourist Officers at Bombay, Delhi, Madras and Calcutta ; and foreigners resident in India from the Secretary, Ministry of Defence, New Delhi.

COMM. Srinagar, the capital of Kashmir, can be reached by air or road. There are daily air-services between : (i) Delhi and Srinagar touching Amritsar and Jammu on the way (time— 4 hours : fare—Rs. 99/8/-), and (ii) Pathankot and Srinagar (Time—1 hour : fare—Rs. 40/-).

There are through mail trains from Calcutta, Bombay and Delhi for Pathankot (1160 m. from Calcutta. 1258 m. from Bombay and 306 m. from Delhi) which is the rail-head for Kashmir. But the most convenient train is the Kashmir Mail which leaves Delhi at 9.30 p.m. and arrives at Pathankot in the morning, in time to catch the motor coach and aircraft for Srinagar. The 267-mile bus journey from Pathankot to Srinagar takes about 1½ days with halts at Jammu Dak Bungalow (67 m.) for lunch and at Banihal Pass Dak Bungalow (half way between Pathankot and Srinagar) for night stop. These Dak Bungalows are well equipped to receive visitors although they are usually over-crowded and can not afford adequate sleeping accommodation. Food and lodging in the Dak Bungalows are charged according to fixed schedule. Apart from affording an ever-changing view of the mountains, rivers and rushing torrents, the road journey from Pathankot to Srinagar takes one through the new Banihal Tunnel (1-3/4 miles long), which is one of the longest and the most modern road tunnels in the world. Bus fare for Srinagar is Rs. 20/- per seat. For big parties it is advisable to book transport in advance by remitting 15% of the fare to the Manager, J. & K. Government Transport, Pathankot.

ACCOM. Of the Western style hotels Oberoi's Palace Hotel (Rs. 25/- daily) is best in Srinagar. Others are Nedou's (Rs. 20/-) Golf View (Rs. 12/-), Park (Rs. 11/-) and Boulevard (Rs. 12/-). Indian style Hotels are : Grand, Mejestic, Odeon, Khalsa, Kashmir Hindu, River View etc. with charges between Rs. 6/- to Rs. 10/. daily.

HOUSEBOATS. Charges in "A" and "B" class houseboats vary with the size and furniture of the boat from Rs. 500/- to

229

Rs. 600/- per month including the services of four servants, cook, bearer, bhisti and sweeper and lighting charges. Daily charges (including boarding and lodging) on contract basis range from Rs. 20/- to Rs. 25/- for a single person. 'B' and 'C' are still cheaper.

CONVEYANCE. Taxis and tongas are usual transport. Buses of the Kashmir State Transport ply to almost all the places of interest around Srinagar.

There may be occasions for complaint against the house-boat keepers, art dealers and transport men, for they are known to be hard bargainers. Such cases should be reported to the Director of Tourism, Srinagar, who takes immediate and drastic action. He also becomes helpful in a hundred other ways.

SHOPPING. Kashmir shawls, woollens, and wood carvings are famed throughout the East. Prices must be verified before an article is bought.

# KANGRA & KULU VALLEY

Lying at the foot of snow-capped mountains of the colossal Daula Dhar Range are the two valleys of Kangra and Kulu which for the mellow beauty of their landscapes, studded with hamlets and richest cultivation, irrigated by streams which descend from the perennial snows, are unequalled in the Outer Himalayas.

Kangra is known as the home of exquisite paintings which for their ageless beauty continue to throb with passion even after the lapse of two centuries. As places of ancient human habitation the valleys abound in ancient relics and beautiful temples which contain some of the noblest specimens of Kangra paintings. Jawalamukhi, Kangra and Baijinath are important centres of Hindu pilgrimage. Even more picturesque than these temples are the ancient, impregnable Rajput Forts like the forts of Haripur, Nurpur and Kangra. "Coupled with the beauty of the landscape is the beauty of humanity ; in the mysterious forests of the Daula Dhar wander the very lovely Gaddi maidens (shepherds), unconscious of their beauty, living a life of extreme pastoral simplicity."

Pathankot is the gateway to the beautiful valleys. A 102-mile narrow gauge line runs from there to Jogindarnagar, at the end of the Kangra valley. But for those who are in quest of beauty, motor road is ideal. The main Kangra-Kulu motor route from Pathankot passes through a variely of scenery and historic sities of the two valleys. The bus journey from Pathankot to Kulu (175 miles) through Kangra can be made in a day. But it is advisable to spend a few days in the Kangra valley visiting the beauty spots and temples. There are cheap hotels and Dak Bungalows on the way where tourists are given priority. Cottages are available in Dharamsala, Palampur (Kangra Valley) and at Katrain and Malani (Kulu Valley) for longer sojourns. The District Tourist Officer, Dharamsala, supplies all information and arranges for transport.

**Dalhousie :** 50 miles from Pathankot by bus is Dalhousie (6678 ft.) a celebrated hill station and sanatorium to the south-east of Kashmir. The best hotels at Dalhousie are Dalhousie Club, Grand View Hotel and Metro Hotel, all charging Rs. 8/- daily. About 20 m. from Dalhousie is Chamba, beautifully laid out on a terrace, 300 ft. above the water of the river Ravi. There are many temples, ancient and impressive.

**Nurpur :** 19 m. from Pathankot, on the Kangra-Kulu main road, is Nurpur named after Empress Nurjahan who visited the place with Jahangir and was charmed by its beauty. Towering over the town is the ancient fort which amiably mingles with the fine landscape. There is a Forest Rest House (no cook).

**Dharamsala :** 56 m. from Pathankot, along the Kangra-Kulu bus road, is Dharamsala, a popular hill station and the headquarters of the Kangra District. Dharamsala is ringed by the snowy ranges of the Daula Dhar. The scenery around is fine. It can also be reached from Hoshiarpur by road. The P.W.D. Dak Bungalow (permission from Deputy Commissioner, Kangra), provides food at actual expense.

**Kangra** : 50 m. from Pathankot by bus is Kangra, (2,500 ft.) an ancient town named after the Rajput fort which dominates the majestic landscape around. Of the various temples that of Debi Vajreswari still draws pilgrims from far and near. The temple was sacked by Sultan Mahmud in 1008 and again by Firoz Shah Tughlakh in 1360. The main street is like a moving garden where the colourful, lovely gaddi maidens mingle with a wondrous variety of hill people including men from the plains. Kangra can also be conveniently reached by train. The Civil Rest House provides food. There are hotels.

21 miles south of Kangra lies the holy temple of Jwala Mukhi, picturesquely built on the crest on a hill. Inside the temple are half a dozen natural flames which are regarded as divine glows emerging out of the fiery mouth of the Goddess (Sati, consort of Siva). The temple is one of the most famous in all India.

**Baijinath** : 82 m. from Pathankot by bus and 10 m. from Palampur, which is another popular holiday centre, is Baijinath (4,150 ft.) which contains the celebrated temple Vaidyanath dedicated to Siva. The panorama around is beautiful. Baijinath marks the end of the Kangra valley, and Kulu lies from beyond the ridge that separates the two valleys. There is a Dak Bungalow where visitors are easily accommodated (permit not necessary).

**Mandi** : Leaving Baijinath one reaches Jogindarnagar and thence Mandi (2,500 ft.) the gateway to Kulu, 132 miles from Pathankot. Situated on the bank of the Beas, Mandi itself is an old town. Its temples of rock carvings on the edge of the river lend an archaic charm to its bazars and beautiful gardens. There is a P.W.D. Dak Bungalow and a Rest House (permission from Executive Engineer, P.W.D., Mandi).

**Kulu (Sultanpur)** : From Mandi to Kulu (4,000 ft.) the distance is 43 miles. The one-way narrow road ascends speedily to Ghatasani (6,000 ft.), the highest point on the road to Kulu. Beyond Aut the valley opens out and the final stretch through the lovely Kulu Valley offers an entirely different scenic grandeur. The scenery is sublime and presents delightful contrasts. "Kulu is so pretty and yet so unspoiled. Here life moves gently, here simplicity is as natural as the rugged hills". Kulu is a hiker's paradise. There are glorious sights around the wooden glens of Soja and Seraj ; there are hot water springs at Manikaran. Kulu is also reached from Simla via Jalori Pass (122 m.). There is a bus service up to Narkanda (40 m.) whence the journey upto Aut (Kulu) is made by foot or jeep.

About 8 m. north of Kulu is **Nagar** (5,800 ft.), where the famous Russian painter-philosopher, Nicholas Roerich, lived and painted the snow capped peaks of Kulu.

Visitors to Kulu can stay at the Dak Bungalow (permit not necessary) and Civil Rest House (permit from Sub-Divisional Officer, Civil, Kulu).

**Malani** : The motor road ends at Malani (6,000 ft.), the farthest point of the Kulu Valley, 48 m. from Kulu (Sultanpur). Malani, set amidst typical Alpine scenery, is regarded as the queen of the Kulu Valley. Visitors can stay at Sunshine Orchards and at Civil Rest House (Permission from S.D.O. Civil, Kulu), or at Banon's Hotel (daily charge Rs. 12/8/-). There is the Tyson Hotel at Katrain.

**Season** : Climatically the best seasons in Kangra and Kulu are from March to May, then again from September to the end of November. June, July and early August are pleasantly warm. Woollen clothings are necessary for higher altitude stay in the Kulu Valley.

# Chapter III

# RAJASTHAN

\* \* \* \* \* \* \* \* \* \* \* \* \* \* \* \* \* \* \* \* \* \* \* \* \* \*

*Rajasthan, an administrative unit of the former States of Rajputana, is largely a land of rock and sandy desert, of hills and lonely lakes sometimes shaded by dark forests where, it is said, "the tiger, bear and panther take the waters, and the arrogant boar jostles them aside and drinks first".*

*In this land of living tapestries and vivid frescoes which will never change, live the Rajputs of ancient lienage, brave and chivalrous, proud and to the manner born, with a stirring history of battles heroically fought and noble deeds magnificently done. Much of the glamour and fascination which Tod saw in Rajasthan is still there, for the age of chivalry is not yet quite over in Rajputana. Even today the "poorest Rajput retains all his pride of ancestory, often his sole inheritance; he scorns to hold the plough, or use his lance, but on horse-back". Here, on a spur of the Araballi hills, is historic Chittor, where the Rajput made great stand, and the great sacrifice—the historic Johar.*

*Nowhere in India the visitor will see so much of real Hindu manners and fashion, colour and pageantry as in Rajputana, for of all the people of India today none are more typically Indian or prouder of Indian culture and tradition than the Rajputs.*

\* \* \* \* \* \* \* \* \* \* \* \* \* \* \* \* \* \* \* \* \* \* \* \* \* \*

## JAIPUR

Jaipur, 180 miles south of Delhi, is the capital of Rajasthan and a fascinating city built almost wholly of rose-pink stones. Known as the rose-pink city, it has an interesting history and many sights worth visiting. A noble example of fine town planning, the city takes its name from the famous Maharaja Swai Jai Singh II, who built it in 1726. A brave warrior, an accomplished diplomat and, above all, a great scholar, Jai Singh would have been a remarkable man anywhere and at any time. He was a mathematician, an astronomer and a town-planner and was interested in the study of history. He built big observatories at Jaipur, Delhi, Ujjain, Mathura and Banaras; and his career shows that the spirit of scientific enquiry was not dead even in an age we call the Dark Age of India. In his passion for town-planning, the Maharaja collected the plans of many European cities of the time and then drew up his own. The result is the city of Jaipur. Laid out in the beginning of the eighteenth century it might well have been designed by a progressive architect of the twentieth century. As Kipling puts it : "Many years afterwards, the good people of America builded their towns after this pattern, but knowing nothing of Jai Singh, they took all the credit to themselves". Here, almost every building is pink or mauve which, with their latticed windows balconies and pavilions, lend that touch of colour to the scene which at sunset makes it almost magical.

In the centre of the city stands the Maharaja's palace which is a noble example of Rajput architecture. The Chandra Mahal which dominates the vast palace enclosure is a seven-storied building built by Jai Singh. Close by are the Dewani-Khas, which was used for State ceremonies, and the beautiful Jai Niwas garden, fairy-like with its fountains and running water. In one corner of the palace is a museum which is the repository of rare manuscripts and priceless specimens of Rájput and Moghul paintings.

The Hawa Mahal ("the Palace of Winds"), an adjunct of the palace which rises over a principal street of the city, is a nine-storied pink-coloured edifice of fanciful architecture. It has no inner apartments. Described by Sir Edwin Arnold "as a vision of daring and dainty loveliness" it was built by Maharaja Iswari Singh to enable the ladies to watch processions. To the east of the Chandra Mahal is the famous observatory built between 1718 and 1734 by Maharaja Jai Singh. At the back of the palace is the celebrated temple of Gopal which is the principal centre of worship in the city. A good view of the palace and its gardens can be had from the temple.

Other objects of interest are : the Albert Museum situated in a vast, beautiful garden named Ram Niwas; the School of Arts; the cenotaphs of the Maharajas at the base of the Nahargarh fort a little to the north of the city; and the temples at Galta (1½ to the east), a notable beauty spot situated in a depressed valley surrounded by hills on all side. The panorama around is pleasant.

**Ambar :** About seven miles north of Jaipur city, on a slope of hill skirting a beautiful lake, is Ambar the capital of the State till 1728 and now a deserted palace. It was built by Maharaja Man Singh in 1600. The Jai Mandir or the "Hall of Victory" is delicately ornamented with panels of alabaster with fine inlay work of soft colour and other fine workmanship for which Jaipur is famous. It 'literally glows with bright and tender colours'. Crowning the summit of the hill, 500 ft. high, rises the fort of Jaigarh, amazing in its beauty and its loneliness. Here are the cenotaphs of the former rulers. Service buses go to Ambar at regular interval from the Hawa Mahal square.

At the foot of the hills below, round the entrance to the palace, there are many temples, but most of them are now in ruins. To these temples, were removed the sacred images of Mathura and Brindaban when Aurangzeb demolished their temples. The Jagat Siromaniji temple is a fine building famous for its beautiful carvings, and white marble gateway, and above all, for its association with Mira Bai.

**Sanganur :** 7 miles south of Jaipur is Sanganur containing beautiful temples and palaces dating to the 11th century. The chief among the objects of interest is the shrine of Sanghiji which for its sculptural grandeur is considered next to the famous Dilwara temples at Mount Abu.

*　　　*　　　*　　　*

COMM. Jaipur lies on the metre gauge line of the Western Railways which directly connects it with Delhi, Agra and Ahmedabad. It is also connected by air with Delhi.

ACCOM. The chief among the Western style hotels is the Jai Villas Hotel which was till recently the principal palace of the Maharaja. Then there are the Circuit House, the Kaiser-i-Hind Hotel and New Hotel. Edward Memorial Hotel, outside the Ajmer Gate, provides cheaper and yet comfortable accommodation to middle-class Indian tourists. Polo Victory Hotel, a a good middle class Indian style hotel, excels in food and service. There are a number of cheap and yet clean hotels near the Hawa Mahal Chawk (Bara Chawk) where is also situated the main bus stand. Taxis, and Tongas are transport.

SHOPPING : Jaipur is noted for its arts and crafts. Its porcelain pottery, enamelled jewellery, engraved and embossed brass articles, ivory and sandalwood are prized throughout India. The main shopping centre is around the Hawa Mahal square.

# AJMER

Picturesquely situated at the foot of the Taragarh hill, 85 miles south-west of Jaipur, Ajmer is a city of great antiquity and a place of great pilgrimage of the Muslims. Historically, the city was regarded as the "Gibraltar of India". This gives the clue to its stormy past, for this key to Rajputana had changed hands many times during its long and chequered history.

The city first came into prominence early in the 12th century, when the Chauhan king Ajayaraja made it his capital and beautified it with palaces and temples. In 1536, Akbar annexed the city and made it a place of royal residence ; the fort of Taragarh built by him dominates the city. In the Ana Sagar Lake with its picturesque surroundings the visitor finds a real beauty spot of India. In later years, Shah Jahan added to its glory by buildings on its embankments five marble pavi-

237

lions of exquisite beauty which still adorn its shore. To the west, beyond the hills, lies the holy lake of Pushkar.

To the Muslims of India Ajmer is unusually holy for the Dargah Khawaja Sahib, the tomb of the famous saint Main-ud-din Chisti who came here from Iran in 1195 A.D. and died in 1255 A.D. Like Surdas and Kabir, Khawaja Sahib was one of the great Bhakti Saints of India who, even in his life time, attracted to his person a great number of people belonging to all the religions. Ever since, for the last 700 years Ajmer has been a great place of pilgrimage for kings and commoners alike. As is well known, Akbar came to Ajmer to pay respect to the Darga of Khawja Saheb on many occasions, several times on foot. Today, as in the past, the shrine draws thousands of Muslim pilgrims from all parts of India and Pakistan. Inside the shrine are seen the large drums taken by Akbar at the siege of Chittor, and two mosques, one built by Akbar and the other by Shah Jahan. Of the objects of archaeological interest the most remarkable is the Arhai-din-ka-Jhompra, a mosque built in 1235 A.D., and described by Fergusson as "one of the most remarkable architectural objects in India".

\* \* \* \*

COMM. 276 miles from Delhi and 85 miles from Jaipur, Ajmer lies on the Delhi-Ahmedabad main lime (metre gauge) of the Western Railway. A fine road connects Delhi with Ajmer through Jaipur.

ACCOM. There is no good hotel in the town. Marina Hotel is a middle class hotel which serves both in European and Indian style (Rs. 9/- daily). Retiring Rooms at the station however are very comfortable (daily rent : Rs. 3/-) ; excellent meals can be obtained from the attached Refreshment Room. For longer stay there is the Edward Memorial Hostel near the station (daily rent-single room : Rs. 2/-; double room ; Rs. 4 to Rs. 6/-).

CONVEYANCE. Tongas are main transport ; there are taxis. From the station stand buses go to many places including Pushkar (7 miles).

# PUSHKAR

Seven miles to the west of Ajmer lies the holy Lake of Pushkar, one of the most sacred in all India and an eminent place of Hindu pilgrimage. Vast crowds of pilgrims attend the annual fair held in October-November and bathe in the holy water of the lake. On the southern shore of the lake is the temple of Brahma, supposed to mark the spot where the incarnation of the Gods took place. There are very few Brahma temples in India and hence its unusual sanctity. There are many temples on the shore of the lake and on the hills around. To devout Hindus Pushkar is the Tirtharaj which in holiness must be considered equal to Gaya, Banaras, Garhmukteswar, Kurukshetra and Pravas.

\* \* \* \*

COMM. & ACCOM. Pushkar is connected with Ajmer by a fine road with a regular bus service. There are many Dharamsalas of which the Sindhi Dharamsala is remarkable. Taxis and tongas are transport.

# CHITTORGARH

116 miles south of Ajmer and an equal distance north of Ratlam is Chittorgarh where Rajput bravery has written a golden chapter of history; for, the words "death before dishonour" was not mere phrase to them. Again and again, here the Rajputs made the great stand, the great sacrifice—the historic Johar; and of all the brave stories of Rajput valour and constancy none are more beloved than the tales which hang round the three sacks of Chittor.

Chittor (Mewar), the old capital of the Sisodia Rajputs, was first sacked by Allauddin Khilji in 1303 to secure the hands of Rani Padmini, the Indian Helen, who was famed to be the most beautiful woman in the world. At first the Rajputs gave the invader the rudest shock of his life and routed him completely. Years passed, and once again Allauddin marched against the city. "We will die for Chittor!"—cried the noble Rajput warriors, and when the city was tottering to its fall a funeral pyre was built in an underground vault and to it plunged the Rajput women, singing and dressed in their festal robes. The last to enter the vault of

death was Padmini.   When the last man had died fighting for Chittor, Allauddin entered the city only to find a
wisp of smoke oozing from the silent vault.  This was
the first sack of Chittor.

The second sack came in 1535, when Bahadur
Shah, the Sultan of Guzrat seized the city.  Again the
Rajputs put up a heroic resistance, and when the
garrison of Chittor saw that their city must fall, they
remembered the first sack and all resolved to die in
the same way.  The Queen-Mother succeeded in getting
her little son, the infant Udai Singh, away to a place
of safety; and then she led the women to the
funeral pyre. The Johar was again performed and
thirteen thousand Rajput women gave themselves to
the flames.  The flower of the Rajput perished : 32,000
were dead.

The third sack of Chittor came in 1567, when the
Rajputs and the Great Moghul came to blows.  Akbar
led a powerful army against his foes ; and though Akbar
triumphed, the honour rested with the Rajputs and
particularly with the two vassals of Mewar—Jaimal and
Patta.  Jaimal took the lead when Patta fell, but was
killed by a shot fired by Akbar himself.  Again all the
clans lost their brave chiefs. Johar was again performed in which 1700 Rajput women laid down their
lives to save the honour of Chittor.  This was the last
sack.  But the conqueror was of right royal stuff and
knew how to treat brave men.  So when the final
consummation was once more reached, Akbar left the
city levying no ransom ; and on the place where his
camp had stood, he raised a white marble tower from
whose top a light might shine to cheer the darkness of
Chittor.

## Objects of Interest

The ancient Chittor with its ruined walls still stands
on its ridge 2 miles east of the station.  Over this rise two
beautiful and lofty towers, one called the Kirti Stambha
(Tower of Fame) and the other, the Jai Stambha (Tower

of Victory). The Jai Stambha was erected by a Jain merchant, probably in the 12th century, and dedicated to Adinath, the first of the Trithankaras. About 80 ft. high, 30 ft. in diameter at the base and fifteen at the top, the tower consists of seven storeys and is covered with figure sculptures belonging to the Jain pantheon. Nearby is seen the ruined palace of Rana Ratan Singh and his wife Rani Padmini—a large building overlooking a tank.

Beyond the palaces of Jaimal and Patta, is the Kirti Stambha, raising its slender columns towards the sky. The Kirti Stamba, a nine-storeyed structure, somewhat similar in design, was built in 1449 to preserve the name and fame of the Rajput chiefs and is equally remarkable for its surface ornamentation and exquisite figure sculpture. Statues and ornaments decorate it inside out, and every Hindu deity with name inscribed below is there represented. The sculptures, in fact, constitute an illustrated dictionary of Hindu mythology.

Nearby is the Mahasati, a small wooded terrace, which was the cremation place of the Ranas ; and close to it is a cave where Rani Padmini and the Rajput ladies are said to have performed the historic Johar. To Rana Kumbha (1428-1468), the most glorious and powerful of the kings of Mewar, we owe several other noble works which still adorn the brow of Chittor. The temple of Krishna, the Kurma Sagar Lake and the temple of Mahadeo were also built by him. The two temples of Krishna are of considerable interest because of their association with the saintly songstress Mira Bai, the widowed wife of Rana Bhojraj. It is said that "the God descended from his pedestal and gave her an embrace. 'Welcome, Mira, said Krishna, and her soul was absorbed into His'. The odes and hymns of Mira Bai have become the most beloved of the devotional songs of India.

*　　　*　　　*　　　*

COMM. Chittorgarh lies on the Ajmer-Khandwa (M. G.) section of the Western Railway and is best reached from the south and west via Ratlam. Travellers can stay at the

Railway Retiring Room at Chittorgarh station. Meals are served by the attached Refreshment Room. There is also a Dak Bungalow where Khansama serves food at actual expenses. The ancient fort is about 3 miles from the station. Carriages and tongas are transport.

# UDAIPUR : THE "CITY OF ENCHANTMENT"

About 69 miles west of Chittorgarh lies lovely Udaipur, the capital of former Mewar since 1558. Rana Udai Singh, who had been saved from being murdered as a baby by the supreme devotion of his nurse Panna (who sacrificed her own child to save the little king in the third sack of Chittor by Akbar), abandoned Chittor and founded Udaipur. To his son, the immortal Rana Pratap, also goes credit for adding to its grandeur.

Udaipur, the most romantic city in all India, has been variously described as the "City of Sun-rise", the "Venice of the East", the "City of Dreams" and by similar other terms of eloquent homage as the fancy of the satisfied traveller could imagine, for its beauty is of that order which is associated with the scenes from Fairyland. "Alone at Udaipur is there, in its perfection the fairy palaces of one's childhood, just such a long cataract of marble terraces and halls falling into the water of a mountain-encircled lake, as the illustrator of an Andrew Land fairy book delights to draw".

Picturesquely set amdist the wooded slopes of a dimpling hill, this "City of Enchantment" owes its principal charm to its situation. On the low wooded ridge, skirting the water's edge, rise the historic marble palaces, glistening in the sun shine ; and crowning the summit is the Maharaja's palace within which the visitor sees the magnificent East in the peacock mosaic of the Choti Chitra-Shal, the mirror of the Moti Mahal, glittering like diamonds and in the oriental grandeur of the marble halls leading to the roof garden which affords thrilling views of the grand panorama around.

Here one may roam through miles of courts, saloons, corridors, pavilions, balconies, terraces, all a fairy land of splendour in which every room, every gallery is decorated with art of exquisite beauty.

To the north and the west, the palaces extend to the bank of the Pichola Lake. In the middle of the lake stands two island palaces, the Jag Mandir (1625) and the Jag Niwas, gleaming like myriad gems and containing in its mirrored halls the vanishing glimpses of the mystery and magnificence of the East. At one bank of the Pichola lake is the Odi Khas, a tower from which the wild pigs and elephants were fed every evening ; almsgiving to animals was traditional with the Udaipur Kings.

After you have seen the fairy palaces of this wonderful city your highest aspirations are satisfied ; then you naturally want to be left alone to picture what your eyes have seen. But there are some other interesting objects in Udaipur. There is the great temple of Jagannath, set high among hills, built by Maharana Jagat Singh in 1655 ; the sculptured gateways between the Bari Pol and the Triple Gateway under which the Maharanas were weighed against their weight in gold which was then distributed to the poor ; and if you like, an ascent to the summit of the Sujangarh hill which affords a wonderful view of Udaipur below.

Two miles from Udaipur are the cenotaphs of the Maharanas, where one can also see the Sati stones commemorating the heroic self-sacrifice of women on fire on the death of their lords. Fourteen miles from Udaipur through a picturesque hilly country is the magnificent temple dedicated to Mahadeo here worshipped as "Eklingaji". The bus goes up to Nathdwara, another beautiful spot in the inner reaches of the Aravalli hills, 18 miles beyond Eklingaji. About 30 miles from Udaipur is the Jai Samand lake, one of the loveliest lakes in India. It has hills rising sheer from the water's edge a thousand

feet, and charming little wooded islands; and picturesque fishing hamlets, temples, palaces and pavilions are
scattered all along its beautiful shore. To anyone loving
huge spaces under varying colours of nature, Udaipur
is fascinatingly beautiful and endlessly interesting.

*    *    *    *

COMM. Udaipur, a terminus station on the metre gauge
line of the Western Railway, is 69 miles from Chattorgarh via
Mavli junction which connects it with the Ahmedabad-Delhi
section of the Western Railway. Ratlam is the most convenient
point to reach it from the south and west, and Ajmer from north.

ACCOM. Travellers can stay at the Anand Bhawan
State Guest House (Rs. 12/8/- per day). There is also a Dak
Bungalow and a private hotel, named Lake View Hotel. Taxis,
buses and tongas are transport. Buses run to Nathadwara
(32 m.) via Eklingaji.

# JODHPUR

191 miles to the west of Jaipur, on a low sandstone
hill, stands the city of Jodhpur, the one-time capital of
the State of Marwar. Beyond the confines of the city
spreads the sands, 35,000 square miles of them, for this
largest of the Rajput States, like Bikaner, is almost entirely a desert. The city is shut in from the desert by a
colossal wall, guarded by towers and pierced by seven
fortified gateways.

Dominating the city and the entire countryside
rises a massive, mediaeval fortress, 400 ft. above the
city, crouching almost half-way to the sky. Named
after Rao Jodha, who founded it in 1459, Jodhpur city
has many houses and temples of richly carved stone; but
its fort, the finest in Rajasthan, is its jewel. A picturesque road meanders up the slopes to a massive
gateway and then winds a zigzag course through
several other gates and inner walls built for purpose
of defence. Within the fort, crushed into a space of
some 500 by 250 yards, is an inchoate mass of palaces,
decorated with beautifully carved panels, lattice windows

244

of delicate design, and here is the treasury containing a fantastic collection of jewels of inconceivable value, and the armoury which comprises a rare collection of mediaeval arms. A bird's-eye veiw of the city nestling around the imposing fort can be obtained from the battlements.

A fine view of the Fort can be had from the Gulab Sagar lake, within the city. There are several lakes in and around the city : the most picturesque of them is Kailana, the headquarters of Jodhpur Yacht Club. Among the fine buildings in the city are the temple at Dhan Mandi (grain market), and the Tailati Mahal, now the Jaswant Female Hospital. At Mahamandir, a walled town $1\frac{1}{2}$ miles north-east of the city wall, stands the Great Temple, the massive roof of which is supported by one hundred pillars. The inside is decorated with exquisite carvings.

About five miles to the north of Jodhpur is Mandor which was the capital of Marwar before the foundation of Jodhpur. Here are the cenotaphs of the former rulers of the State, some of which are imposing and architecturally beautiful, notably the one dedicated to Maharaja Ajit Singh who died in 1724. Another object of great interest is the Hall of Heroes containing a row of gigantic painted figures of divinities and heroes hewn out of a single rock. There are peaceful, old gardens too at Mandor, which are in keeping with the sanctity and the old-time glory of the place.

**Osia :** Not far from Jodhpur is Osia, the temple city of Rajasthan. Between the 8th and the 10th century, Osia was a great centre of religion and abounded in many fine temples. The finest of them is the 10th century Surya temple which for its richly carved plinths and niches shows close affinity to those of the Khajuraho temples. Speaking of the great artistic excellence of the Osia School an eminent authority says that "in course of time this process culminated in the elaborately sculptured temples of Abu, Modhera, Khajuraho and Bhubenaswar".

*      *      *      *

COMM. Jodhpur is reached by through trains from Delhi and Jaipur from the North, from Khandwa in the South and Agra in the East. It is also connected with Delhi by air.

ACCOM. The Circuit House or the State Hotel (Rs. 12/8/- daily) provides the best amenities of a western style hotel. Besides there are Retiring Rooms at the station and a few middle class hotels in the city. Taxis are available but tongas are popular transport. Buses go to important places.

# MOUNT ABU

Mount Abu, an ideal place for combining the pleasures of a charming hill resort with the interests of an archaeological excursion, lies on an isolated plateau near the Aravalli Range in southern Rajasthan. A place of pilgrimage of Hindus and Jains, Abu is no less so for the archaeologist; for in the high valleys between the rocky peaks are a number of shrines of which the two Dilwara temples (Jain) stand out as astonishing pieces of virtuosity and intricate stonework in the history of sculpture. And if technical skill of an almost terrifying competence in stone carving in India is to be seen, the Dilwara group of temples— Vimalashah and Neminath—must be visited. The main shrine, Vimalashah, which contains the most fantastic specimens of stone carvings in all India was built in 1030, while the second great Dilwara temple dedicated to Neminath was built by the two brothers, Vastupala and Tejpala, in 1231 A.D. Both are of pure white marble and carry to its highest perfection the Indian genius for the invention of graceful patterns. "In their ormate ways", says Dr. Benjamin Rowland, "they can be counted among the architectural wonders or curiosities of the world". To look at the ceilings of the Dilwara temples is to 'behold a dream-like vision'; for they contain some of the world's masterpieces of intricate sculpture.

Eastward from the Dilwara temples a track way leads to the shrines of Achaleswar at the foot of the hill-fort of Achalgarh some five miles away, which are worth visiting for their interest and the beauty of their surroundings. Near the temple is a big lake called Mandakini the shores of which are studded with statues, the most remarkable of which is that of Adipal.

The pre-eminent beauty spot of Abu is the Nakki Talao, a lake of idyllic beauty, surrounded by shrines and princely mansions. With its superb landscape and beautiful shrines Mt. Abu is indeed a fitting place for an inspiring holiday. The best season is from March 15 to June 15, then again from October to November.

\*      \*      \*      \*

COMM. Mount Abu is reached from Abu Road station on the Ahmedabad-Delhi metre gauge line of the W. Rly. The station is 117 m. north of Ahmedabad. From Abu Road station to Mt. Abu the distance is 18 miles by bus through a charming hill road. Bus fare is Rs. 1/3/6 plus Rs. 2/- toll tax.

ACCOM. Mount Hotel caters in European style. Other good hotels are Hill View (Rs. 8/- to 10/-), Central (Rs. 7), Guzrat Hindu Hotel and others. There are six Govt. Dak Bungalows of which the Rich View' (Central P.W.D. Dak Bungalow) is the best. Application for advance booking in "Rich View" should be made to the Executive Engineer, Central P.W.D. Ajmer or Sectional Officer, C.P.W.D. Abu.

# BHARATPUR

33 miles west of Agra and 21 miles from Mathura, on the Delhi-Bombay main line of the W. Rly., is Bharatpur, one of the chief cities of Rajasthan, famous for its historic fort which in 1803 repulsed successive British onslaughts.

The Jat ruler Suraj Mal (1733), who founded Bharatpur, was an outstanding military figure of the eighteenth century. He successfully fought the Mahrattas and the Moghuls and occupied Agra. His

successors were equally powerful and gave the British
tough fights for many years till 1825, when the inner
fortress was dismantled by the victorious British.
Objects of interest in the fort are : the Jowahir Burj
which was the coronation pavilion of the rulers and
the Kamra-Khas or the Durbar Hall. 3 miles north-
west of the city is the great marsh, Keola Deo, famous
for duck shooting.

\* \* \* \*

ACCOM. There is no good hotel at Bharatpur. The Circuit House offers all comforts of a western style hotel. The
Punjab-Sind Hotel caters for the middle class.

CONVEYANCE. The beautiful palaces of Dig including
the tomb of Suraj Mal mentioned under Mathura section may
be visited from this place. Dig is 23 miles from Bharatpur :
there is a regular bus service between the two places.

# ALWAR

57 miles south of Delhi (via Rewari) lies Alwar on
the metre gauge section of the Western Railway.

The town is dominated by the mediaeval fort which
crowns a conical rock with a range of hills as its back-
rest. There is nothing much to see in the fort except
that it affords a good view of the surrounding countryside interspersed with lakes and forests. Overlooking
the beautiful Sagar tank stands the palace of the
Maharaja which contains within it an extensive
library, rich with rare Sanskrit and Persian manuscripts.
The cenotaph of the late Raja Bhakteswar Singhji
(1781-1815), and the tomb of Fateh Jang, a minister
of Shah Jahan, are of considerable archaeological interest.
The Sagar Tank at the foot of the fort is a beauty spot
which attracts large crowds.

\* \* \* \*

SPORTS. There is plenty of game in the neighbouring
forests. Antilope and gazelle which are rare in other forests
can still be seen in the forests of Alwar.

ACCOM. There is no good hotel in Alwar. The Circuit House (Rs. 12/8/- daily) offers all conveniences of a western, style hotel. Tongas are usual transport.

# KOTAH

291 miles from Delhi, on the Delhi-Bombay main line of the W. Rly., is Kotah situated on the right bank of Chambal river. A historic city, surrounded by an old wall, it contains a number of objects of interest, the chief among them being the public gardens on the shores of a beautiful lake ; the royal cenotaphs ; the old palace ; and Umed Bhawan, the new palace. The Circuit House (Rs. 12/8/- daily) caters both in European and Indian style. A regular bus service runs to Bundi and thence to Ajmer.

# BUNDI

About 28 miles north-west of Kotah is Bundi, reached by road from Kotah or from Bundi Road railway station (288 miles from Delhi) on the Delhi-Bombay main line of the Western Railway.

Beautifully situated amdist a wooded hill, the city is surrounded by a huge wall and contains an impressive palace which according to Colonel Tod "must be acknowledged to be in the first rank for which it is indebted to situation not less than to the splendid additions which it has continually received". Crowning the summit of the hill (600 ft.) rises the fort of Taragarh built by Rao Bar Singh in 1354 A. D. The Circuit House caters both in European and Indian style (daily charge : Rs. 12/-).

# BIKANER

Bikaner, capital of the State of that name, is, like Jodhpur, a city of the desert. Built on an eminence, it has an imposing appearance being surrounded by a fine battlemented wall. Bikaner possesses many fine buildings. The Fort, built between 1588 and 1593, by Raja Raj Singh, contains the old palaces ; it has an interesting Sanskrit and Persian library, and a very fine armoury. There are several other interesting buildings in Bikaner—Jain monastries, temples and mosques. The Lallgarh Palace with its indescribable profusion of latticed arch and pagoda roof and the Lakshminarayan temple, built early in the sixteenth century, are the outstanding edifices of the city.

Ganga Golden Museum is worth a visit. It contains a valuable collection of mediaeval Rajput sculpture. The marble images of Bikaner are among the finest specimens of Hindu art.

\*       \*       \*       \*

COMM. Bikaner is reached by through trains from Delhi (277 m.) and Jodhpur (172 m.). There is also a Dak Bungalow near the station. There are cheap middle class hotels in the town.

ACCOM. The Circuit House (Rs. 12/8/-) caters in Indian and European style. Conveyance consisting of taxes, tongas and buses.

# CHAPTER IV

# CENTRAL INDIA

\* \* \* \* \* \* \* \* \* \* \* \* \* \* \* \* \* \* \* \* \* \* \* \* \* \* \*

*Occupying the very heart of India and blessed with the three great rivers—the Chambal, the Narbada and the Godavari—and thickly wooded forests with plenty of game, is Central India for which legend, romance and history combined to write a glorious history dating back to the dawn of Indian civilisation. Rich as it is in history and artistic treasures, Central India has also been enshrined India's early literature which reached its perfection in the dramas of Kalidasa during the reign of King Vikramaditya of Ujjain Other great giants of the age were Bhabavuti, Banabhatia and Vasavadatta, to name only a few. Through the ages the cultural tradition of Central India continued unabated and the proof of its great height is seen today in the exquisite carvings of Sanchi, mural paintings of Bagh caves, temples of Khajuraho, the ruined splendour of Mandu, the fine architecture of Gwalior and in the palaces of Orcha on the Betwa river.*

\* \* \* \* \* \* \* \* \* \* \* \* \* \* \* \* \* \* \* \* \* \* \* \* \* \* \*

## INDORE

Indore, 74 miles south of Ratlam and 87 miles north of Khandwa, was built by Rani Ahalya Devi Holkar (1765-96) ; it is now a flourshing centre of industry and education.

Indore has several beauty spots and buildings, mostly palaces built by the successive rulers of the

Holkar family. Among the palaces, the Old palace (or Juna Rajawara), with its many-storeyed gateway at the main square of the city, is historic. Here lived the Holkars of Indore. The modern Lal Bagh palace on the river Saraswati is also notable. The Maharaja stays at the Manick Bagh palace near Piplia Pala tank. The magnificent Jain temple built by Seth Hukamchand in multi-coloured glass and mirrors is the show-place of the town. At Chattri Bagh there are the cenotaphs erected to the memory of the members of the Holkar family of which the Chatri of Malher Rao Holkar I is remarkable for its sculptural embellishments. Close to it is another raised in honour of Rani Ahalya Bai of hallowed memory.

Lying on the outskirts of the city are the Piplia Pala Tank and Naulakha gardens, ideal for picnic and holidaying. The sylvan surroundings of the Sukh Nivas palace, picturesquely set on the edge of a lake with forests all around, have a charm all their own. Five miles south-east of Indore is Kasturba Gram, the headquarters of the Kasturba Trust.

**Dhar:** 40 miles west of Indore is Dhar, a historic city associated with that great patron of Sanskrit literature and art, Raja Bhoja (1000-1055), who ruled over Malwa from Dhar and who is celebrated in bardic poetry as an ideal Hindu monarch. Dhar was the capital of the Paramar Rajputs up to the thirteenth century. Raja Bhoja, the greatest of the Parmar rulers, was the author of numerous works on astronomy, architecture and poetry. He adorned Dhar with many fine buildings, among which was a Sanskrit College, the 'Bhojasala (later turned into a mosque), in which is found inscribed on black slates the fragmentary texts of Parijata Manjari. In the temple was installed a beautiful image of Vagdevi by Raja Bhoja in 1034 A. D. The image (now in the British Museum) is regarded as one of the finest specimens of Hindu Art.

The old fort, the temple of Goddess Kali and the shining lakes are other attractions. Dhar is the road junction for trips to Mandu and Bagh.

**Mhow :** Mhow, a well known military station on the high road to Bombay, is only 14 miles south of Indore. The new Swargashram temple is worth a visit. Mhow is a convenient base for trips to Mandu and Bagh by bus, via Dhar. There is a well furnished P. W. D. Dak Bungalow about a mile west of the station with cooks and amenities.

**Omkareswar :** About 50 miles from Indore, on the main line to Khandwa, is the Omkareswar Road station. From there a seven-mile bus journey through green forests takes one to the celebrated temple of Omkareswar situated on an isle of the holy Narbada. In an ancient temple on this picturesque river-island is enshrined the holy lingam of Omkareswar, one of the twelve Jyotir-lingams of Lord Siva. This is one of the leading places of pilgrimage in India ; and thousands of pilgrims flock to the holy shrine every year, especially on auspicious occasions in the months of Sravana and Kartick. There is a Dak Bungalow at Omkareswar.

\*　　　　\*　　　　\*　　　　\*

COMM. Indore lies on the Ajmer-Khandwa metre gauge line of the W. Rly. The Agra-Bombay high road passes through Indore (370 m. from Bombay).

ACCOM. Western style hotels are : Indore Hotel (Rs. 12-). and Lantern Hotel Rs. 14/-). Viram Lodge (from Rs. 6/- to 10/-) and Central Lodge, both near Rly. Station, are good Indian style hotels. There is a Dak Bungalow about 1½ m. from the station (inclusive charge Rs. 9/- daily).

CONVEYANCE. Taxis and tongas are available. Madhaya Pradesh State buses are available for hire. Long-distance bus services connect almost all the places of interest, such as, Mhow, Maheswar, Mandsaur Ujjain, Bhopal, Bhar, Mandu and Bagh.

# MANDU

62 miles west of Indore and 55 miles south-west of Mhow (reached by bus via Dhar from both places) lie the beautiful buildings of Mandu, the historic pride of Madhya Bharat, occupying 37 sq. miles of ground on a picturesque tableland of the Vindhyas.

Mandu saw great days of prosperity and pomp from the beginning of the fifteenth century, when Dilawar Khan (1401), the then Gevernor of Malwa made himself virtually independent of the Delhi empire, shifted his capital from Dhar to Mandu and laid the foundations of the celebrated fort. His son, Hoshang Shah (1405-1434), a great soldier and a builder, added to the architectural beauties of the fort, erected the great Jama Masjid, a fine specimen of Pathan architecture, and the mighty marble mausoleum in which he lies. It was, however, left to the next ruler, Mohammed Khilji, to erect the finest monuments of Mandu including the Ashrafi Mahal which even in their decay overwhelm the visitor with solid majesty and rare beauty. His son, Giasuddin, built the great Jahaz Mahal, the "Hall of Pleasure" with its swimming baths, turrets and cupolas.

If Mohamed Khilji gave splendour and fame to Mandu, a touch of romance was lent by the last Sultan of Malwa, Baz Bahadur, who was captivated by the peerless beauty and charm of Rupamatiti, a Hindu songstress of great fame. The saga of their romance, marriage and their tragic death still holds the imagaination of millions throughout Malwa. Indeed, the first building that strikes the visitor to Mandu is the Rupamati Mahal, the pavilion in which Baz Bahadur and Rupamati 'spent many hours singing of their love amid the wonders of nature which the hills of Mandu provide.'

In 1560, Adham Khan, Akbar's general, invaded this fertile kingdom and laid siege to the fortress of Mandu. Baz Bahadur was routed and Rupamati fell a captive to the general. The beautiful queen, however, disappointed lascivious Adham Khan by poisoning herself. Akbar himself visited Mandu several times to participate in its splendours ; and Jahangir stayed there for months leaving behind a glowing description of the beauties of Mandu, the 'City of Joy'.

*  *  *  *

COMM. Mandu (now a small village) is reached by service buses, both Government and private, from Mhow and and Indore (55 & 62 miles) via Dhar. There is a bazar at Dhar where refreshments are available. Bus fare is Rs. 2/- from Mhow and Rs. 2/4/- from Indore.

ACCOM. A former palace of the Sultana has been converted into a Rest House. It is ideally situated in the fort near the Jahaz Mahal. Khansama prepares food and charges actual expense. There are 4 rooms. Rent Re. 1 per day for each room.

## BAGH CAVES

82 miles from Mhow, 96 miles from Indore (to the west and reached by bus from both) are the famous caves of Bagh which for their beautiful frescoes are regarded as extension of those at Ajanta. There is a great deal of similarity between these caves and those at Ajanta ; in point of time also the Bagh caves belong to the same period as the later Ajanta caves though some of them date as far back as the fifth century A.D. The nine caves of Bagh, set in a single row with a frontage of 750 yards, stand on the bank of the river Baghini, hence the name Bagh. The caves, known as Pancha Pandavas, are 4 miles away from the Bagh village. The damaged fragments of decoration in the verandah of Cave IV (Rang Mahal) display the finest surviving examples of Gupta wall-painting.

Unfortunately not much remains now. The rock, out of which the caves were cut, has mostly succumbed to the ravages of time. The greater portion of what has escaped has been largely obliterated by the smoke of cooking of the hill tribes who in later years made the caves their homes. Only a few of the images within the

255

caves and a colossal figure of Yaksharaja in front of one of them, are really intact. Even in their damaged condition Bagh points to the high level which the art of painting had attained in the Gupta age. "The picturesque setting of the caves and the pleasant calm that permeates the whole atmosphere easily convince the visitor that the Buddhist monks could not have chosen a better site to hold communion with nature and delve deep into the self in search of enlightenment, on finding which nothing remains to be sought".

\*            \*            \*            \*

COMM. The village of Bagh (56 m. from Dhar, 90 m. from Mhow and 97 m. from Indore) is reached by bus via Dhar. The buses of the Indore. Alirajpur service pass through Bagh. The caves are five miles from the village where the bus stops. Bus fare from Mhow is Rs. 3/- and Rs. 3/8/- from Indore. The nearest railway station is Dohad, 94 m. east of Baroda.

ACCOM. There is an Inspection Bungalow at the village where the care-taker can arrange for food. Room rent Rs. 1/8 per day. For reservation Oversear, P.W. Kukshi may be contacted. There is another Dak Bungalow near the Caves. The Head Care-taker, Bagh Caves, arranges for food on previous intimation.

# UJJAIN

About 44 miles north of Indore, on the banks of river Shipra, is legendary Ujjain or Avanti of yore. A city of great sanctity having been the seat of a Jyotirlingam, (Mahakal) which is held in great veneration by all Hindus, Ujjain is also the Indian Greenwich from which the early Indian astronomers calculated the first degree of longitude. One-time capital of Malwa hallowed by the memories of the great Asoka as Governor of the Province, the city in later years witnessed the "Golden Period" of Indian history, when the great Vikramaditya made it his temporary capital. He gathered around him the 'Nine Jewels' headed by Kalidasa who combined to make their age for India what the days of Pericles had been for Athens and the reign of Augustus for Rome. In particular, the city was the traditional place, where at the spring festival, the poet laureate Kalidasa presented his dramas before the king.

It was again a favourite with king Harsha under whom India continued to be the focus of world attention. Ujjain again saw great days under the Paramara King Bhoja who eventually removed his capital to Dhar.

The ancient shrine of Mahakal, which was destroyed by Altamash in 1253 and later rebuilt at this site, is the principal attraction of the city. The show-place of the town is the Ram Ghat on the legendary river Sipra (2 miles north-west of the railway station) which is the popular bathing ghat. The ghat is paved all along and is lined with many temples. The temple of Mahakal is about a mile from the ghat. Other objects of interest are : Raja Jai Singh's Observatory on the railway line, outside the town ; Datta-Ka Akhra which is the meeting place of sadhus ; the Chattri Ghat ; and the Arts and Crafts Emporium. Seven miles from the city is Kaliadeh, a beautiful water palace of the Sultans of Mandu, picturesquely situated on an island in the Sipra. Tongas can be hired for a trip to Kaliadeh.

\*　　　　\*　　　　\*　　　　\*

COMM. & ACCOM. Ujjain, on the broad guage line of the W. Rly. is a railway centre which connects Bhopal to the east by broad gauge and Khandwa to the south by metre gauge via Indore and Mhow. The road route via Dewas (on the Agra-Bombay main road) is fine. Grand Hotel (Rs. 12/-) offers excellent food. There are fine Railway Retiring Rooms at the Station (Rent Rs. 3/- daily). Food can be had from the attached Refreshment Room. Besides there is a Dak Bungalow and a Dharamsala.

# BHOPAL

Bhopal, 521 miles from Bombay and 437 miles from Delhi, on the Delhi-Bombay main line of the Central Railway, is a picturesque city built around a huge lake. From mediaeval days women of the Nawab family played a predominant part in Bhopal's history. Today, Bhopal the capital of Madhya Bharat, is increasingly gaining in importance ; many fine public buildings have been built, all dominated by the Nawab's palace from which can be obtained a splendid view of the sprawling city and the country-side for miles around. Bhopal is the popular base for trips to Sanchi, (44 miles by road ; 28 miles by rail) and other important places of Buddhist remains such as Bhilsa (6 miles from Sanchi) and near-by Besnagar and Udaigiri caves.

*      *      *      *

ACCOM. The Circuit House (Rs. 12/-) caters in Western style. It's 2 miles from the station. Ruby Hotel (close to the station) also caters in European style (Rs. 10/-). New Bhopal Hotel (Rs. 8/-) caters for the middle class.

CONVEYANCE. Buses ply between Bhopal and Sanchi (28 m.). Upper class fare Rs. 3/-. Lower class Rs. 2/-. Taxis are available. Tongas are popular transport. There are frequent trains for Sanchi.

# SANCHI

28 miles to the north-east of Bhopal, on the Bombay-Delhi main line of the Central Railway, is the famous stupa of Sanchi which is undoubtedly the most perfect and the most beautiful of all Buddhist monuments of the early school.

The stupas were built to mark some spot sacred to Buddhism or were meant to contain some relics of the Buddha himself. Here, stupas, rails and monasteries are nobly set on a low, flat-topped hill commanding wide and beautiful views. The most important of them all is the Great Stupa originally built by Asoka, though it bears later embellishments. The Great Stupa is a stupendous structure which commands attention on account of its size (the diameter of the solid stone dome is 121 ft. at the base and height 56 ft.), artistic work and antiquity. The base of the stupa is enclosed by a massive stone railing with four gateways (toranas) and on these are found all the exquisite carvings for which Sanchi is famous. Carved in relief on the sides of the pillars and architraves are scenes from the life of Buddha and stories from Jatakas. The way in which these carvings depict the life of Buddha without ever representing him in person is an outstanding achievement in the sphere of iconography. Queen Maya, surrounded by elephants pouring water over her, represents the Nativity ; the damsels before the empty seat depict the scene of Temptation ; and the riderless horse represents the Great Departure. There are, in addition, scenes of historical interest. A panel shows king Bimbisara, leaving Rajagriha to visit the Buddha, while the other showing the journey of Asoka to the sacred tree of Bodhi Gaya contains probably the only known image of Asoka. Other objects of interest are the Stupa No. 2 which contains remains of the saints who took part in Asoka's foreign mission ; the newly-built Buddhist Vihara ; the Museum ; and Stupa No. 2, a modern renovation, which originally contained the remains of Sariputta and Moggalana, the foremost disciples of the Buddha.

The site of Sanchi seems to have found favour with Asoka for the Great Stupa for a somewhat sentimental reason. Sanchi was on the outskirts of Vidisa, the birth-place of his queen Bedesa Devi whose son Mehendra went on a mission to Ceylon. Around Sanchi itself there are many more stupas and the whole area within five to ten miles of Sanchi is rich in Buddhist Hindu and Jain relics ranging from 2nd. century B.C. to the fifth century A.D. The shrines of Bhilsa and the Udaygiri caves (belonging to Hinduism and not Buddhism) and the monolithic pillar at Besnagar, erected by Heliodoras, a Greek ambassador at the court of Vidisa in 90 B.C. are well known. Bhilsa lies a few miles to the north of Sanchi on the main railway line. There is a Dak Bungalow at Bhilsa.

ACCOM. There is a well equipped Government Rest House at Sanchi (cook attached). Advance booking should be made with the District Engineer P.W.D. Bhopal or with the care-taker, Asoka Cottage, Sanchi. There are fine Railway Retiring Rooms at the station.

# GWALIOR

About 73 miles of Agra, and 195 m. from Delhi, on the Delhi-Bombay main line, is the historic city of Gwalior which contains one of the most impressive and renowned of the mediaeval strongholds of India. A splendid example of Rajput architecture, the Gwalior Fort has been described as the "Pearl in the necklace of Hind", a testimony borne out by its proud history of about 1500 years and by the numerous monuments and antiquities found within its extensive limits. The hill on which the fortress is built is honeycombed with caves and cells which contains several enormous figures of Jain Tirthankaras and representations of elephants, peacocks and other birds in green, blue and gold mosaic which lighten and enhance the massive contours of the fort. The ascent to the fort is like that of some fabled palace of the Arabian nights.

Superb among the many palaces crowning the fort is Raja Mansingh's palace (1486-1516) with its tall towers standing like lilies amidst foliage of richly carved balconies. The Gujari Mahal, another beautiful palace built by Man Singh for his favourite queen, now houses the archaeological museum. Among the temples of the fort the most outstanding is the Sas Bahu temple which stands on richly carved plinths and dates from the eleventh century.

The Jai Vilas palace, the magnificent modern residence of the Maharaja, contains a splendid carpet which is said to be the largest and the heaviest in the world.

Among the other objects of interest are the tomb of the Muslim divine, Mahammad Ghaus, a fine specimen of early Muslim architecture ; the mausoleum of Tan Sen, at the entrance to the Fort, where thousands of musicians gather once a year to pay homage to the prodigy of Indian music ; and the memorial of Rani Lakshmi Bai of Jhansi of revered memory who at her twenty-two threw a mighty challange to the British and proved to the world that Indian women at times can become the best of generals.

Gwalior is an industrial centre which contains many mills and factories. A visit to Gwalior Pottery factory may prove interesting. There are a number of educational and cultural institutions in the town.

*   *   *   *

COMM. Gwalior is reached by through trains from Delhi, Agra, Bombay and Madras. The Agra-Bombay trunk road passes through Gwalior. It is also connected by air with Delhi.

ACCOM. Gwalior Hotel, opposite Railway Station, (W.S.) provides excellent food and accommodation. Hindu Lodge, Laxmi Hotel and Maharastra Lodge, all at Lashkar, are good Indian style hotels. Transport consists of taxis, tongas and buses. Government buses ply to all the nearby places of interest.

# SHIVPURI

73 miles south-west of Gwalior, at a height of about 1,609 ft. above sea-level, lies Shivpuri, an ideal summer resort renowned for its scenic beauty, water-falls and delightful lakes. Sports include facilities for yachting and shooting including such big game as tiger, bear, sambhar, blue bull, spotted dear and a wide variety of birds.

Shivpuri lies on the Agra-Bombay trunk road. Buses of Madhya Bharat Roadways and a narrow gauge line of the Central Railways connect Shivpuri with Gwalior. Shivpuri Hotel, near the Railway Station, provides excellent food and accommodation. Besides, there is a Dak Bungalow, an Inspection House and a

Circuit House. For reservation one has to apply to Executive Engineer, Shivpuri.

# KHAJURAHO

About 150 miles west of Allahabad (via Manikpur and Banda) is the ancient town of Mahoba on the Jhansi-Allahabad section of the Central Railway. From Mahoba, the village of Khajuraho (Chattarpur State) is 61 miles to the south reached by bus. Tourists coming from Jhansi have to detrain at the Harpalpur Station whence buses go to Khajuraho via, Nowgong and Chattarpur (62 miles).

The magnificent group of Hindu and Jain temples at Khajuraho, built between the 10th and the 11th century by the Chandelas of Bundelkhand, bear the highest expression of the Gupta Classic art ; they are unrivalled for their profusion of ornate detail and the perfect balance they represent between two the forms of art—architecture and sculpture. The Kandaraya Mahadeva temple, the largest of the group, alone contains in its walls 800 beautiful statuettes, each a masterpiece of sculpture.

"Like jewels encrusted on a beautiful casket, these renderings in stone of life and love blend beautifully with their background imparting vibrant texture to the temples. An animated array of womanhood stands in an endless procession round the temple walls. From every niche a nymph looks down, vaunting her voluptuous charms in an infinite variety of attitudes : one applying make-up, another picking a thorn from her foot and yet another in the embrace of her lover". The frankly erotic nature of much of the sculpture at Khajuraho might well have seemed in succeeding centuries incompatible with the sanctity of the shrines and led to their abandonment as places of worship.

The Chaturbhuj temple stands on a high base , profusely ornamented, with smaller shrines at its four corners. The Jain temples and the Ghantai temple are equally remarkable for their architectural and sculptural splendour which are definitely individual in character, different from that in any other part of the country.

Architecturally, the temples are more compact than the Orissan temples. Of the eighty-five temples that once adorned the proud capital of the Chandelas only twenty now remain, representing a world of joy in which men and women, *apsaras* and *apsaris* indulge in a mystic 'rapture typifying the ultimate union of the soul with the Divine'

The splendid temples of Khajuraho, though no longer the resort of the devout, certainly mark out a pilgrimage spot for the aesthete and the lover of art who will gasp at the wonderous beauty of the temples and their images—each a perfect piece pulsating with life.

\*       \*       \*       \*

COMM. Mahoba, itself a historic city with many relics, is the base for trip to Khajuraho (61 m. by bus via Chattarpur). There is a Dak Bungalow at Mahoba where the visitor can stay. Advance booking may be made with the District Magistrate, Hamirpur. Access is also gained from Harpalpur station, on the same line, from where Khajuraho is 62 miles away by bus or car. From both stations—Mahoba and Harpalpur—the road to Khajuraho passes through Chattarpur which is 29 miles below Khajuraho. There is a Circuit House and a Dak Bungalow at Chattarpur where food is charged at fixed rates. Advance booking should be made with Dy. Commissoner, Chattarpur. At Khajuraho there is a well-equipped Circuit House (occupation charge Rs. 5/- per day). Khansama supplies all types of food at actual expense. Advance booking should be made with Dy. Commissioner Chattarpur, or with Care-taker, Circuit House, Khajuraho Madhya Pradesh.

# JUBBALPORE

224 miles west of Allahabad and 616 miles east of Bombay, on the Allahabad-Bombay main line of the

Central Railway, lies Jubbalpore, an important civil and military station and a large city of Madhya Pradesh.

**Marble Rocks :**   13 miles to the south-east of Jubbalpore are the famous Marble Rocks in a gorge of the river Narbada.   Near the popular view-point stands the old Madanpur temple surrounded by sixty-four Yoginis (female ascetics) and a little beyond the temple is the point where the river Narbada plunges down in cascades of mighty rage to the bed of the rocks below. Further down, the mass of water settle down in a broad recess of the river surrounded by wooded forests on all sides which affords enjoyable boating and fishing, and picnicking on the shores.   There in the midst of the calm river the boatman points to a curious rock rising above the deep waters—the "Elephant Foot"—which provides a pleasant observation point.

4 miles from Jubbalpore is Madan Mahal, an ancient fortress of the Gond Kings built on the crest of a huge boulder.

\*         \*         \*         \*

ACCOM.   Jackson's Hotel (Rs. 8/- to 12/-) caters in European style.   Other good hotels are Royal Hotel and Cecil Hotel. There is a comfortable Dak Bungalow near the Rocks in beautiful surroundings : there the visitor can enjoy a few day's holiday.

CONVEYANCE.   Taxis and tongas are available at Jubbalpore.   A fine metalled road connects Jubbalpore with the Marble Rocks.

## PACHMARI

A delightful hot-weather hill station on a plateau of the Mahadeo hills in the Satpura range (3,500 ft.) reached via Itarsi or Jubbalpore, Pachmari is steadily taking its place among the hill-resorts of India.   Apart from its salubrious climate, natural scenery and numerous picnic points, Pachmari has all the amenities of a modern hill station.   It has a progressive club—the

Pachmari Club—equipped with an 18 hole golf course, a fine swimming pool, a spacious lounge, a good library and ample facilities for indoor and outdoor games. The bathing pools of Pachmari, fashioned in natural settings, are great attractions. The largest and most favoured of these is the Bee Dam, about half a mile from the Government House, at a picturesque spot on the Bee stream. Other attractive bathing pools are Waters Meet, Pansy Pool and Pathar Chatta, all on the Denwa river. During the season, these spots continually hum with life and excitement.

To the shikari plenty of big game is available in the Jharia block forests within 20 miles of Pachmari on the Piparia road. Permits for shooting can be obtained from the Divisional Forest Officer, Hoshangabad.

\*　　　　\*　　　　\*　　　　\*

COMM. Pachmari is 32 miles by car or bus from the Piparia station on the Jubbalpur-Itarsi section of the Central Rly. There is a regular bus service between Piparia and Pachmari.

ACCOM. Pachmari Hotel, near Pachmari Club, caters both in European and Indian style (Rs. 8/- daily). There are a number of boarding houses and furnished bungalows for tourists. Besides, there are Government bungalows, a Circuit House and a Rest House where Government officials are given priority. Taxis and station waggons are available.

# CHAPTER V

# WESTERN INDIA

\* \* \* \*\* \* \* \* \* \* \* \* \* \* \* \* \* \* \* \* \* \* \* \*

*From the northern peninsula of Saurastra to Mysore in south, Western India spreads a long narrow strip of fertile land lapped by the Arabian Sea. The steep mountain wall of the Western Ghats which runs almost parallel to the coast for about 600 miles shelters on its flat-topped peaks the impregnable Mahratta fortresses which played a glorious part in the history of the nation. These lowlands gave the first glimpse of India to foreigners in early times as the Bombay harbour does in the present day. It was on them that the foreigner first set his foot with his curious merchandise; and the India known to the West for centuries was but the narrow margin of fertile territory which lay below the ranges of the Western Ghats. Beyond the ghats are the plains and great cotton-growing tracts feeding the textile mills of Bombay and Ahmedabad, the Lanchashire of India.*

\* \* \* \* \* \* \* \* \* \* \* \* \* \* \* \* \* \* \* \* \* \* \* \* \*

## BOMBAY

"To the vast majority of European travellers Bombay is the gateway to India. It is here that they get their first glimpse of the bewildering variety of races, of colours, of types, of customs, which make up India". Lying on the shores of a beautiful sea, sparkling in the sunshine, glorious in the monsoon and sheltering a great variety of sea-going vessels, is the city of Bombay—"the beautiful". The transition of Bombay from a cluster of fishing villages of 'pestilential swamp' into one of the greatest cities of the world has been distinguished by a human endeavour that is almost romantic. The story is primarily one of continued struggle against the sea—an unparalleled struggle for reclamation in which many men played the noblest part.

Today, Bombay boasts of a port that is the third largest in the world, an imposing array of public and mercantile buildings, broad thoroughfares and fine parks and gardens where move the most beautifully dressed ladies in the world. Its miles of docks and railways roar continually with activity ; for the city is the centre of a gigantic industry and thriving commerce which earn for it fabulous profits. It is again a city in which almost every race in the East is represented, and in that strange diversity of creed and language, of tradition and ideals, there has, as a rule, been marked concord.

If Bombay is proud of its port and its great industry it is equally proud of two other institutions which have a long and honourable history—its University and its Municipality. One of the three oldest universities of India, the Bombay University has played a conspicuous part in the educational history of the country. Similarly, the Municipality has been one of the pioneers in the development of local self-government in India ; it has done splendid work in beautifying the city and promoting that feeling of citizenship which has long distinguished Bombay. Along the rocky ridges, and on the slopes of the Cumballa and Malabar Hills are the charming homes of Bombay's aristocracy. From this eminence the visitor gets a superb view of the city which is almost magical at night. Here, too, are the famous Hanging Gardens and the Parsee Tower of Silence.

## Objects of Interest

A magnificent sight in the city is the Marine Drive, a crescent-shaped promenade by the sea flanked on one side by beautiful buildings and on the other by a fine sheet of water. Nearby is Chowpatty, a wide sandy beach which attracts large crowds every evening. Of the many beautiful gardens and parks the Victoria Gardens takes pride of place. It accommodates the Bombay Zoo which contains almost every representative of the animal kingdom. Inside the Gardens is the Victoria Albert Museum containing many objects of industrial and agricultural interest.

Near the Victoria Gardens is the pride of Bombay, the Prince of Wales Museum, holding priceless treasures of Indian Art, Archaeology and Natural History. In its grounds is the Jahangir Art Gallery where Art Exhibitions are frequent events. The Museum in open daily, except on Mondays, from 10 a.m. to 6 p.m.

Other buildings of interest are the Rajabai Tower which rising above the University dominates the entire Fort area; the "Gateway of India" at the Apollo Bunder, a beautiful arch which was used for ceremonial landings and departures of the British Viceroys ; the Mahalaxmi temples facing the Arabian Sea at the north-west end of the Cumballa Hills; and the nearby Mahalaxmi Race Course which is reckoned to be one of the finest in the East. The other objects of interest are the Crawford Market at the northern end of the Hornby Road Brabourne Stadium near the Church Gate ; Taraporevala Aquarium containing a huge variety of exotic fish from the Indian Occean ; and the Haffkine Institute ($5\frac{1}{2}$ miles from Flora Fountain) which is the principal centre of medical research in western India.

There are many more beauty spots in and around Bombay which has the additional advantage of a picturesque lake district.

**Juhu :** 13 miles north of Bymbay is Juhu Beach with its wide expanse of golden sands, waving palms and the blue waters of the Arabian Sea dotted with the sails of fishing boats, reminiscent of an idyllic South Sea Island. Known as the Brighton of India it provides refreshing sea bathing from November to May. The nearest station is Santa Cruz whence cars and buses provide transport to the Beach. The local hotels and restaurants provide all types of food.

**Kanheri Park & Caves :** Twenty miles from Bombay and reached in 40 minutes by local trains is Kanheri Park, the Mecca of holiday makers. Occupying an extensive area of 5000 acres and equipped with numerous picnic cottages the Park is a veritable heaven of shady trees, water channels and colourful birds. A delightful walk of three miles through the Park brings the visitor to the Buddhist Caves—100 in number—which are believed to have been excavated between the 2nd and the 8th century A.D. Situated on an eminence on the coast, the Caves command a superb panorama of the surrounding countryside. Caves 3, 10, 35 and 56 are the most interesting.

The Park and the Caves are reached from the Borivli station (W. Rly.) whence the Park is one mile and the Caves 4 miles reached by car or foot.

**Elephanta :** Six miles south-east of Bombay, on a small wooded island reached by ferry launch, are the famous cave temples of Elephanta. The name no longer applies ; for the huge stone elephant after which the Portuguese once named the island has disappeared. That stone elephant now adorns the Victoria Gardens. On a 250-ft-high rock, two miles beyond Elephanta Ghat are five caves which date from the middle of the eighth century. In the central hall (about 130 ft. square) are fine sculptures depicting the various aspects of Shiva—as a dancer, as a destroyer of evil, as a husband and as an ascetic. But the highlight of interest is the colossal three-headed bust of Siva which for its sheer beauty, superb plastic quality, concentrated vigour and latent energy has been justly acclaimed as one of the finest sculptures in all India. The image has been, mistakenly though, called a Trimurti ; in reality it is a representation of Siva as Mahesh.

Nowhere has the monotheistic tendency of Hinduism found a more moving expression than here ; the central head stands forth royally representing Siva as Brahma, the lord of creation, the one on the left is the terrible form of Siva as Rudra, the god of destruction and one on the right is the benevolent expression of Siva as Vishnu, the preserver.

Further around the caves the visitor is attracted by what originally must have been a superb piece of work, depicting the wedding of Siva and Parvati. Unfortunately much of its beauty has been damaged by the ravages of time.

The Bombay Steam Navigation Co. (100 Frere St. Phone : 25061) runs a ferry service on Sundays and charges Rs. 2/4/- per head. On week days launches can be hired at Ballard Pier at a charge of Rs. 60/- for parties up to 21. There is no launch service between June and September.

*       *       *       *

COMM. Bombay, the second largest city of India, is connected by through mail trains and a net-work of air services with almost all the cities of India. A number of international airlines directly link the city with the countries of the West.

ACCOM. A list of hotels appears in the General Information Section. The Railway retiring rooms at Victoria Terminus station also provide comfortable accommodation at cheaper rates.

CONVEYANCE. Bombay boasts of the best transport system in the East. Luxurious motor coaches, taxis and tram cars provide a comfortable and cheap transport throughout Bombay and Greater Bombay, while fast, electric trains connect the city with the surrounding areas. Transport is plentiful and cheap.

# BOMBAY : GENERAL INFORMATION

## HOTELS

Ambassador,
    Chruchgate Extn.
Grand
    Ballard Estate
Green's
    Apollo Bunder
Ritz
    Chruchgate Reclamation
Tajmahal
    Apollo Bunder
West End
    Marine Lines

### Indian Style

Empire Hindu Hotel,
    Bori Bunder
Madhavashram
    Girgaum
Sardar Griha Hotel
    Crawford Market
Welcome Hindu Hotel
    Bori Bunder

## NEWSPAPERS

Times of India
Bombay Chronicle
Free Press Journal
Indin Express

## BOOK-SELLERS

Popular Book Depot
    Lamington Road
New Book Co,
    Hornby Road
Taraporewalla & Co.
    Hornby Road

## INFORMATION

The Regional Tourist Officer,
123 Queens Road, Charchgate
(Telephone : 32446) supplies all
information on travel and sight
seeing. He also arranges for
liquor permits for overseas
visitors.

## TRAVEL AGENTS

American Express Co. Inc,
    Hornby Road
India Travel Service
    Sir Phirozshah Mehta Rd.
Jeena & Co.
    10 Veer Nariman Rd.
Mercury Travels
    Hornby Road
Thomas Cook & Son.
    Hornby Road
Trade-Wings
    Rampart Row

## ART DEALERS

Gazdar Ltd.
    Tajmahal Hotel
Indian Textiles Co. Ltd.
    Tajmahal Hotel

## HANDICRAFTS

Bombay Swadeshi Store
    Sir Phirozshah Mehta Rd.
Kashmir Art Emporium
    Sir Phirozshah Mehta Rd.
Bombay Cottage Industries
    Sir Phirozshah Mehta Rd.

## RESTAURANTS

Eros Restaurant
    Churchgate Reclamation
Parisian
    Marine Drive
Gordon's Restaurant
    Churchgate Street
Mongiri's
    Churchgate Street
Rendezvous
    Tajmahal Hotel
Purohit's
    Churchgate

*Bombay is dry. Liquor is served
only to overseas visitors on production of Liquor Permits.*

271

# MATHERAN

67 miles from Bombay and reached in three hours from Victoria Terminus, is Matheran, a charming hill-station near Bombay, much frequented during the hot season and after the rains. Besides its lovely scenery and salubrious climate the other attractions of Matheran, often described as the 'Daisy of the Hills', are its wooded walks and the thirty-three points of vantage which offer excellent views of the panorama around. Visitors to Matheran can have a wonderful holiday wandering around these beautiful points. Other attractions are : the Olympia Race Course ; Charlotte Lake ; the Sunday Bazar ; and the beautiful gardens.

\*     \*     \*     \*

COMM. Matheran is reached from the Neral station (54 miles from Bombay) whence Matheran is 13 miles by a light railway. Train service is suspended during June-September due to monsoon. From Neral, Matheran is only 7 miles by road.

ACCOM. There are Rly. Rest House and Retiring Rooms at the Neral station. Western style hotels of Matheran are Lord's and Rugby Hotel. Of the Indian style hotels Brightland, Cecil, Pinto and Luxmi Hindu Hotel are popular.

# KARLA AND BHAJA

About 80 miles from Bombay, on the Bombay-Poona line of the Central Railway, is Lonavla station which is the best base for trips to the celebrated rock-cut caves of Karla, Bhaja and Bedsa.

The rock-hewn sanctuaries of the Bhor-Ghat—*chaityas* and viharas of early Buddhism—are scattered in the secluded hills and glens around the Poona-Bombay road. A marvel of consummate architectural skill and the most perfect specimen of early Buddhist art, these caves along with some in other parts of Western India are the earliest examples of rock architecture that reached its climax in the great cave temples of Ajanta and Ellora and played a decisive role in the development of mediaeval sculpture. Among the earlier chaitya halls datable between the second and the first century B.C. are the caves at Bhaja, Pithalkhora, Bedsa and Karli. "The finest example, undoubtedly", says Sir John Marshall, "is the hall at Karli which is at once the largest, the best preserved and the most perfect of its type".

Karli (1st century A.D.) is only 6 miles from the Lonavla station, while Bhaja (2nd century B.C.) is very close to the Malvali station. Lonavla itself is a fine hill station with amenities of accommodation and transport. There are refreshment rooms at the station and Dak Bungalows and rest houses in the vicinity. Taxis are available for trips to the caves.

## POONA

Poona, the Queen of the Deccan, is reached by one of the most interesting hill journeys either by rail or by road from Bombay. One of the best and fastest trains in India is the 'Deccan Queen' which covers the 118-mile distance between Bombay and Poona in 3 hours. Poona has always been a seat of power, first of the great Indian hero, Shivaji, who founded the great Mahratha Kingdom, and then of his successors, great Peshwas (Prime Ministers). With the beginning of the British rule it has been the Headquarters of the Army's Southern Command. The National Defence Academy is situated at Khadakvasla, 11 miles from Poona.

The climate of Poona provides a welcome relief from the humidity of Bombay. Poona has several places of interest, such as the Bund Gardens, the Aga Khan's palace on the river bank, the Parvati temple on top of a hill, the Shanwarwada palace inside the old city, the Khadakvasla Lake (11 miles) and the historic Sinhagarh Fortress, four miles beyond it. The historic Purandhar Fort, 24 miles south-east of Poona, is now used as a sanatorium. Poona is the leading centre of Oriental Culture in Western India. There are a number of famous institutions of which the Deccan College and the Bhandarkar Research Institute are famed throughout India

*     *     *     *

ACCOM. There are many hotels. Napier Hotel, Poona Hotel and Wellesly Hotel cater in European style. Visitors can also stay at the Fergusson College Hostel. Transport consists of taxis, auto-rickshaws and tongas.

## MAHABALESWAR

75 miles from Poona, reached only by bus, is Mahabaleswar (4,500 ft.), the premier hill-station of the Bombay State. It has a dry and invigorating climate during summer and winter, but very heavy rains during the monsoon. During the monsoon (June-September) everything shuts down and buildings are muffled up in hay to protect walls from collapsing.

The gayest season is from April to May, and then again from October to December when Mahabaleswar becomes a favourite resort for holiday makers. There are beautiful drives and walks, and lovely parks and gardens. As in Matheran there are a number of picnic points such as Bombay Point and Falkland Point. Delightful excursions may be made to the historic Maratha fortresses at Pratapgarh (10 miles), Raigarh (43 m.) and Satara (33 miles).

*     *     *     *

COMM. The State transport runs buses and de-luxe coaches during the March-May season between Poona and Mahabaleswar. Charges are : Rs. 5/6/- per seat by luxury coach and Rs. 3/9/- by ordinary bus. The road to Mahabaleswar passes through Panchgani, a charming all-the-year hill resort with moderate rains.

ACCOM. Western style hotels are : Frederiks and Race View (Octo-June). Among the Indian style hotels Fountains (Rs. 14/-), Granville (Rs. 10/-) and Paradise (Rs. 10/-) are popular. Besides, there is the Mahabaleswar Holiday Camp (October-June) situated in the compound of the Government House which provides excellent accommodation and food. Application for

274

accommodation should be made to the Executive Engineer, Poona.

# AJANTA

The Buddhist rock-hewn monuments at Ajanta, not far from Jalgaon, need no introduction. They are the most outstanding and internationally famous monuments of Indian art which in the opinion of Laurence Binyon have for Asia 'the same outstanding significance that the frescoes of Assisi, Siena and Florence have for Europe'.

"The paintings at Ajanta consist of the considerable remains of series of wall and ceiling ornaments to a group of rock-cut shrines of the Buddhist faith, architecturally remarkable in themselves and cut in a beautiful and remote river gorge in the Deccan. The shrines range in date from about the second century B.C. to the middle of the seventh century A.D. ; the paintings, with the exception of a few dating from the mid-first century B.C., belong almost entirely of the early seventh century A.D., probably around 620 to 640. They include elaborate figure compositions which may contain life-size human forms and, especially on the ceilings a wealth of floral and other conventional decorative motifs. Time, damp, decay, the fires of peasants and the ill-advised use of varnish to preserve them in the last century have contributed to their mutilation, but enough remains to justify Laurence Binyon's estimation of their importance. They are, undoubtedly, major works of art". (Stuart Piggot)

The rock-hewn caves of Ajanta consist mainly of two parts : chaityas or chapels and viharas or monasteries. There are twenty-nine of them, but the principal paintings are in caves 1,2,16,17, and 19. The subjects are taken from Jataka stories, scenes from court and domestic life and the life of the Buddha. It is impossible to describe the exuberance of paintings and sculpture that distinguish these caves, and Havell rightly tells us that

275

very rarely in world's history has there come together such a true symphony of the three arts—painting, sculpture and architecture—as at Ajanta. These paintings, he asserts, constitute India's claim to the respect and gratitude of humanity.

Here in vivid colours a whole age comes to life. "On the hundred walls and pillars of these rock-carved temples, a vast drama moves before our eyes : a drama played by princes and sages and heroes, by men and women of every condition, against a marvellously varied scene, among forests and gardens, in courts and cities, on wide plains, and in deep jungles, while above the messengers of heaven move swiftly across the sky". And despite the long intervals which separates these paintings in time there is a unity of conception and design which is quite remarkable.

**Location** : Aurangabad (in former Hyderabad State) is the base for trips to Ellora and Ajanta (18 and 65 miles respectively). The Railway Hotel, Aurangabad, provides good amenities. There are bus services to all places and cars are also available on hire. Ajanta is only 31 miles from Jalgaon station on Allahabad-Bombay main line of the Central Rly. There are comfortable transport buses plying between Jalgaon and Fardapur (in the Ajanta village) which is only 3 miles from the caves. The State Guest Houses at Fardapur charges Rs. 5/- per head per night—Rs. 1/8/- for breakfast and Rs. 3/8- for lunch or dinner. Advance booking should be made either with the Collector, Aurangabad or Special Officer, Archaeological Dept., Ajanta Caves.

## ELLORA

About 18 miles from Aurangabad, around a crescent shaped hill, are the stupendous cave temples of Ellora—Brahmanical, Buddhist and Jain—containing elaborate carvings of gods and goddesses and remarkable memorials of the three great faiths they represent. There are nearly fifty caves of which only 33 are important.

The most remarkable of these, the Kailasa temple, is not a cave temple. It is a great monolith, 164 ft. in length, 109 ft. in breadth and 96 ft. in height hewn entirely out of solid rock. With its massive pillars and colonades, intricate galleries, painted ceilings, and huge sculptures the Kailasa temple is the supreme creation of Indian sculptors, unique both for the boldness of conception and perfection of execution.

"It is estimated that the task of quarrying its 3,000,000 cubic feet of rock must have occupied at least one hundred years". As one of the earliest European visitors remarks, "it is a wonder to see so great a mass in the air which seems so slenderly underpropped that one could hardly forbear to shudder on first entering it". There is no nobler achievement of Indian architects and sculptors, and no greater marvel of Indian sculpture. This and the superb sculptures of Elephanta, which register the consummation of the same style, are the offerings of the Rastrakutas, who succeeded the Chalukayas in Western Deccan in 753 A.D. The temple itself was constructed by King Krishna I of the Rashtrakuta dynasty in 760 A. D.

## AURANGABAD

Aurangabad, a flourishing trade centre and the base for a trip to the world famous caves of Ajanta of Ellora, is itself a historic city. This was Deogiri, the old capital of the Yadava kings. The visitor should not miss seeing the Bibi-ka-Muqbara—the mausoleum of Aurangzeb's wife—modelled on the Taj Mahal at Agra. The graveyard, the marble screen and the carvings are of the same pattern as at Agra. This is perhaps the finest Moghul building in the Deccan now standing.

The Panchakki or watermill is historically important. The water flows down through clay pipes based on the siphon system from a distance of 7 miles. The mill was formerly used to grind corn for the poor in memory of the famous saint, Baba Shah Mazaffar. The mill is situated in a garden attached to the shrine of the saint who was the spiritual preceptor of Emperor Aurangzeb. Six miles from Aurangabad, near Rabia Daurani's mausoleum, are the caves of Aurangabad cut between the 6th. and the 8th. century and containing exquisite Buddhist sculptures. 16 miles from Aurangabad past Daulatabad and near Ellora, is the Rouza or "the place of tombs" which contains amongst others the simple tomb of Emperor Aurangzeb. The Emperor died at Ahmednagar, but had particularly desired to be buried at Khuldabad, in the courtyard of his patron saint Jainuddin.

30 miles south of Aurangabad, reached by bus, is Piathon, an ancient city visited by the Greek traders from 400 to 200 B.C. Today it is the centre of the ancient industry of gold and silver thread embroidery for which the motifs are derived from the Ajanta frescoes.

**Daulatabad :** Nine miles from Aurangabad on the road to Ellora rises the famous hill-fort of Daulatabad which was for a short time the capital of Mohammad Tughlak, Sultan of Delhi. The citadel—the original Hindu fortress of Deogiri—is a 600-foot-high rock mass and a landmark for miles around. The most remarkable features of the fort are the moat, the scarp and the spiral passage all hewn out of a solid rock. The chief buildings of interest are the Chand Minar, the Chini Palace and the Nizam Shahi Palaces at the foot of the inner fort. The story of the terrible forced transference of the entire population of the Jahapanah city on three day's notice, and the terrible forty day's march southwards and the unforgettable picture of the Sultan standing on the roof of his palace at night and looking out over Delhi 'where there was neither fire nor smoke nor lamp' and saying 'Now my mind is tranquil and my wrath appeased' throws a lurid light on mediaeval tyranny.

COMM. Aurangabad, the centre for excursion to Ajanta. Daulatabad and Ellora is 315 miles from Secunderabad (Hyderabad) by the metre guage of the C. Rly. and 233 miles from Bombay changing at Manmad from broad guage to metre. Visitors from Calcutta and Delhi detrain at the Jalgaon station, on the Itarsi-Bombay section of the C. Rly., whence Fardapur (in the Ajanta village and 3 miles from the caves) is only 31 miles by bus. There is a regular bus service between Jalgaon and Fardapur, and cars and station wagons are also available. The comfortable State Guest House at Fardapur accommodates visitors to Ajanta. After seeing Ajanta the visitors proceed to Aurangabad (65 miles) by bus or car for tripes to Ellora and other places.

ACCOM. The Railway Hotel, Aurangabad, is famous for comfort and cuisine. Besides, there are the Greens Hotel and Dak Bungalows. There are also Government Bungalows at Rouza, near Ellora, but the visitor to Ellora usually returns to Aurangabad for the night.

CONVEYANCE. Comfortable transport buses ply to Ajanta, Ellora and other places from Aurangabad. Taxis, station wagons and tongas are also available. It is advisable to carry torches to the caves.

# BARODA

Baroda, 244 miles from Bombay, is one of the most progressive and beautiful cities of India. It is a lovely city containing many fine gardens, shady avenues, palaces and public buildings. Of the many objects of interest Lakshmivilas Palace, one of the finest and most beautiful in India takes pride of place. Others are the Museum and the beautiful 125-acre public park on the bank of the river ; the University with its famous Oriental Institute ; and the old Nazar Bagh Palace with a fine collection of jewellery and antiques.

\*　　　　\*　　　　\*　　　　\*

ACCOM & COMM. Baroda lies on the Bombay-Delhi main line of the W. Rly. (244 m. from Bombay). Baroda Hotel on Race Course Road caters in European style. There are Retiring Rooms at the station. Krishna Nivas Hotel and Coronation Hotel cater for the middle class. Transport consist of taxis, tongas and buses.

# AHMEDABAD

Ahmedabad, the second largest city of the Bombay State and one of the finest cities in Western India famous for its handsome buildings, lies on the river Sabarmati. The city was built by Ahmad Shah (1411-1441), the Sultan of Gujrat as his capital. Standing as she does in the midst of fertile plains of Gujrat, Ahmedabad, with her looms for the weaving of fine silks and cottons and gold thread, and her easy access to the sea, became the Venice of Western India in the middle ages. Contemporary visitors averred that "no city on earth was so beautiful, so charming and so splendid".

A great centre of textile industry, Ahmedabad is also noted for its splendid mosques, tombs and palaces with which the Sultans of Gujrat adorned their capital. The Jama Masjid with its dome supported on triple tiers of columns, its gateway flanked by two highly carved minarets and its richly decorated interior, is probably the most imposing of the Muhammadan buildings in Western India. This great mosque was build by Sultan Ahmed Shah, the builder of Ahmedabad in 1424 A.D. Its prayer hall contains 256 carved pillars and its courtyard covering 87,096 sq. feet is one of the largest in India.

The palm goes to the exquisite little tomb of Rani Sipri (1474) which has been described as a building "which only a 'Hindu queen could order, and only Hindu artists could carve". The Sidi Sayyidd mosque is noted for its magnificent perforated windows which are regarded as the climax of the stone-cutter's art. Other objects of absorbing interest are the Baoli (well) of Dada Hari ; Rani Rupamati Masjid with its unsurpassable stone carvings ; the Leaning Towers resembling the Leaning Towers of Pisa ; and the old palace at Sarkhej built by Mahmud Bighara on a huge tank, five miles outside the town. Kankaria Lake is a popular picnic spot. The adjoining Hill Garden which has a small aquarium, zoo and aviary is a show-place which attracts many visitors.

On the banks of the Sabarmati is the famous Ashram of Mahatma Gandhi. It was from here that he started the historic Dandi March in 1930.

*  *  *  *

COMM. 306 miles from Bombay and 539 miles from Delhi, Ahmedabad lies on the broad gauge of the W. Rly. A metre gauge line of the same railway connects Ahmedabad with Delhi via Ajmer. It is also linked by air with the principal towns.

ACCOM. Western style hotels are : Ritz, Barnett's and Royal. Among the cheaper hotels are : Grand Hotel, (near Lal Darwaja), Bombay Hotel (near Ellis Bridge), and Anand Niwas (near Krishna Cinema). Conveyance consists of taxis auto-rickshaws and tongas. There is a city bus service.

## BHAVNAGAR

Bhavnagar, 167 miles from Ahmedabad, is an important port on the Gulf of Cambay and a busy trade centre for export of cotton.

Bhavnagar is an industrial city; it has many modern buildings, factories, hospitals and educational institutions. The Samaldas College, Sir Prabhashankar Pattani Science College, the Bhavsingh Polytechnical Institute and the M.J. College of Commerce are some of the notable institutions. A Salt Research institute, one of the several national laboratories recently established in India, is also located here. A number of textile mills, vegetable oil, salt, match, pottery factories have also grown up in recent years. The tourist would do well to visit the Gaurishankar Lake, the Victoria Park, the marble temples of Takhtshwar and Gangaji and the Roopvani temples. The ancient University town of Valabhi (modern Vala) is about 20 miles from Bhavanagar by bus.

*  *  *  *

COM. & ACCOM. Bhavanagar is easily reached by air from Bombay. By rail it is 167 miles from Ahmedabad via Viramgam.

There is a State Guest House (Rs. 12/8/-daily) and a number of middle class hotels. Buses go to many places of interest including Vala (20 miles) and Palitana (32 miles).

# PALITANA

Palitana, 18 miles by rail from Sihor and 32 miles by bus from Bhavanagar, is famed for its Jain temples which adorn the top of the Satrunjaya hill rising above the town. Perched on the foot of the sacred Satrunjaya hills (1977 ft. above sea level), Palitana is the most sacred of the five holy hills of the Jains. It has been described as the "first of all places of pilgrims, the bridal hall of those who would win everlasting peace."

For centuries temples were built on this ancient site by the devout Jains who believed in the efficacy of temple-building as a means of spiritual salvation, thus making it a city of temples. There are now as many as 863 temples dedicated to various Jain Tirthankars, the earliest among them being that of Adinath dating back to 960 A.D. A great many of the present temples are modern as the earlier ones were destroyed in the wake of Muslim iconoclastic zeal which swept the country during the 14th and 15th century. Among the more important and famous temples on the sacred hills are those of Adinath, Kumar Pal, Vimal Shah, Sampati Raja, and Chaumukh (four faced). They are all remarkable in detail and exquisite in finish, but lacking in conception and sculptured figures.

The holy spot at the top of the hill is not inhabited by man—only the gods dwell there. "No mortals not even the priests are allowed to sleep within the walls, and no food must be cooked on this holy ground. Before nightfall, both priests and pilgrims must leave the gods to their meditation, and watchmen are placed at the gateways to prevent intruders disturbing them." Other places of interest to the visitors are the Maharaja's Hava Mahal, Temple of Bhavanath, and monuments of warriors.

COMM. The railway journey from Ahmedabad through the desert-like peninsula of Kathiawar to Palitana is a long and hot one. It is, therefore, advisable to take a plane at Bombay for Bhavanagar which is the best base for a pilgrimage to Palitana. Since the holy city does not have any hotel it is best to arrive in the morning from Bhavanagar by rail or bus for the climb to Satrunjaya Hill and return to Bhavanagar in the afternoon. There is a P W.D. Rest House at Palitana where all types of food are provided. Advance booking may be made with the Engineer, P.W.D. Palitana. There are many Dharamsalas for the Jains.

Tongas are available at the Palitana station for the journey to the base of the Satrunjaya Hill (2 miles). The climb up to the top (2000 ft.) is quite arduous although there are well dressed steps all the way up. The ascent takes nearly two hours ; dolis are available.

# JUNAGARH

Situated near the base of the famous Girnar Hills is Junagarh, one of the most ancient cities of India. Junagarh is accessible by air from Bombay, Porbandar, Jamnagar and Bhuj, and by rail from Rajkot which is only 66 miles. Junagarh is the natural base for trips to the well-known Gir Forest, the only remaining haunts of the Indian lion, and to the historic temple of Somnath.

The sacred Mount Girnar (3,500 ft.), east of the city, consists of five peaks, rising one above the other. It is crowned by many temples among which are a large number of Jain temples and Hindu temple of Ma Ambaji. There one can also see the hallowed footprints of Gorakhnath and Guru Dattatraya. The Jain temples on the Girnar hills are noted for their ornate beauty and architecture. The site is known for its anceint past and the famous inscription of Asoka with its famous edicts dating as far back as 250 B.C. Junagarh is also associated with the life of the well-known Vaishnava poet Narsinh Mehta.

Other places of interest in Junagarh are Silekhana, and Darbar Hall, containing the royal regalia and weapons of its former rulers, the Willingdon Dam, Saker-bagh, and the Khapra Khodia and the Bawa Piara caves.

There are a State guest house and a Dak bungalow which provide accommodation to visitors and tourists.

**The Gir Forests :** The Gir Forest is a veritable paradise for game hunters ; for in its dense growth, one may get a very close view of the beautiful Girnar lion, the only one to be found anywhere in Asia. Big game like *nil gai* (blue bull), spotted dear, panther, wild boar, antelope and gazelles, and the like are plentiful here. The forests abound in smaller game too such as jungle cats, monkeys, porcupines, hyaenas, jackals and foxes, pigeons, partridges, quails, etc., which are too nume-rous to mention in detail.

No shooting is allowed in the forest during the monsoon (June to September). The best time to visit it is during the months of March, April and May. The way to Gir Forest is from Junagarh from where a train goes up to Sasangir via Veraval. There is also a motor road leading to Sasan from Junagarh. The guest house in the heart of the forest accommodates parties. Intend-ing visitors should obtain prior permission from the Chief Conservator of Forests, Junagarh, who also arranges other facilities for shooting and sight-seeing.

## PORBANDAR

Porbandar, the only centre of commerce and indus-try in Sorath is 191 miles from Bhavnagar, and 131 miles from Rajkot ; it is a beautiful seaside resort on the west coasts of Saurashtra. It can be reached by plane from Bombay from where the journey is only of two hours. From Jamnagar, it takes only half an hour to reach Porbandar by air. Porbandar is also known as Sudamapuri, named after Krishna's great friend Sudama of legendary fame.

This old city of hoary memory which has main-tained old contacts with Basra, the Gulf of Persia, Arabia and the African coast, has a beautiful beach with fine villas along the coast. Its salubrious climate in summer soothes the jaded nerves of overworked men and women who resort to them for a restful holiday. Porbandar has acquired great importance on account of its being the birth-place of Mahatma Gandhi, the Father of the Nation. In Kirti Mandir, an imposing building erected to commemorate his memory, one can see the room where Gandhiji was born.

The training college situated in a palatial on the coast facing the turbid ebb and flow of the waters of the Arabian Sea and "its melancholy, long, withdrawing roars." Arya Kanya Gurukul is situated on the coast of the farther tip of the city where girls are trained according to the ancient ideas of Aryan culture.

## SOMNATH (Veraval)

A sea-port on the south coast of the peninsula, Veraval is only 51 miles from Junagarh by rail. According to Hindu mythology, it was here at Bhalaka Tirtha that Shri Krishna, the hero of the Bhagavad Gita, breathed his last; a small temple with a reclining statue commemorates his death. The Triveni Sangam, (Dehotsarga) is the confluence of the three rivers—Kapila, Saraswati and Hiranya—where he was cremated; and Pranchi Pipla is famous for Shradh ceremony. The presence of some Buddhist caves nearby (at Una, about 59 miles from Veraval) testify to the belief that the town was known during the Buddhist period. The celebrated town of Somnath, known by several names—Deo Pattan, Prabhas Pattan or Pattan Somnath—which it acquired during its long and chequered history, is only three miles to the south-east of Veraval. The history of the temple of Somnath is a house-hold story.

The original temple of Somnath, according to legend, was built by Siva, as the Lord of the Moon or Moon-God, himself. Somnath's glory and fame is legendary. It has one of the twelve pre-eminent Jyotirlingas which has a special sanctity for all Hindus. A huge amount of money collected from 10,000 villages was spent on its maintenance, 2,000 Brahmans served the temple ; and people from all parts of the country come to worship there.

The famous Somnath temple is believed to have been built by the Vallabhi kings between the fifth and eighth century. It was destroyed by Mahmud Ghazni in 1025 A.D. which is an important event in Indian history. The present temple is a small but impressive underground structure.

A large new temple is being eracted on the site where the original building once stood. On May 11, 1951, Dr. Rajendra Prasad, the President of the Republic of India, installed the Jyotirlingam, in the presence of a large gathering.

Veraval also provides a fine beach. Visitors can stay in the Dak Bungalow with the prior permission of the Collector, Veraval.

## RAJKOT

Rajkot, the principal city of Saurashtra, is like a provincial capital with spacious houses, gardens and Government houses. It is known throughout India because of its association with the early life of Mahatma Gandhi.

Objects of interest include : the Gandhi Museum and the Hall situated in the Jubilee Gardens, Rajkumar College which produced the great cricketer Ranjit Singhji (Ranji), Dharvindra Singh College and Vallabh Kanya Vidyalaya.

There are the Sardar Bagh Guest House and the State Guest house at Rajkot. Permission for use of which can be obtained from the Collector, Rajkot. Transport consists of taxis, tongas and public buses. Rajkot is a natural base for trips to the places of interest in Saurashtra.

# JAMNAGAR

Jamnagar (former Nawanagar) is one of the most modern towns of India famous for its silk and golden embroidery; it is also known as the jewel of Kathiawar. It has several Jain temples; the Ranjit Sagar Lake is situated only six miles from the city. It has a radium institute, an Aeronautical School and a solarium, the only of its kind in the East. At important Hindu festivals, particularly during Navratri, the tourist will be regaled by the garba dancing of the village folk. There is a guest house which caters for visitors.

# DWARKA

Situated on the extreme north-west tip of the peninsula, Dwarka is 85 miles from Jamnagar, 135 miles from Rajkot and 248 miles from Viramgam by train. Dwarka is one of the seven most important holy places of the Hindus. It is associated with Shri Krishna, who spent the later part of his life here. The two temples of Gomati Dwarka and Beth Dwarka are remarkable for their architecture and a attract pilgrims from all parts of India in large numbers every year. Dwarka has also been one of the four regional seats of the Jagatguru Sri Sankaracharya. There are three Dwarkas : (i) Gomati Dwarka, (ii) Beth Dwaraka (iii) the original Dwaraka of Lord Krishna now under the sea. This invisible Dwaraka is said to have been Krishna's original capital. Beth Dwaraka, situated on a small island in the Ocean, is reached by sailing boats from Gomati Dwaraka. The inhabitants are colourful and the town shows an unusual Dalmatian-like architecture.

There are P.W.D. rest houses for visitors.

# BIJAPUR

The city of Bijapur which was for two hundred years the capital of the powerful Adil Shahi dynasty (1484-1656) stands on a barren plateau, 345 miles south-east of Bombay midway between Bhima and Krishna rivers.

The Adil Shahi Sultans had a great passion for architectural construction and they adorned their capital with many striking buildings which are characterised by a distinct form known as the Bijapur style. Of the multitude of buildings of which the great city once boasted, the most renowned is the Gol Gumbaz, the mausoleum of the last great sultan Muhammad Adil Shah (1626-1656). Its gigantic dome, the second largest in the world, dominates the city. Its internal height is 178 feet and it covers an area of 18,337 square feet—an area larger than the Roman Pantheon. Like St. Paul's Cathedral and similar domed structures, it has a whispering gallery. The slightest sound is heard from one side to the other, the ticking of a watch being distinctly audible while a single clap is echoed over ten times. The austere dignity of the Gol Gambuz with its plain massive walls, and its four corner-turrets, is in striking contrast to the Ibrahim Rauza, the tomb of his father, Ibrahim II. The Rauza stands in what was once a garden, with its richly decorated walls and its perforated stone widows, filled with Koranic texts. The Jama Masjid is one of the finest mosques in India, remarkable for its perfect proportions, the beauty of the graceful minarets, the construction of its bulbous domes and the execution of ornamental details. There are many more Rouzas and Mahals scattered in all directions within the walled city and many of the buildings were decorated with mural paintings, which have been sadly mutilated by that fanatical iconoclast, the Emperor Aurangzeb. But, inspite of the ravages of time and men, Bijapur even today presents a splendid sight.

Among the scholars who flourished at Bijapur, the most famous was the historian Muhammad Kasim Firishta. His *History of the Muhammadan Power in India* is a classic of its kind, scrupulously fair and accurate and free from courtly subservience of other writers. It is the chief authority for the period up to the year 1612.

COMM. Bijapur (on the Hotgi-Gadag metre gauge section of the Southern Railway) is reached from Bombay changing broad gauge for the metre at Hotgi station, 292 miles from Bombay, on the Bombay-Madras main line of the C. Railway. From Hotgi Bijapur is 53 miles south on the metre gauge of S. Rly.

ACCOM. Travellers's Bungalow (1 mile from the station) caters for visitors. There are Railway Refreshment Rooms at the station. There is a Dharamsala (1½ m. from station) and a middle class hotels known as Arogya Nivas.

# BADAMI

73 miles due south of Bijapur, on the Sholapur-Gadag section of the S. Rly., is Badami well-known for its cave temples belonging to the 6th. and the 7th. centuries. It is a picturesque spot nestling in the lap of red sandstone hills with a pretty lake, surrounded by jungle ; its caves and temples bear testimony to its former eminence. Some of the temples are Brahmanical while others are Jain. Vatapi, the modern Badami, was the first capital of the Chalukya kings of whom the greatest monarch Pulikesi II (608-642) repulsed an attack of Emperor Harsha in a remarkable feat of arms. About 6 m. from Badami is the village Pareshgad with its famous temple of Sri Banasankari. In the Durga temple at Aiholi, some 12 miles from Katgeri railway station, can be seen some of the most beautiful carvings.

*      *      *      *

ACCOM. The town is about 3 miles from the station. There is a Rest House near the station and a P.W.D. Dak Bungalow near the town. The Station Master of Badami arranges for conveyance on previous intimation.

# CHAPTER VI

# SOUTHERN INDIA

\* \* \* \* \* \* \* \* \* \* \* \* \* \* \* \* \* \* \* \* \* \* \* \* \* \* \* \*

*Occupying what is geologically the oldest landmass of the Indian sub-continent, Southern or Peninsular India is a land of variegated natural beauty, great rivers, waterways, peaceful lagoons, and a cocoanut palm-fringed shore, and has a cultural tradition going back to pre-historic times. Seat of the ancient Dravidian civilisation and Dravidian still in speech, this is the most ancient part of India, and early developed a culture essentially its own to which it largely adheres even today. Broadly speaking, the great uplands of the Deccan and the country stretching down to Cape Comorin developed their own lines of culture, uninterrupted and uninfluenced by the turmoils of the North.*

*Rich in historical and archaeological remains and possessing the most magnificent temples of India, Southern India is the land where visitors can still have a glimpse of India's traditional way of life.*

\* \* \* \* \* \* \* \* \* \* \* \* \* \* \* \* \* \* \* \* \* \* \* \* \* \* \* \*

## HYDERABAD

Hyderabad, the capital of Andhra Pradesh, is one of the most important cities in India. The population of the State is predominantly Hindu, but the Nizam who till recently governed the former state of Hyderabad is a Muslim. The present Nizam is the seventh of his line and a lineal descendant of the first Nizam Asaf Jah, a most distinguished general of Emperor Aurangzeb, who founded the house in 1725. The Nizam is one of the richest men in the world. The value of his jewels is anybody's guess, but legend insists that he possesses in his palace more than the wealth of the mines of Golconda. But the present Nizam is averse to any form of ostentation and leads a life of excessive frugality. An English observer has remarked that he "does not entertain if he can possibly avoid it. His Guest Houses are often empty, his magnificent tigers left to their own devices".

## Places of Interest

The outstanding monument of the city is the 16th century Char Minar, a stately gateway with four minarets in the heart of the city, under which the principal street runs. The Nizam's magnificent palace lies to the south of Char Minar. Other buildings are : the Osmania University ; the High Court ; the State Library ; the great Mecca Masjid ; the Zoo ; the far-famed Salar Jung Museum (Friday closed) ; and the public gardens. Some six miles distant is **Secunderabad.** The road from Hyderabad crosses a picturesque bridge across the beautiful Hussainsagar Lake which separates the two cities. Secunderabad is one of the largest military cantonments in India. It is a fine, modern city well supplied with hotels which makes it a suitable base for sight-seeing in Hyderabad city and its environs. Rastrapati Nilayam, the Southern headquarters of the President of India, is situated at Bolorum in Secunderabad.

Five miles to the west of Hyderabad lies the historic fort of Golconda, picturesquely perched on a low hill. Founded in 1518 A. D., it was the capital of the Kutab Shahi dynasty and an extensive market for Turkish, Persian and Arab traders. The nearby tombs of the Kutb Shahi kings are of considerable archaeological interest. 14 miles from Hyderabad city is the beautiful

Osmansagar Lake formed by a dam built across the river Musi. On its shores are charming gardens and walks which are favourite spots of holiday makers at weekends. Three miles beyond it is another beauty spot— the Himayat Sagar lake. 36 miles to the east of Secunderabad, on a precipitous hill, stands Bhongir Fort, one of the earliest in the Deccan, whilst some 82 miles from Hyderabad is the pleasant little hilltown of Bidar with the ruins of the beautiful buildings of the Bahamani time and the tombs of Bahamani kings.

**Hanam Konda :** 90 miles east of Hyderabad is Kazipet, an important railway junction, around which can be seen a number of ancient Dravidian temples with pyramidical *Shikaras*. The most famous of them is the Hindu temple at Hanam Konda, situated on the main road to Warangal. According to an inscription it was built in 1162 A.D. by Pratap Rudra Deva, the last reigning sovereign of Telingana. Altogether the temple has one thousand pillars. Architecturally, it is perhaps the finest specimen of Chalukyan art in the Deccan.

Further up is Warangal which was the old capital of the Andhras. Marco Polo visited the court of the Rani and left a glowing account of the prosperity of her realm. In the fortress there are four magnificent gateways, the main interest of which to quote Fergusson "lies in their being the lineal descendants of Sanchi".

\*       \*       \*       \*

COMM. 548 miles from Bombay and 350 miles from Nagpur, Hyderabad is reached by through trains of broad gauge line of the C. Rly. from both places. Visitors arriving from Delhi by the Grand Trunk Express have to change train at Kazipet while those coming from Calcutta by the Madras mail reach Hyderabad changing at Bezwada. Secundrabad is the popular and convenient railway station for Hyderabad.

ACCOM. There are a number of good hotels at Secunderabad and Hyderabad to suit all pockets. Hilfort Palace (Rs. 25/-) and Ritz Hotel (Rs. 21/-) at Hyderabad, and Percy's Hotel at Secunderabad cater in European style. Conveyance consists of taxis, tongas and rickshaws. Buses ply to all places.

# MADRAS

Madras, the third largest city in India and the chief port of the Eastern Coast, is the gateway to the South and the land of magnificient and awe-inspiring temples. Though the site of the earliest important British settlement in India it is perhaps least affected by foreign influence and maintains its ancient character. It was in 1639 that the Raja of Chandragiri, a descendant of the Rayas of Vijaynagar, gave Francis Day the site of the city of Madras; and Fort St. George, built in the following year, soon became the chief centre of activity of the East India Company.

Within the Fort is St. Mary's Church, the oldest Protestant place of worship in India (1678). Here Lord Clive was married; here was buried Lord Piggot who defended the Fort against Lally; here, too, lies the mortal remains of Governor Nicholas Morase, a great grandson of Cromwell. From the harbour and business quarters around the Fort in the north, to the garden suburb of Adyar in the south, the city of Madras covers an area of fifty square miles containing a large number of parks, tree-shaded avenues, garden houses and old buildings which lend to the city an atmosphere of old-world charm and spaciousness.

## Places of Interest

Madras is justly proud of the Marina which is reputed to be the second best beach in the world, of the long drive that runs parallel to it for miles, and glories in the fact that it is unspoilt by big hotels, restaurants and shops. At the southern end of the Marina is the Roman Catholic Cathedral of San Thome, founded by the Portuguese in 1504 around the site of the ancient church founded by St. Thomas, the Apostle who is believed to have come to India after the martyrdom of Jesus Christ and settled at Mylapore. He, too, is said to have been martyred at Madras and his mortal remains lie buried at St. Thomas Mount near the airport at Meenambkkam.

Mylapore is hallowed by the memory of the greatest of Tamil poets and the author of the *Kural*, Tiruvallavar who lived about 100 A.D. The *Kural* is regarded as the "most venerated and popular book south of the Godavari...the literary treasure, the poetic mouth-piece, the highest type of verbal excellence among the Tamil people". Its couplets are still enshrined in the hearts of the common folk.

Other places worth visiting are the strikingly picturesque Mylapore temple with its sculptured dome and the sacred tank, and the ancient Triplicane temple where worship is offered according to ancient customs and rituals; the headquarters of the Theosophical Society at Adyar; the Kalakshetra at Adyar, a school for the revival of classical dancing and music, founded by Srimati Rukmini Debi; the Museum and Art Gallery at Egmore; and the People's Park and Zoo. Also worthly of visit is the Integral Coach Factory at Perambur, a giant Government of India undertaking for production of railway coaches.

The Port of Madras, one of the largest in India, is equipped with the most up-to-date means for handling passenger and freight traffic. The principal exports are groundnut and raw skins. Industrially, Madras is still severely handicapped by the absence of coal, although in every field today there is progress and improvement. Her cotton mills are among the best and most prosperous in India.

"Madras is truly the microcosm of the Presidency. Here may be seen sturdy men and handsome women from Coorg, the gaily decorated gypsies from the Agencies ; the bright, alert, and capable Malayalees; the placid fellow from the Andhra country. Pilgrims from the north and distant Burma, journeying to the great shrines of Rameswaram and Srirangam or going

294

to bathe in the sacred Cauvery, jostle one another in the streets. Madras University attracts students from all parts of India. The bazaars are a feast of colour. Here it is always warm; a disgruntled resident has described the climate as "three months hot and nine months hotter". And yet the people are, on the whole, cheerful. They love a *tamasha* and loose no opportunity of being present at one. Scarcely a night passes without some temple procession with the blaze of lights, the blare of trumpets, the whine of conches, the throbbing of drums, the thunder of rockets, and the shrill note of the flute. All these combine to produce noise, yet not an unpleasing noise if one enters into the spirit of the festival. And such scenes are typical of the city's life". ("The Times" Book of India.)

*    *    *    *

COMM. 1032 m. from Calcutta, 794 m. from Bombay and 1361 m. from Delhi. Madras is reached by through mail trains and planes from almost all the important cities of India.

ACCOM. Hotel Ambassador, Connemera Hotel and Hotel Oceanic View are good European style hotels. Good Indian style hotels are : Hotel Dasaprakash, Woodland (Mylapore), and Modern Cafe.

CONVEYANCE. Taxis and motor rickshaws are popular transport. There is a net-work of efficeint bus service in the city and beyond it to the places of interest. Service buses go to Mahabalipuram and Kanchipuram.

# MAHABALIPURAM

53 miles from Madras by rail (via Chinglipet) and about forty miles by a good motor road along the coast is Mahabalipuram famous for some of the most wonderful architectural remains in South India. Mahabalipuram or Mamallapuram, says Prof. Rawlinson, was named after the Pallava King Narasimhavarman (625-645 A.D.) who enjoyed the title of Mamalla or great Champion on account of his victories over the Chalukyas. He excavated many cave temples, decorated with fine reliefs. Most remarkable of all, however, are the seven monolithic

Rathas or temples known as the Seven Pagodas, each carved from a single granite boulder standing upon the sea-shore, somewhat in the manner of the Kailasa temple of Ellora. These are undoubtedly the supreme example of Pallava sculpture. One of these works, a tableau representing the Goddess Durga subduing the baffalo demon, has been considered to be the most animated piece in the whole range of Hindu sculpture. Another magnificent piece is the open-air bas-relief known as Arjuna's Penance, carved on a slab of rock 96 ft. by 43 ft. and covered with numerous figures of deities, including a whole menagerie of animals. "What we have before us", says Grousset, "is a vast picture, a regular fresco in stone".

Apart from their grace and beauty of workmanship, these buildings form an interesting link between the Buddhist cave temple and the later structural Dravidian temple. These superb monuments laid the first foundations of Dravidian architecture and later played an important role in spreading the model of Indian art and culture across the Ocean to Java and Cambodia.

\* \* \* \*

COMM. Chinglipet, 35 m. south of Madras, is the railway station for Tirukkalukunram, or the Hill of the Seven Kites, and Mahabalipuram. The former is 9 miles from Chinglipet by road and latter is 18 miles. Buses run between Chinglipet and Mahabalipuram via Tirukkalukunram. There is a P.W.D. Inspection Bungalow at Mahabalipuram which may be used by the visiting parties. Advance booking may be made with the Collector of Chinglipet. Tourists are advised to take a picnic lunch from Madras. Mahabalipuram is an excellent place for sea bathing.

# TIRUKKALUKUNRAM

On the way to Mahabalipuram an inevitable halt is Tirukkalukunram which lies midway (9 miles) between Chinglipet and Mahabalipuram and is associated with a mysterious phenomenon. There is a famous Shiva temple in the village, but the chief attraction is the small temple on the top of a 500-ft-high hill reached by a flight of steps. Every day, just before noon, two white kites come to this hill to partake of the food kept in readiness, from the hands of an hereditary priest. Legend has it that the two kites are actually the spirits of two saints and that they have been visiting the hill from time immemorial on their daily journey between Rameswaram and holy Banaras.

A crowd always collects and watches the feeding of the birds with reverent delight. The birds are punctual and arrive an hour before noon. Since ascent at noon is rather arduous, the visitor would be well-advised to climb the hill-top before the sun is high.

## KANCHIPURAM

Kanchipuram, the Golden City of a thousand temples and one of the seven sacred cities of India, lies fiftyseven miles south-west of Madras. The sacred city is regarded as the Banaras of the South, for throughout the ages the city has been a great centre of Hindu learning and worship. Hiuen Tsang, who spent the 'rain rest' of A.D. 640 at Kanchi, tells us that the various sects— Hindus, Jains and Mahayana Buddhists—flourished side by side. The great Hindu philosopher Sankaracharyya, the great Buddhist Bikku Bodhidharma and the great exponent of the Bhakti cult, Ramanuja, who blended in full harmony the highly intellectual 'unqualified monism' of Sankara with the 'qualified monism' of worhipping a Supreme Being of infinitely blessed qualities, lived and taught at Kanchi.

There are a number of temples dedicted to Shiva and Vishnu, prominent among which are those dedicated to Kailasanatha, Ekambarnatha, Kamakshi and Varadaraja. The temples contain beautiful specimens of Pallava art and it is said that the builders of the rock temples at Badami and Ellora derived their inspiration from them. In its heyday Kanchipuram was the capital of the Pallava kings who built the beautiful monuments at

Mahabalipurum. Most of the temples were built by them between the 4th and the 8th centuries. When the Cholas occupied Kanchi in 740 all building activity stopped. The Cholas and the Rayas of Vijaynagar who ruled after them, however, made minor contribution to the artistic wealth of Kanchi.

*       *       *       *

ACCOM. Kanchipuram is 22 miles from Chinglipet and 57 miles from Madras on the Chinglipet-Arkonam section of the Southern Rly. The city is easily seen in a day's trip by bus from Madras. There are a number of small hotels in the city besides the Municipal Travellers' Bungalow (no cook) in which accommodation may be reserved with the Commissioner, Kanchipuram Municipality.

## CHIDAMBARAM : THE DANCING CITY

Chidambaram, famous for the great 9th century temple dedicated to Nataraja or Siva in His aspect as the Cosmic Dancer, lies 151 miles south of Madras city on the Madras-Trichinopoly main line of the S. Rly. This is one of the foremost places of pilgrimage in South India and the rival cults of Siva and Vishnu are worshipped side by side in the temples of Nataraja and Govindaraja. The great Nataraja temple stands on a plain between two rivers covering an area of 32 acres. The *gopurams* of the inner walls contains perfect sculptural representation of the 108 postures illustrative of the Natya Sastra or the Science of Dancing. In the sanctum reposes the great Nataraja or Siva Dancing—an image of uncommon beauty and significance—cast in an alloy of five metals. The numerous mandapas and fine temples are endowments of devotion of the Pallava, Chola, Pandya and Naik rulers. The Arudra Dharsan in December-January, and the Thirumanajanam in June-July are great festivals.

A mile to the south Chidambaram Railway station is the campus of the Annamalai University, one of the leading centres of education in the south.

298

# TANJORE

118 miles from Madras, in the delta of the Cauvery river is Tanjore, the home of Dravidian music and the garden of Southern India. Tanjore was the capital of the great Chola kings under whose patronage it grew in name and fame as a great centre of culture.

The Cholas, who reached the zenith of their power under Rajaraja the Great (985-1018) and his son Rajendra Chola Deva 1 (1018-1035), established a great empire stretching from sea to sea, built a powerful navy, despatched an overseas expedition which conquered Ceylon. The invincible Chola army marched as far as the Gangas, where they inflicted a defeat on Mahipala, the King of Bengal. The Cholas were great temple builders and all their work was on a stupendous scale. The great Brihadeswara temple built during the reign of Rajaraja Chola, is regarded as "the grandest temple in India" and is undoubtedly the best specimen of early Dravidian style. The tower of the temple rises pyramid-like to a height of 190 ft. in thirteen successive storeys and is surmounted by a single block of stone estimated to weigh at least 80 tons. To place this in position by means of an inclined plane starting 4 miles away was a remarkable feat of engineering. There are two gopurams to the temple, the second one giving entrance to the spacious courtyard of the great temple which dominates the flat countryside for miles around. A black granite monolith bull about 13 ft. high and 16 ft. long—the second biggest in the country—guards the portals of the temple.

More graceful, if less imposing, is the Subramanya temple, a much later construction, which has received eloquent appreciation for its superb ornamentation. There are altogether 70 temples in the city and in them there are contributions from the Naiks and the Mahrathas who came after the Cholas.

The palace of Tanjore comprising two blocks—Naik's Court and Mahratha Court—is a vast edifice of masonry (of no architectural merit), containing statues and pictures and a library of some 30,000 manuscripts in Sanskrit, Tamil, Telugu, Marathi and the European languages on a variety of subjects of which 8,000 manuscripts are written on palm leaves.

The Schwartz Chruch, built in 1779 by Raja Sarbhoja as a token of affection and esteem for the Rev. C.V. Schwartz of the Danish Mission, who was his teacher and guardian, contains a very fine group of figures in white marble, by Flaxman, representing the death of the aged missionary, Schwartz.

\*　　　\*　　　\*　　　\*

COMM. Tanjore lies on the Madras-Trichinopoly section of S. Rly., 218 miles south of Madras. Visitors can stay at the Rly. Retiring Room or at the Govt. Inspection Bungalow in charge of the District Collector, Tanjore. Ananda Lodge near railway station and Mangalambika Lodge opposite Clock Tower cater for the middle class.

CONVEYANCE. Taxis and jutkas are popular transport.

## TIRUCHURAPALLI

249 miles from Madras and 35 miles from Tanjore is Tiruchurapalli a flourishing educational and commercial centre on the banks of the Cauvery. The city has been of strategic importance throughout the centuries and was the seat of the Chola kings and later the scene of struggle between the English and the French for supremacy in South India.

The city is built round a rock and the most interesting object is the Great Rock which rises abruptly from the Fort (now dismantled) to a height of 273 feet. On the top is a celebrated Shiva temple built by the Pallava kings in the 11th century. Right on the top of

300

the Rock is a small temple dedicated to Ganesha, from where one can have a panoramic view of the town lying along a meandering river.

**Srirangam** : About 3 miles north of Tiruchurapalli is Srirangam which contains the largest temple in India dedicated to Vishnu. The Temple is unique in design having well preserved ceilings and ornaments of precious stones in one of the pavilions. In the court is the so-called Hall of the Thousand Pillars (there may be half a hundred or a few more). A famous Vaishnava centre, it attracts pilgrims from all parts of South India. The Vaikuntha Ekadasi festival in December attracts a great concourse of pilgrims.

About a mile to the east of this celebrated temple is the famous shrine of Jambukeshwar (Siva). The deity is popularly known as Apulinga or the water-phallus, because the deity in the adytum is always in water. Architecturally far superior to the temple of Srirangam, the Jambukeshwar temple comprises five courtyards, the mandapam representing in carvings early legends relating to the deity.

*    *    *    *

COMM. & ACCOM. 240 miles from Madras, Tiruchurapalli is a big Railway junction. The Railway Retiring Rooms, Roberts Hotel (W.S.) in the Cantonment and the Inspection Bungalow (no cook) in charge of the District Collector accommodate visitors. Ashoka Bhavan, Modern Hindu Hotel and the New Modern Hotel cater for the middle class. Transport consists of taxis and jutkas. Buses ply to all places of interest.

# MADURA

Madura, the 'City of Festivals' and the second largest city in Madras State, has been aptly described by European scholars as the "Athens of South India"; from times immemorial it has been the abode of South Indian culture, religion and trade. Ramayana speaks of it as being adorned with gold and jewels. The fabulous profits made by overseas trade in spices, silks and precious

301

stones contributed to the prosperity. The vast number of Roman coins found at Madura point to the fact that there was another Roman colony at the ancient Pandiyan capital. This is confirmed by the celebrated Roman writer, Pliny, who was alarmed at the drain of Roman wealth to India for purchase of Oriental luxuries. Strabo tells us that in 25 B. C., on the accession of Emperor Augustus, a Pandiyan king of Madura sent an embasay to congratulate him. Madura had been the capital of the Pandyan rulers who ruled from the era before the Christ to the 16th century when the Vijaynagar dynasty extended its sway over the far south.

Madura had been an important centre of architecture before the fall of Vijaynagar (1565), and on the fall of Vijaynagar it became the principal seat of Hindu architecture mainly due to the efforts of the Nayaka rulers of the 16th and the 17th centuries of whom Tirumala Nayaka proved to be the greatest builder.

Tamil architecture reached its climax in the 17th century temples of Rameswaram and Madura, and the famous Meenakshi temple of Madura contains some of the most exquisite pieces of temple sculpture and architecture. The great hall with its pillared hippogryphs and other mythological monsters "in which the sculptor's imagination has run riot" is a remarkable structure.

The palace of Tirumala Nayak records a landmark in the development of Indian architecture. "It makes a great example where Hindu architecture in a masterly way had assimilated the principles of Saracenic and Gothic architecture". The great hall in the palace is 140 ft. long, 70 ft. wide and 70 ft. high and contains a carved dome which is an architectural feat.

There is the famous Teppakulam (tank) with a picturesque island temple, about 3 miles from Madura station. About 11 miles from Madura and reached by road is Alagar Koil, ideally situated at the base of the Alagar Hills, which contains a well-known Vaishnavite shine with exquisite sculptures. Four miles south of Madura is Tiruparankundram, at the foot of "Skandamalai". There is a cave t e m p l e dedicated to Subramanya. Madura's handloom textiles and silks are famed throughout India.

\*      \*      \*      \*

COMM. Madurai, in the heart of Tamiland, is 249 m. and 99 m. from Madras and Tiruchurapalli respectively. Visitors can stay at the Rly. Retiring Rooms or in the Circuit House (cook attached) with permission from the Collector of Madurai. Udipi Boarding Lodge at West Tower Street and Mani's Cafe on the Town Hall Road caters for the middle class.

CONVEYANCE consists of Taxis, motor-rickshaws and jutkas. There is a city bus service and transport buses ply to all places of interest.

## RAMESWARAM

On an island in Palk Straits, 414 miles from Madras, stands the most venerated temple of Rameswaram amidst idyllic surroundings lapped by the Indian Ocean.

The place is so holy that every particle of sand on the island is regarded as part of the Sivalinga, and to millions of devout Hindus the fondest dream is to visit Rameswaram after a visit to holy Banaras. Legend has it that Shri Rama here offered worship to Lord Siva to expiate his sin in having killed Ravana in the fight to rescue Sita.

The great temple of Ramaswaram built by a prince of Ceylon over a period of 350 years is the finest example of Dravidian architecture. Its glory lies in its vast pillared corridors, each 700 ft. long and carved out of solid granite, covering a total length of 4,000 ft. For sheer beauty and sculptural magnificence it stands unsurpassed in India. The lingam is said to have been installed by Shri Ramchandra himself. The temple stands near a lake with a circumference of about 3 miles.

23 miles further ahead by rail is Dhanuskodi, the southernmost terminus of the S. Rly., connected by ferry service with Ceylon. Pilgrims from all over India visit Dhanuskodi for bathing in the sea. The rail journey from Pamban to Dhanuskodi running along a narrow promontory separating the Bay of Bengal and the Arabian Sea is one of the finest imaginable.

\*          \*          \*

COMM. A branch line from Pamban, on the Dhanuskodi route, runs to Rameswaram (8 miles). From Paban Dhanuskodi is 16 miles. There are a number of comfortable Dharamsalas and a number of middle class hotels. There are Rly. Retiring Rooms at Pamban and Dhanuskodi.

# KODAIKANAL

Kodaikanal, one of the healthiest hill stations of South India, lies on the southern crest of the upper Palni Hills admidst scenic grandeur at an elevation of 7000 feet. It is easily reached by a short motor journey from the Kodaikanal Road Station, on the Tiruchurapalli-Madura section of the S. Rly.

Apart from its fame as a haven of ease and comfort to recoupe and rejuvenate, free from the heat of the plains, Kodaikanal offers all the amenities of a modern hill station. There is sight-seeing a plenty, then there are excellent opportunities for hiking, golfing, tennis, boating, fishing, picknicking and shooting. The star attraction of Kodai, however, is its pretty lake with a boat club offering boating and angling facilities. Beautiful bridal paths around the Lake present many vantage points for viewing delightful scenery. Other beauty spots are the Fairy Falls, the Silver Cascades, the Bear Shola Falls, the Glen Falls, the Pillar Rocks, the famous Observatory on the Palni Hills, Pig Falls and Ampthill Downs.

April to June is the best season when the average temperature is 64° maxi. and 51° mini. The station has a mean annual rainfall of about 65 inches, a major por-

tion falling in the month of October, November and
December.

*      *      *

COMM. An overnight train journey from Madras brings
one to Kodaikanal Road station (320 miles) whence an excellent
road winds its way up to Kodaikanal, 5 miles away. There is a
regular bus service, and the 2½ to 3 hours' journey is bound to
prove most enjoyable.

ACCOM. Carlton Hotel (Rs. 15/-) and Holiday Home
(Rs. 18/-) are good European style hotels. Modern Cafe and
Tourist Home cater in Indian style.

# TRAVANCORE-COCHIN (KERALA)

The most beautiful and most fertile region in all
southern India, Travancore-Cochin has a whole world
of charm to offer visitors. It has scenery ranging from a
countryside of lakes and canals, to undulating down land
with low hills and shallow valleys, entirely covered with
forests of coconut and areca palms, with a heavy under-
growth of pepper vines and rice fields. The dominant
note in this beautiful land, in the beautiful setting of the
Tropics, is one of luxuriant vegetation and picturesque waterways. And as the boat carries the traveller
along the rivers and lagoons of this slumberous and enchanted land, he may well ask the question, "why should
life all labour be?"

It has also a wonderful highland zone—the region
of Periyar with mountains ranging of from 5,000 feet to
over 8,000 feet, and through the boulder-strewn valleys
of which dash foaming torrents. The hills are covered
with the dense virgin forest, the home of great herds of
wild elephants, bison, tiger, bear, black panther and
wild boar, and where lies the lovely Periyar Lake with
fairy-like islands, behind which the ranges of high hills
form a magnificent background. Here one may cruise in
a delightful setting, and have an opportunity of seeing
the wild animals of the Game Sanctuary coming down to
the lake to quench their thirst.

305

Kerala has an area of 14,937 square miles, mostly covered with forest, and a population of over nine million which works out to something like 1,000 persons to the square mile. This is enormous compared with the rest of India. Enormous again is her figure of literacy : in Kerala about half the males and a forty-sixth of the females are literate. There is a school for every two square miles and there is a good deal of co-education in the colleges where the girl students share in all the men's activities except football.

**Trivandrum** : Situated on a low hill, some two miles from the sea, Trivandrum, the beautiful capital city, has some fine, well-illuminated avenues and public buildings of artistic pattern. It is also a great religious centre, attracting pilgrims from all over India ; its temples which are monuments of art are open to all Hindus, without any distinction of caste. Chief among the objects of interest are the Picture Gallery which is housed with the State Museum in the Public Gardens ; the Palace Picture Gallery within the Fort ; the Kaudiyar Palace (the residence of the Maharaja) ; and the Observatory. The Zoo and the Aquarium, said to be the best in the East, contain attractive specimens rarely found in any other parts of India.

Trivandrum, also known as 'Anantasayanam', is a celebrated place of pilgrimage. The temple of Shri Ananta Padmanabha in which adorns the family deity of the Maharajas of Travancore, is a much venerated shrine maintained in its pristine purity.

### Excursions

Ten miles south of Trivandrum is Kovalam, a pleasant seaside resort, with good facilities for bathing. 33 miles south of Trivandrum, on the way to Cape Comorin, is Padmanavapuram which was the capital of Travancore till 1338 A.D. Here stands the ancient palace of the Maharaja, a monument of architectural beauty, famous for mural paintings eloquently illustrative of the art and culture of the Malabar coast. Two miles above Padman-

306

avapuram is the ancient fort of Udaigiri which contains
the tombs of De Lannoy, a Flemish officer, who served
the ruler of Travancore with conspicuous success in the
eighteenth century and consolidated what was till recently
known as Travancore.

**Kanya Kumari** : 51 miles from Trivandrum and
19 miles south of Padmanavapuram and reached by a
fine, coconut-lined avenue is Kanya Kumari, the Land's
End of India—southernmost apex of the triangular sub-
continent—a veritable beauty spot. To see the sunrise
and sunset at Kanya Kumari and to bathe in its waters
is a most thrilling experience. This is a sacred spot to
the Hindus, being the reputed abode of Kanniymambal,
the 'Virgin Goddess' to whom the exquisite temple is
dedicated.

The journey is made by car or bus (service) halting
at Udaigiri and Padmanavanuram on the way. The Cape
Hotel caters in European style (Rs 12/-). Visitors can
also stay at the Sea View Hotel or at the Government
Satrams. Buses ply to Tinnevely, Palgam Kottah and
to the neighbouring places of interest.

\* \* \*

COMM. 779 miles from Madras by the metre gauge line of
S. Rly., Trivandrum is the south western-most terminus of the
Railway. Trivandrum is connected with Cochin by steamer, road
and air.

ACCOM. Mascot Hotel (Rs. 17/8/- daily) caters in European
style. Among the Indian style hotels, Hotel Aristo and Palm-
lands are popular. There is a Government Rest House and a
Satram.

CONVEYANCE consists of horse carriages, taxis and buses.
There is a bus service in the city and beyond it to the neighbouring places of interest.

# QUILON

40 miles north of Trivandrum, reached by rail or
road, is the ancient town of Quilon where 2,000 years
ago the Phoenicians, the Grecians and the Romans did

enormous trade. Quilon today is an important industrial centre and port ; some of the factories are worth visiting. There is a Government Rest House and a number of middle class hotels.

## ALLEPPEY

About 50 miles from Quilon, reached by bus or boat along the delightful backwaters of the Malabar Coast, is the busy seaport of Alleppey, which, for its network of canals that intersects the town, has won for it the proud term of "the Venice of the East". One can stay at the Government Rest House by the beach and see the Alleppey Port and Lighthouse. Between Quilon and Alleppey the famous bridge at Meendakara is seen.

## COCHIN AND ERNAKULAM

45 miles north of Alleppey by bus or launch is Cochin and adjoining it is Ernakulam situated in the backwaters of Cochin Harbour. Between the two ancient towns is a beautiful lake opening to the sea, and over it is a bridge connecting Cochin and Ernakulam with both rail and road over it.

The historic port of Cochin, next to Bombay on the western coast of India, is known as the Queen of the Abrabin Sea for her pretty location and landscape of memorable beauty. On one side of the delicious island-flecked lagoon, surrounded by palms, there is the strange town of Ernakulam with its streets of the Black Jews and on the other side of the water is Cochin, pleasantly medi-aeval, with its quarters of the White Jews. The traveller can never forget the charming backwater scenery of the two towns, the beautiful Cochin Harbour, the Bolghatty Island on the north of the Lake and bridge on the south, all wearing a mystic robe in the night's illumination.

**The People**

"In Cochin it seems that everyone lives on the

water. Boats take the place of houses. On the hundreds of backwaters leading to the magnificent harbour, house-boats cluster, close as the buildings in a village street. Apart from the woodcutters, carpenters and other forest workers, Cochin is given up to fishermen. Fishing supports something like 30,000 people in the lovely land of Cochin. There are no rules...except to catch as many fish as possible, whatever their size and shape".

One of the earliest European settlements in India, Cochin has many vestiges of the past. Of the many foreign communities who have made the land their home for centuries, the White Jews and the Black Jews of Cochin arrived here in the reign of the Solomon and since then the two communities have lived apart.

## Places of Interest

The Mattancherry Palace, the Synagogue in Cochin, the Santa Cruz Church and the St. Francis Church in Fort Cochin are worth visiting. In the latter is the tomb of Vasco-de-Gama. The High Court and other public buildings at Ernakulam are also worth visiting. A few miles to the east of Ernakulam is Trippunithura and a few miles beyond it is the Hill Palace, the residence of the Maharaja of Cochin.

\*       \*       \*

COMM. Cochin-Ernakulam is reached from Trivandrum by rail or road up-to Quilon and from there by bus or launch via Alleppey. One can go direct by bus or rail from Kottayam also From the rest of the country Cochin is reached by the broad gauge line of S. Rly. of which it is the terminus. It is also reached by sea and air.

ACCOM. Sea View Hotel, Hotel Terminus and Hote Atlantis are among the good hotels of Ernakulam. There are also a Government Travellers' Bungalow and a Municipal Satram. At Cochin Harbour (Willingdon Island), the Malabar Hotel (Rs. 15/-) caters in European style. Comfortable rickshaws are the popular mode of conveyance. Taxis are also available.

# PERIYAR LAKE AND WILD LIFE SANCTUARY

From Trivandrum, or from Cochin, to Thekaday (the road terminus for Periyar Lake and Wild Life Sanctuary) through the hills of Travancore is a long but fascinating journey through fathomless depths of palms and dense forest inhabited by a strange variety of men and cattle and with the lower slopes carpeted with tea. Periyar, the "Kingdom of Elephants", offers the most exciting holiday of one's imgination amongst the variegated tropical flora and fauna. Here in the bosom of the hills, cruising safely on the waters of the Periyar Lake on a fast moving motor boat, the visitor can see at close range the majestic Indian elephant—wild herds of 15 to 20 disporting themselves on the hill-side of the lake, or the lone tusker in splendid isolation ; he will also see bison, wild boar and sambhar and, at a lucky chance, even a tiger or a leopard coming down to quench their thirst in the waters of the Lake, or moving away into the heart of their dense, dark forest home.

The lake is about 3000 ft. above sea-level and skirts the Game Sanctuary which is bounded on three sides by precipitous cliffs. Apart from the thrill which the visitor may feel on seeing wild life in its natural home, the scenery all around is magnificent. In no other spot on this earth do men and wild beasts flourish side by side free from fear as in Periyar.

For a quiet picnic in idyllic surroundings, there is Crusoe island in the Periyar Lake where there are ample facilities for boating and rowing. Aranya Nivas, situated at Thekaday in the heart of this enchanted jungleland, provides for visitors to the Game Sanctuary the best amenities of a western style hotel. The hotel is owned by the Government and is well furnished and electrified. For those desirous of travelling to Periyar by car the Aranya Nivas makes necessary arrangements on request.

COMM. Thakaday (Periyar) is 135 miles, 170 miles and 71 miles by bus from Cochin, Trivandrum and Kottayam respectively. Kottayam, the road junction for Periyar, is equipped with a comfortable Government Rest House where excellent food and accommodation are available. Periyar can also be reached from Kodaikanal Road by bus (70 miles). Visitors to Periyar should possess a Certificate of "No objection to visit the Periyar Dam Area" issued by the Inspector General of Police, Travancore-Cochin or the S. P. of Police, Kottayam.

## NILGIRI HILLS

The Nilgiris or the Blue Mountains are, in many ways, a Land of Enchantment—the mountain-home of variegated tropical flora and fauna. With a bracing climate and plentiful rainfall the abundance of material flower growth is the glory of the Nilgiri hills. In its inner lap are situated the beautiful hill stations of Ootacamund, Coonor and Kotagiri. There are magnificent landscapes, and on the slopes of the descending hills are great forests in which big game abounds. Situated between Coimbatore and Mysore this is an ideal ground where one can have a wonderful holiday, shooting and hunting or hiking in the hills, holding his breath at the wondrous natural beauties.

## OOTACAMUND

Of the three hill stations the palm goes to Ootacamund—named "Ooty" for short—situated 7,429 feet above sea level, on a plateau amidst marvellous scenery. This is the most loved hill station in the Madras State, Although 11 degrees from the Equator, its climate is akin to that of a fine summer in England. The temperature seldom exceeds 69° and never falls below 50°. The best season is between April and June.

Ooty has the appearance of a vast park, and motoring, which can be enjoyed in very few of India's hill stations, is one of the many attractions that Ooty provides in ample measure. Its many miles of roads are not only picturesque but excellent in construction, for Ooty has no high mountains or deep valleys. Another pretty feature of Ooty is its rolling "Downs"— 55 miles of them where one can play golf on one of the finest golf courses, hunt panthers and leopards, and walk mile after mile through fascinating forest scenery. Ooty has a lovely lake, surrounded by beautiful trees, which offer amenities for lounging, boating and even fishing. On the opposite bank is Fern Hill which provides wonderful walks. The Botanical Garden where the Flower Show is an annual event, the Race Course, and several dales and hills nearby are worth visiting.

Ooty is surrounded by hills and many delightful excursions can be made to their wooded slopes. Doddabetta (9690 ft.), the highest peak in the Eastern and Western Ghats, is one of the attractions for visitors to Ooty. The Snowdon (8,299 ft.), Elk Hill (8,000 ft.), and Cairn Hill (7,583) are the other nearby hills usually ascended.

Sixteen miles from Ooty (ten miles by a short road) are the famous Pykara Falls which are harnessed to generate electricity for many districts of South India. With its 300-ft-high falls, a picturesque lake and a dam, Pykara is a magnificent theatre of nature's beauty.

\*　　　　\*　　　　\*　　　　\*

COMM. Ooty is reached by a picturesque mountain railway (30m) from Mettupalayam which is the terminus of the Blue Mountain Express from Madras via Jallarpet and Erode. To reach it by plane one has to fly up to Coimbatore and thence proceed to Ooty by car or bus (53 miles). The most enjoyable journey to Ooty is perhaps by bus from Mysore—a 100-mile joy ride through some of the best scenery of the world.

ACCOM. Hotel Cecil (Rs. 12/-) and Savoy Hotel (Rs, 17/8/-) are good European style hotels. Other good hotel are : Modern Hindu Hotel, Modern Lodge, Willingdon Hotel and Tajmahal Hotel. Beside, there are a number of European style boarding houses. Taxis and rickshaws are transport.

# CONOOR

An ideal hill station on the Nilgiri Hills, Conoor is 12 miles from Ootacamund by road and 6,000 ft. above sea level. Conoor has a more equable climate than Ooty—neither too hot in summer nor too cold in winter—and has, therefore, become popular as a residential hill station. The town has a good water supply and is one of the cleanest towns in South India.

Sims Park, a lovely, shady garden containing a rare collection of plants is the predominating beauty spot in Conoor proper. The Pasteur Institute is famous throughout India for research work and effective treatment of various diseases.

There are many places for excursion in and around Conoor which are famous for their scenic beauty. The most beautiful of them is Lady Canning's Seat, a vantage point, about six miles away from the town and in the heart of the woods. The panorama around is superb. Three miles from Conoor is Wellington, the famous military town with its row of barracks first built in 1862.

\* \* \* \*

ACCOM. Conoor lies on the Mettupalayam-Ootacamund narrow gauge line of the Nilgiri Railway, and is connected by road with Ootacumund (12 miles) and Kotagiri (13 miles). There are regular bus services between these places.

ACCOM. Hampton (Rs. 15/-) and Hill Grove (Rs. 13/-) are good western style hotels. Good Indian style hotels include Mysore Lodge, Ganesh Bhavan, Bharat Cafe and Royal Cafe. Besides there are a number of European style boarding houses and a P. W. D. Dak Bungalow. There is a bus service in the town and beyond it to the neighbouring places of interest. Taxis are the chief means of conveyance.

# KOTAGIRI

13 miles from Conoor and 18 miles from Ootacamund by bus is Kotoagiri, "a little pearl in the ear of the Nilgiris". It is the oldest hill station in the Nilgiris and has a climate which is said to be superior to that of Ootacamund and Conoor. The natural surroundings are even more beautiful, and for those who desire rest in seclusion Kotagiri is an ideal resort.

A circular trip of Kotagiri and Conoor can be made from Ootacamund along a narrow, winding motor road up the Dodabetta returning to Ooty by way of Conoor.

\* \* \*

ACCOM. Blue Mountain Hotel caters in European style. Besides there are number of comfortable boarding houses on the Queen's Hill.

# MYSORE

Mysore, the land of fertile plains and virgin forests, of simmering cascades and majestic waterfalls, of charming cities and ornate temples, presents to visitors a wealth of interest that is almost bewildering.

Mysore, the 'City of Garden and Light' and is one of the cleanest in India. Beautifully situated beside a rocky hill, 2,500 feet above sea level, which lends a pleasing picturesqueness to the place; the city has a number of inviting wide roads which are splendidly illuminated every night. The traditional pageantry of India can be seen at its most magnificent in September or October when the festival of Dussara is observed, attracting huge crowds from far and near.

## Place of Interest

The Palace of the Maharaja, picked out every night with 50,000 electric lights, is one of the most handsome in India ; the brilliant frescoes and ivory fittings inside are breath-taking in their splendour. The Jagmahon Palace houses an exquisite Art Gallery. Lalita Mahal is another magnificent mansion reserved for distinguished guests. The Zoological Gardens, the Palace Stables and the Garage are well worth a visit. Other places of interest are : the University, the Oriental Research Institute, the Sandal Oil Factory and Sri Chamarajendra Technical Institute. The Chamundi Hill, two miles south-east of the Fort, is well worth climbing (motorable), for it contains a colossal figure of Nandi, the Sacred bull, carved out of a solid rock.

314

COMM. Mysore lines on the metre gauge of S. Rly. and is 308 and 86 miles from Madras and Bangalore respectively. Bangalore, the principal city of Mysore, is the natural starting point for a tour of the Mysore State. One of the largest and most beautiful cities of India, it is replete with fine parks, beautiful avenues. modern buildings and palaces and is well supplied with hotels of all categories. Bangalore is connected by air with the principal cities of India.

ACCOM. Hotel Metropole (14/-), managed by the Government and Carlton Hotel (Rs. 9/-) are the principal European style hotels. The Railway Retiring Room where Spencers cater are superbly fitted with all modern comforts. Modern Hindu Hotel, Dasaprakash Hotel, Anand Bhavan and Krishna Bhavan are good Indian style hotels. Taxis and two-seater horse cabs are popular transport.

## Sight-Seeing from Mysore

**Srirnagapatnam :** About 10 m. from Mysore by bus or rail (seen by way of a round bus trip of Krishnarajsagar from Mysore), is Srirangapatnam, the old capital of the Mysore kings situated on a small island on the Cauvery river. The fortress here, considered impregnable by Tipu Sultan, was stormed and captured by the British forces at the battle of Srirangapatnam in 1799. The huge temple of Sri Ranganatha-swami and the big mosque of Tipu Sultan with two tall minarets are conspicuous landmarks. At the eastern end of the island are the Darya Daulat Bagh, the favourite garden retreat of Tippu, the water-gate in which he died fighting, and the mausoleum of Tippu and his parents.

**Krishnarajsagar :** Twelve miles north-west of Mysore is Krishnarajsagar, the second biggest artificial lake in the world, with a water area of fifty square miles. Just below the walls of the dam are the enchanted "Brindaban" gardens glowing with lovely flower beds, fragrant shrubs and shady walks, cascades and countless fairy fountains playing delightfully in a riot of colour in the night's illumination presenting a scene of sublime wonder and beauty that is almost magical. A wonderstricken foreign visitor has rightly observed : "I can imagine what the great Moghul Emperor, Shah Jahan, would say if he could come back to earth and see this artistic creation of modern engineering ingenuity—if there is a Tourist Paradise on earth, it is this, oh yes, too right this is it !"

Hotel Krishnarajsagar, situated amidst the unearthly beauty of Brindaban gardens, is a Government-owned luxury hotel and is undoubtedy an ideal holiday resort.

Melcote, 34 miles north of Mysore by road, is a sacred place for the Hindus, for the great philosopher Ramanuja lived and preached there in the eleventh century. "Vairamudi", an important festival, takes place about April every year.

**Somnathpura :** Those who are interested in art and antiquity may proceed to Somnathpura, 34 miles west of Mysore by road, where the Chalukyan temple style reached its zenith under the Hoysala dynasty. Of the many noble temples of the period, the most notable are at Somnathpur, Belur and Halebid. The Somnathpur temple, erected by king Vinaditya Balala in about 1043 A.D. is the earliest and in many respects the best. The temple, an elaborately carved structure, with exquisitely carved ceilings, idols and other figures, bears witness to the marvellous skill and imagination of the master builders of by-gone days ; it is one of the few places indeed where one can feast on the marvels of stone carving.

## BELUR & HALEBID

There are three other places of very great interest to the tourist—Belur, Halebid and Sravanabelgola, and the centre for seeing them is Hasan, a district headquarters, about 74 miles by train from Mysore city.

The Hoysalas of Halebid (1047-1327 A.D.), an offshoot of the Western Chalukyas, were originally Jains, but in the eleventh century the Hoysala kings returned to the Hindu fold, marking their return by erecting a number of remarkable temples.

The Chena Keshava Temple at Belur, 25 miles from Hasan, is one of the most exquisite specimens of Hoysala architecture, built 800 years ago by the munificence of the Hoysala King Vishnuvardhana. Ten miles from Belur is Halebid, an unpretentious village which marks the spot on which once stood the flourishing capital of the Hoysala Kings. Here is the latest and the most elaborate temple, an imposing shrine, which was still unfinished when the Mahammedans under Malik Kafur occupied Halebid and imprisoned the Hoysala ruler. Even in its unfinished condition the temple of Halebid ranks among the masterpieces of Hindu art ; and according to Fergusson "may probably be considered as one the most marvellous exhibitions of human labour to be found even in the patient East."

## SRAVANABELGOLA

Sravanabelgola, 30 miles south-east of Hasan and 50 miles north of Mysore, is famed throughout India for its Jain temple and its colossal Gomateswara statue. Here on a rocky cave, on the small hill, the great Emperor Chandragupta Maurya, having taken vows of renunciation, spent his last days as an ascetic ; and on the other and larger hill, there was erected, in the year 984 A.D., the largest known statue in the world. Carved out of a single boulder, it represents the Jain saint, Gomateswara, who stands above all earthly pursuits, in constant meditation of the Supreme Being on realising whom nothing else remains to be sought.

\*　　　\*　　　\*　　　\*

ACCOM. There is a Travellers Bungalow at Hasan in addition to a number of small hotels. Buses run from Hasan to Belur, Halebid Sravanabelgola and other places. As it is not possible to do full justice to Belur and Halebid in one day, one full day should be devoted to Belur and another to Halebid. Sravanabelgola may be visited on the third day en route

Mysore. All these are grand sights and visitors would not appreciate their magnificence and spirit if they attempt to 'do' them in the compass of a day or two.

## GERSOPPA FALLS

62 miles from Simoga and 19 miles from Sagara Railway station by bus are the world-famous Jog falls which are unrivalled for their majestic beauty and scenic grandeur. The falls are formed by the river Sharavati falling into a mighty chasm about half-a-mile wide and 930 feet deep. They are four in number and are framed in a wonderful setting, wild and mountainous, and are perhaps the most beautiful in the world. As an enchanted traveller has said : "What more perfect morning with coffee with the Dame Blanche of Gerosappa".

The four cascades are known as the Rajah or Grandfall, the Roarer, the Rocket and La Dame Blanche. The most popular spot from which to see the falls is Watkin's Platform and from this point, a descent can be made to the foot to the Cliff.

"Probably it is in the evening after sunset, that the sight is most fascinating...Sitting in the increasing darkness and gazing into the obscurity of apparently bottomless depths, from which issue volumes of steam-like clouds, accompanied by an endless roll of thunder, one cannot but feel profoundly impressed by the scene, a fit subject for the brush of a Dore, and recalling his illustrations of Dante's Inferno."

The best season for visiting the Falls is between November and January. There are two bungalows at the falls which provide all amenities to tourists. Sagara is an important place, and in addition to regular bus services to Jog, cars are available for hire. Through bogies run between Bangalore city and Sagara. There is a Refreshment Room at the station.

# INDEX

## Population

The population of India (according to the census of 1951) is 361.15 million or about 1/6th of the population of the world. 17.3 per cent of the population live in cities and 82.7 per cent in villages. Of the self-supporting population of 104.4 million 68.1 per cent is engaged in agriculture and the rest in non-agricultural professions. The density of population per square mile varies between 907 persons in Kerala and 10 persons in Andaman and Nicobar islands.

There are 3016 towns and 5,5S,089 villages in the country. There are 78 cities in India, each having a population of over one lakh.

According to 1951 census, there were 5.93 crore literate persons in India of whom 4.56 crore were men and 1.37 crore women. The proportion of literate persons to the total population works out to 16.61 per cent. Kerala has the highest population of literate persons (40.68 per cent) followed by Delhi (38.36 per cent).

## Occupational Distribution of Working People

| | |
|---|---|
| Agriculture, Animal husbandry, Forestry, Fishery and ancillary activities. | 72.4 percent |
| Factory establishments and Mining | 2.6 ,, |
| Small enterprises | 8.0 ,, |
| Communications (Posts, Telegraphs and Telephones, Railways and commercial transport) | 7.7 ,, |
| Professions and liberal arts | 4.5 percent |
| Government services | 2.7 ,, |
| Domestic services | 2.7 ,, |

## The Chief Cities

| | Population |
|---|---|
| Greater Calcutta (West Bengal) | 45,78.071 |
| Greater Bombay (Bombay) | 28,39,270 |
| Madras (Madras) | 14,16,056 |
| Delhi (Delhi) | 13,84,211 |
| Hyderabad (AP) | 10,85,722 |
| Ahmedabad (Bombay) | 7.93,813 |
| Bangalore (Mysore) | 7,78,977 |
| Kanpur (U.P.) | 7,05,383 |
| Poona (Bombay) | 5,88,52 |
| Lucknow (U.P.) | 4,96,861 |
| Nagpur (M.P.) | 4,49,099 |
| Agra (U.P.) | 3,75,665 |
| Madurai (Madras) | 3.61,781 |
| Banaras (U.P.) | 3,55,777 |
| Allahabad (U.P.) | 3,32,295 |
| Amritsar (Punjab) | 3,25,747 |

## Languages

Hindi, the language of about 46.3 per cent of the total population, is the Official language of the Union.

English is the medium of all higher studies, scientific researches and governmental communications and is spoken exceedingly well by the educated sections of the people. It has been the common language of India and the chief medium of inter-state communications.

There are 14 languages recognised by the Constitution. Principal among them are :

| | | |
|---|---|---|
| Hindi, (Hindustani, Urdu, and Punjabi) spoken by | 41.3 | percent |
| Telugu ,, | 10.2 | ,, |
| Marathi ,, | 8.3 | ,, |
| Tamil ,, | 8.2 | ,, |
| Bengali ,, | 7.8 | ,, |

( i )

| Gujarati | ,, | 5.0 | percent |
|----------|-----|-----|---------|
| Kannada | ,, | 4.5 | ,, |
| Malayalam | ,, | 4.1 | ,, |
| Oriya | ,, | 4.1 | ,, |
| Assamese | ,, | 1.5 | ,, |

## Religious Groups

| | |
|---|---|
| Hindu | 84.99 |
| Muslim | 2.93 |
| Christian | 2.30 |
| Sikh | 1.74 |
| Jain | 0.45 |
| Buddhist | 0.06 |
| Zorastiran | 0.03 |

## Naiya Paise

Under India's new coinage scheme as introduced from 1st April, 1957, there are seven new coins :

| One rupee | — | 100 | Naiya Paise |
|-----------|---|-----|-------------|
| ½ rupee | — | 50 | ,, |
| ¼ rupee | — | 25 | ,, |
| 0/10th rupee | — | 10 | ,, |
| 1/20th rupee | — | 5 | ,, |
| 1/50th rupee | — | 2 | ,, |
| 1/100th rupee | — | 1 | ,, |

The rupee remains the standard coin with no loss or gain in its value. The changeover from the old to new coins will be gradual ; for three years both old and new coins will be current.

## Education

The Indian Constitution provides for compulsory education of all children up to the age of 14 by 1961. The average per capita expenditure on education in India during 1955-56 was Rs. 4.9, while the expenditure per student was Rs. 55.9.

## Educational Institutions (1955-56 figures)

| | |
|---|---|
| Universities | 37 |
| Art & Science Colleges | 712 |
| Professional colleges | 346 |
| Broadcasting stations | 28 |
| Special education colleges | 112 |
| Secondary schools | 32,568 |
| Primary schools | 2,78,138 |
| Vocational schools | 3,067 |
| Special education Schools | 50,987 |

Various schools under the old system and schools for the blind, deaf and mentally deficient are not included in the above figures.

## Films

India occupies the third place among the film producing countries of the world. It produced 295 feature films in 1957. Between 1947-48 and 1956-57 India imported 21,466.22 lakh feet of raw films and 1,273.72 lakh feet of exported films.

Early films were based on religious and mythological themes. Then came an era of social themes. Now, musical comedies, social and religious themes, are becoming features of Indian films.

## Press

On December 31, 1956, the number of newspapers and periodicals published in India was 6,570. There are 476 dailies.

## Transport & Communication

With 34,744 miles of track India's railways system is the largest in Asia. Besides, there were at the end of 1955-56, 320,522 miles of roads including three trunk roads which intersect the country from one end to the other. Motorized transport is available throughout India, and at present there are in India about 48,000 operators of commercial transport. Air transport has developed in rapid speed ; 291 lakh miles were flown in 1957 on scheduled and non-scheduled services.

# INDEX

iii

# Carefree Travel with

# MERCURY

## Specialists in Tours in India

GRAND HOTEL : CALCUTTA ● HOTEL IMPERIAL : NEW DELHI
CONNEMERA HOTEL : MADRAS ● SINGLI BANK BLDG. : BOMBAY

*" It costs no more .... its more convenient "*

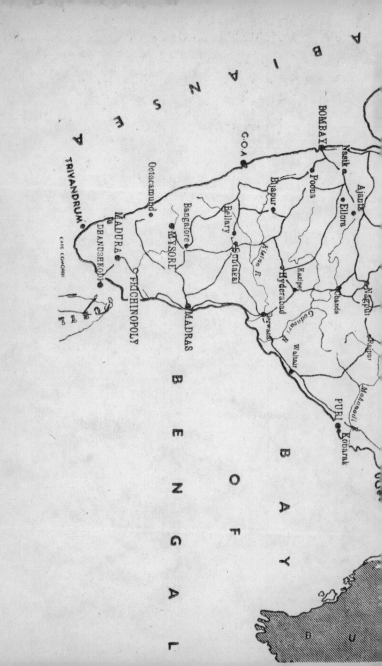